GANDHI'S RELIGIOUS THOUGHT

THE MOST RELIGIOUS THOUGHT

9529

GANDHI'S RELIGIOUS THOUGHT

Margaret Chatterjee

Foreword by
John Hick

UNIVERSITY OF NOTRE DAME PRESS
NOTRE DAME, INDIANA

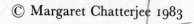

First published 1983 by
THE MACMILLAN PRESS LTD
London and Basingstoke
Companies and representatives
throughout the world

American edition 1983 by
UNIVERSITY OF NOTRE DAME PRESS
Notre Dame, Indiana

Library of Congress Cataloging in Publication Data

Chatterjee, Margaret, 1925–
  Gandhi's religious thought.

  Bibliography: p.
  Includes index.
  1. Gandhi, Mahatma, 1869–1948—religion.   I. Title.
DS481.G3C473   1983   294.5   83–5841
ISBN 0–268–01009–9

Printed in Hong Kong

'Personally, I think the world as a whole will never have, and need not have, a single religion.'

The Collected Works of Mahatma Gandhi, vol. XII
Publications Division, Government of India, Delhi,
30 May 1913, p. 94

'True religion . . . is faith in God, and living in the presence of God, it means faith in a future life, in truth and Ahimsa.'

Young India, 30 Aug. 1928, p. 291

' . . . if we are imperfect ourselves, religion as conceived by us must also be imperfect. . . . Religion of our conception, being thus imperfect, is always subject to a process of evolution and re-interpretation'.

Yeravda Mandir, Navajivan Press, Ahmedabad, 1930, chs X & XI

' . . . I can clearly see the time coming when people belonging to different faiths will have the same regard for other faiths that they have for their own'.

Harijan, 2 Feb. 1934, p. 8

'For me all the principal religions are equal in the sense that they are all true. They are supplying a felt want in the spiritual progress of humanity.'

Harijan, 6 Apr. 1934, p. 59

'Every living faith must have within itself the power of rejuvenation if it is to live.'

Harijan, 28 Sept. 1935, p. 260

Contents

Foreword

The figure of Gandhi is being increasingly recognised as a significant source of light and hope in a world threatened by many kinds of violence, by the erosion of the human environment, and by widespread despair of the future.

There are innumerable biographies of Gandhi: indeed his is possibly the most minutely recorded and scrutinised life that has ever been lived. There are also numerous books on his political, economic and moral teachings. But, surprisingly, whilst there are studies of Gandhi's relationship to Christianity, there are none (known to me) devoted to his religious thought as a whole. Here Margaret Chatterjee presents to the west, in a splendidly balanced way, Gandhi's religious message. Not that his life and thought can ever be separated; for what made Gandhi the centre of so powerful a field of spiritual force was the fact that his ideas were always incarnated in his actions. And so although Professor Chatterjee does not retell the familiar story of Gandhi's life, she does constantly relate his ideas to the Indian culture and the world history of which he was a part.

What we witness above all in the phenomenon of Gandhi is religion becoming creative in human life. The function of religion, as man's response to ultimate Reality, is to transform human existence from self-centeredness to Reality-centeredness. We see this transformation in Gandhi with a clarity which both uplifts and challenges us. His life was a continuous growth in which he became increasingly dedicated to the service of the higher Reality which he thought of as Truth or God. In response to the claim of Reality upon him he renounced the interests of his private ego and became a servant of mankind, transparent to Truth. He loved Truth, or God, with all his heart and mind and soul, and his neighbour as himself; and he did so amidst the pressures, disturbances, ambiguities and confusions of historic liberation struggles, first in South Africa and then in India.

There are at least four areas in which this phenomenon of Gandhi is importantly relevant today, more than thirty years after his death.

One is religious pluralism. Christian theologians are much concerned today with the relationship between Christianity and other religions, with their apparently competing gospels. In this context Gandhi poses a challenge: how could one who lived and died a Hindu have taught so many people, including the great Christian missionary to India, E. Stanley Jones, 'more of the spirit of Christ than perhaps any other man in East or West'. (E. Stanley Jones, *Mahatma Gandhi: An Interpretation*, Hodder & Stoughton, London, 1948, p. 76). It has often been assumed that Gandhi learned of non-violence and self-giving love from Christianity. But in fact he responded so positively to the teachings of Jesus because he found in them a confirmation of what he had already received from his own tradition. He often quoted the verse of a Hindu poet, 'The truly noble know all men as one, and return with gladness good for evil done' (p. 91), and he cherished the traditional Gujarati saying, 'If a man gives you a drink of water and you give him a drink in return, that is nothing. Real beauty consists in doing good against evil' (p. 74). Indeed the Hinduism which provided the supporting framework of Gandhi's life of service affirmed the underlying unity of all mankind, as all being individuations of the same *atman* or soul; from which Gandhi derived the call to renounce egoism and to act in the interests of the whole human community.

Gandhi's own solution to the problem of religious pluralism was learned from the ancient Jain tradition of his native Gujarat. This held that all religious awareness is inevitably partial and incomplete, so that different traditions can complement and enrich one another rather than being mutually exclusive rivals. This world-ecumenical outlook is more widespread today than it was fifty years ago, and we can now proceed with the complex task of working out its epistemological, metaphysical and doctrinal implications.

A second relevance of Gandhi today is to the liberation movements in Southern Africa, South America and elsewhere. Gandhi was perhaps the first practitioner of liberation theology. For he heard the voice of God, which was to him the insistent voice of Truth, calling him to fight, non-violently, for the liberation of the oppressed – in his case, Asians in South Africa, outcastes and the poor in India, and the Indian people as a whole in their struggle for political freedom. This revolutionary activity, rather than any cult or creed, was to him true religion. He said, 'To a people famishing and idle, the only acceptable form in which God can dare to appear is work and promise of food as wages' (p. 229). Gandhi's challenge to the liberation movements of today lies in his profound belief in the ultimate unity of all human beings, *including the oppressors*, and his consequent absolute commitment to non-violence. A study of Gandhi's life shows that *ahimsa* is not mere passivity but a living organism of intense educational activity (or as we say today, conscientisation), highly organised economic and political pressure, and moving symbolic acts. His life and thought should be studied afresh by all who seek to work for human liberation in our contemporary world.

A third area of relevance is the deepening ecological crisis. Although Gandhi was no doubt mistaken in opposing the inevitable industrialisation of India, he was surely right in advocating the production of basic food and clothing rather than wasteful luxuries, and in stressing the dignity of physical labour, the beauty of smallness, the importance of self-sufficiency, and the values of village life. He was not an economist, but he saw the dangers of the modern self-consuming consumer society, with its violent rape of planet earth, with a clarity at which others have only recently arrived. We can profit again today from the human values by which Gandhi lived and the thoughts on human living which he expressed.

And a fourth area of relevance lies in Gandhi's exhibiting – without consciously intending to – a viable style of contemporary sainthood. He was a saint, and indeed a Mahatma, because he was so transparent to the Truth that through his life the claim of Truth was felt and responded to by others. And the Truth that shines through him is both demanding and attractive. For example, in the ashrams and the journeys through India which were among his 'experiments with Truth' Gandhi and his followers lived in freely accepted poverty and constructive hard work. People rose early (prayers at 4.20 a.m.) and worked late. In a land where dirt abounds Gandhi stressed, almost fanatically, cleanliness and sanitation. In a culture in which time is only half real he insisted on punctuality and the stewardship of time. In a society fragmented by caste he deliberately broke all the rules, bringing brahmins, 'untouchables', Muslims, Christians, Sikhs together in the common service of their country. The Truth which grasped him grasped others through him, making great demands on their lives. And yet at the same time everyone who worked with Gandhi has attested that he was full of fun, bubbling over with humour and the joy of living, even in the dark periods of his career.

The pattern of sainthood which we see in him, then, was powered by a complete acceptance of all human beings as ultimately one, and a deep practical love of neighbour which made sacrifice and suffering acceptable. This relationship to the neighbour created a structure of tough political commitment involving careful research, accurate information and prolonged thought. And it overflowed in a continuous delight in human fellowship which won for Gandhi more friends, of more varied kinds, than perhaps anyone else of whom we know. Although he experienced tragic setbacks, hardships and sorrows, and finally met a violent death, Gandhi was a most fortunate person. For his life was a series of experiments with Truth, and the Truth made him free – free from selfishness; free to love and to be loved; free to live creatively, deeply involved in the struggles of his own time and place. Hence he is also a great witness to Truth for other times and place.

Margaret Chatterjee is Professor of Philosophy at the University of Delhi. Born in England and trained at Oxford, she has made India her home since 1946 and has been teaching philosophy there since 1956. She is therefore uniquely equipped, among interpreters of Gandhi to the west, to appreciate the Indian context of his thought and its deep roots in Indian history and religious life. She has succeeded admirably in her aim to discuss 'Gandhi's religious thought in his own idiom so as to present him as a very exceptional personality whose thinking stretches back into the traditional life of India and reaches forward to times which are yet to come' (p. 265).

JOHN HICK

Preface

The following study can only claim to be an introduction to a very vast subject. The source material available on Gandhi is voluminous and no present-day researcher can profess to have been through it all. Students of modern Indian history and political thought have been largely concerned with Gandhi's role in a sequence of events which amounts in fact to the story of the making of modern India. But there is an inner story which has yet to be explored. Having said that, something else must also be admitted. Gandhi himself made no such distinction. He never looked on social, political, economic and religious issues as if they were in watertight compartments. He saw them as a complicated fabric, spun by the hands of millions, to use the idiom of spinning and weaving that he so loved. To try to isolate his religious thought is in a sense to do violence to this most non-violent of men. A full-length study would require constant reference to the socio-economic and political implications of the religious component in his thought. I could not do more, in a book of this size, than indicate from time to time the context in which particular facets of his thought were worked out. The reader will need to fill this out from other sources.

I have tried to keep in mind Gandhi's contribution to religious thought against the broad canvas of India's many – faceted traditions. Where it seemed of interest I have made passing references to matters engaging those concerned with philosophy of religion and theology in the west and elsewhere. My own impression is that Gandhi takes us beyond the language of encounter, and even the language of dialogue, to an approach which I try to characterise at the end of the book. In this respect I believe him to be the man of tomorrow.

I am grateful to a number of people in the writing of this book: first of all to John Hick for his encouraging thought that there may well be an audience for some of Gandhi's ideas about religion in the west and for his recommending this project to the publishers; to the seminarians at 'Vidya Jyoti', Delhi, and successive audiences of

American friends in India and university audiences in England who stimulated me by their questions; to Judith M. Brown for encouragement; to Stephen N. Hay for lively discussions about soul-force many years ago; to Manoranjan Guha and B. N. Ray for patient answers to persistent questions; to Krishna Kripalani for help on the relation between Gandhi and Tagore, useful suggestions for reading and for allowing me to try out some of my wilder hypotheses on him before committing them to print. I owe most, however, to Nirmal Kumar Bose,[1] anthropologist, and secretary to Mahatma Gandhi during a critical period in his life, the source of most of the personal anecdotes in this book and my first teacher in Gandhian thought.

December 1980   MARGARET CHATTERJEE

1 Introduction

When C. F. Andrews met Gandhi for the first time in January 1915, he wrote to Rabindranath Tagore that he felt Gandhi was 'a saint of action rather than of contemplation'. Canonisation was thrust on Gandhi in his lifetime not only by his fellow-countrymen but by his admirers outside India, and the word charisma was bandied about freely in an attempt to explain the enigmatic attraction of this complex personality. Gandhi never failed to feel extremely embarrassed by all this. It distressed him that scores, if not hundreds, came to his meetings to have 'darshan' of a holy man rather than to take up the causes he believed would bring into existence a new India. As for charisma, it was a concept quite foreign to Gandhi's own understanding of his role as a national leader. He drew strength from the people, in his own terminology, the masses rather than the classes, as a great banyan tree roots itself time and time again in the soil, drawing nourishment from them. If, to change the metaphor, he was borne up on wings of faith in his own inward life, he was no less firmly rooted in the world of the common man, that of the poor villagers he knew so well and whose way of life he shared.

Charlie Andrews' comment, written not to a contemplator, but to a poet, reminds the student of Gandhi's thought of a vital point, the extent to which his religious thought runs along as a ground theme, a continuo, to a life of practical involvement. Gandhi warned those who wanted to learn about his ideas not to look only at what he had written but to observe carefully what he did, even better, to take part in his daily routine and his constructive projects. So an earnest inquirer would find himself accompanying Gandhi in the early hours, even before daybreak, in a silent procession across the fields, ending with a cleaning-up operation where thoughtless villagers had left night-soil. Gandhi had a great sense of humour, and while this technique of spiritual instruction must have deterred some, no doubt the point went home to others. He was very patient with those who wanted to draw him into theological discussions, but he often chose a very early hour for this, rationing the time to be allotted, and in his heart of hearts he believed there were better ways of spending the time.

Gandhi's life of practical response to the urgencies of his day is now an open book to all researchers on modern Indian history. In a short book on the religious aspect of his life it will not always be possible to indicate the context in which his ideas were worked out although this is really the way it should be done. Andrews' words, however, need to be kept in mind. Gandhi was extraordinarily sensitive to the idiom of thought of those he addressed whether in private conversation, or in more public gatherings. He had the pedagogue's natural gift for sensing the language which would be intelligible to his listeners. In the vast majority of cases the clarifications of thought which cover decades of a long and extremely active life occurred in very specific contexts, contexts like the day to day running of his ashrams in South Africa and India, the need for bringing about Hindu-Muslim unity, the need for the Hindu community to put its own house in order with regard to its treatment of 'untouchables', or explaining to his Christian friends that men of goodwill could work out their own salvation in the tradition into which they were born and had no need to change their labels unless the spirit so moved them. Gandhi does not belong to the so-called enlightenment stream of eastern thought, as a man like Sri Ramana Maharshi does, but he ever thought in terms of relationship, the relationships between man and man and man and God. Yet even though he sets his sights on a kingdom of 'right relations' he does not look upon human imperfection as a rupture of relation with God (as those do who speak in terms of sin); rather he sees it in terms of an egoity which hampers man's true fulfilment (self-realisation in the language of India's philosophical tradition). Gandhi is a protestant in a challenging sense, protesting against all that makes for fragmentation of life, whether within the individual or in society; catholic in his confidence that his vision of a new society could provide a practical alternative for dehumanised man wherever he may live.

There is a certain danger in hunting in his scattered sayings, which often have an off the cuff character, for keys to matters of immediate relevance to cultures and times other than his own. To take an example, the western reader may well be put off by the numerous references to cow-protection and spinning in his *Collected Works*, both of which Gandhi always referred to as sacred duties. There were reasons tied up with his own people's history why he should have laid such a lot of stress on both of these. Gandhi had a rare gift for picking on symbols which would be readily intelligible to the majority of his countrymen, villagers as they were, and still are. The cow, endowed with special sacredness in ancient times to ensure wise methods of agriculture and animal husbandry, he saw as a symbol of exploited creatures, of gentleness, a poem of pity. It becomes a test case, the occasion of a lesson for the Hindus who resent that Muslims eat beef and yet themselves allow neglected cattle to wander about and die of starvation. Cow-protection was, then, apart from other considerations, a symbol of caring for one's own, a tending of links with nature which gives of her bounty only if she is served by man. Spinning likewise, for Gandhi, apart from being sound economic sense as an occupation for peasants in between crops, becomes a symbol for a common activity which can link men of all castes, a sacrificial act in the sense that it means a giving up of time, indeed a husbanding of time in the interest of bringing men together. Spinning provides him with some of his loveliest metaphors which can be seen as illustrations of his use of religious language. We must spin the 'gossamer string of love', the 'silken net of love being attuned with truth'. Krishna manifested himself in the form of clothes to Draupadi. Spinning and weaving are, then, the Lord's work. The symbolic act of spinning acquires overtones of significance in a community where not all can wear the sacred thread. The thread spun by the lowest of the low in society can be seen as a vehicle of redemption, both economic and spiritual, for the two could not be separated in Gandhi's eyes.

Gandhi warned those who wanted to study his thought to take note of the time sequence in which his sayings found their place and, when in doubt, to look at his later remarks rather than the earlier ones. This is because he was a strong believer in the principle of spiritual growth. His ideas grew, and sometimes we can even say they radically changed. We can, for example, see a clear change in his view of *Varnāśramadharma* (roughly equivalent to the principle of 'my station and its duties'). Once we graft on to this the duties of bread labour, of scavenging, and of each becoming a *śūdra*, the idea of rigid caste duties is effectively eroded. On other topics, for example, the complex elucidation of what he means by truth, we find a steady evolution of insight where the picture is gradually made clearer rather than radically transformed. A nit-picking exercise in finding inconsistencies in Gandhi's thinking misses the mark, for he was well aware of them and gave a clue to lead us out of the labyrinth. Gandhi was ever a seeker. He moved on in quest of light, leaving the dark places behind. Although the language of pilgrimage may not seem to fit the thinking of a man who belonged squarely in a culture which regards time as cyclical, there is considerable warrant nevertheless for finding the word pilgrim not inappropriate in the case of Gandhi. He had read Bunyan's *Pilgrim's Progress* and often quoted from it. Moreover, the Gujarati diary of his early spiritual mentor, Raychandbhai, makes use of the word 'pilgrimage'. He never spoke of himself as having attained the goal of spiritual life, unlike many major figures in the Indian tradition and in modern times. He was acutely sensitive to the approximative character of all human efforts to approach the supreme and spoke with great humility when he compared himself with the figure, say, of Sri Rāmakrishna Paramahamsa.

He had heard the language of marching upward to Zion in the evangelical meetings he attended in South Africa. But for Gandhi the march was not so much upward (Indian cosmology is rather less crude than the cosmology justly satirised by John Robinson) as horizontal, the dusty track of everyday. This in itself marks him out no less from those, in various traditions, who retain the upwards and heavenwards idea, as from one dominant model in his own tradition, the idea of a journey within, to the cave of the heart. Much of the difference of outlook reflected in the famous exchange of ideas between Gandhi and Tagore can be elucidated in terms of Gandhi's own understanding of the pilgrim idea. The traditional *parivrājaka* or wanderer, in the Indian tradition, collects dust on his feet no doubt, but his ultimate goal is the cave of the heart. The cow-dust hour beloved of Indian poets is a thing of beauty, spelling the end of the heat of the day, a home-coming. The dust settles and the benison of night descends. But for Gandhi there was no end to the collecting of dust on his feet, no end to the pilgrimage of day to day living. As long as man is in the flesh he cannot see God face to face. But the further he goes on life's way, his understanding does, or should, deepen. This is the key that Gandhi gives us to sorting out any differences there may be between the reflections of his youth and the more mature insights of his old age.

We need next, perhaps, to suggest a few caveats. It is important to remind ourselves today, from the vantage point of the 1980s, that Gandhi was not, as a religious thinker, fighting a battle against the inroads of secularism as many theologians feel they are doing today.

Gandhi was in fact throughout his life concerned with very secular goals, first, early in his career, the securing of civil rights for Indian settlers in South Africa, and, back in his own country, from 1915 onwards, the gaining of national independence for India. He was not one for whom the dictum 'Render to Caesar the things that are Caesar's and unto God the things that are God's' had much appeal. For one thing the distinction between sacred and profane is not familiar to the Indian mind. Hindu culture sets a pattern which extends from seasonal observances to daily routines to do with bathing, eating and dressing. The kitchen, the bathing place and the *pūjā* room are all, in their various ways, holy. And yet, paradoxically perhaps, Gandhi and his political successor Jawaharlal Nehru, understood that the free Indian *state* needed to be secular if communal harmony was to be safeguarded. What Indian *society* was, and would continue to be, was a different matter. Hinduism is not an institutionalised religion, and the meaning of secularism in India is not what it is elsewhere. Gandhi does not speak out against secularisation or secularism. He does not even speak against atheism, for he finds in many atheists that very desire for truth which he himself believed was identical with the religious impulse. What he does take a stand against is materialism, irreligion, untruth. No doubt, these are not all the same. He found himself pitted against principalities and powers and also against the enemy within the gate; that is, those powers within man himself that tend to drag him down. A greater menace than secularism in his view is the rampant acquisitiveness of industrial civilisation, the worst aspects of which he had seen for himself in South Africa. It was a ruthlessly competitive society which appeared to him to be 'Satanic', much as William Blake and William Cobbett had felt of early industrial England a century before. Like Gustavo Gutierrez, he believes that the 'technological spirit' (in Gutierrez' phrase) actually *limits* man in that it makes man a captive of his own creations. And yet the spirit which seeks to better man's material conditions, to satisfy the minimum needs of all, was not in itself an evil thing. When in his famous tract *Hind Swaraj* he seems to turn his back on all that is modern, he does so out of a reaction at what he has seen of exploitation in South Africa, the lack of response in high places in London to his campaign, and the growing conviction that industrialisation would never be of benefit to the poorest of the poor. All this made him not an anti-secularist but something rather different – a man who increasingly believed that only people who shared a transformed ethico-religious attitude to life would be able to build the Kingdom of Heaven upon earth.

This apparently simple conclusion has in fact far-reaching implications. He was not merely appealing for a transformed *consciousness*. Generations of 'holy men' in India had made this appeal and the impact on the world outside had been minimal if not non-existent. He was not advocating, Quaker-fashion, the slow building up of a society through the transformation of individuals, one by one. The individual and society were to be transformed *pari passu*, and this is as distinct from the Quaker idea as it is from the Marxist clarion call to change the system. And Gandhi believed this could be done here and now, in modest ways, by ordinary people who did not have any particularly saintly qualities, but who, through the combined discipline of non-violent resistance to exploitative structures and constructive work on a modest scale, would gradually learn what the Kingdom of Heaven was all about, and this not through being instructed about it, but in seeing it grow through their very own efforts. That all this took place under the umbrella of an impulse which is at first sight purely political, i.e. the fight for civil rights in South Africa and the national movement in India, cannot be denied. But it does bring out one important aspect of Gandhi's thinking, his belief that the most urgent struggles against injustice can be humanised, so to say, by the persuasive and creative power which is released when men of goodwill band together, with enmity to none, in order to better their lives and those of their neighbours. These are some of the considerations, it seems to me, which mark off Gandhi's thinking on the range of topics which are often brought under the general rubric of secularisation.

Another caveat goes something like this. We shall look in vain in Gandhi's religious thought for the hermeneutical problems which begin with the historical criticism which is built into continental theological scholarship. He is not in search of the historic X, Y or Z. Western scholars have tended to lament the lack of historic sense in the world of Indian scholarship. Gandhi shocks his western readers by often pointing out the *irrelevance* of history. He himself had a rather idiosyncratic view of history.[1] He saw history as a record of departures from the regular stream of events. This ties in oddly with the view of those who understand by history something more than political history. But whereas the latter would like to put social and economic history in its place, Gandhi seemed to think of history as the record of the follies of mankind, of departures from truth as he would put it. If all was proceeding according to *sanātana dharma*, the eternal law of righteousness, then logically speaking, there would be nothing to record. Such an orientation of opinion throws some light on why Gandhi is not concerned with the historicity or otherwise of Krishna and why, as he himself says, it would not matter whether or not the historic Jesus had ever existed, for the Sermon on the Mount would still remain as a shining testimony. The question about the testimony *of whom* thereby becomes subordinate to the question of the testimony *to what*.

And yet there is something very like a hermeneutic to be extracted out of his very unorthodox interpretation of the *Bhagavad-Gītā*, for it is a new interpretation, based again not on a history inspired urge to get at the *Ur*-text, the original, but a rethinking in line with his own very firm commitment to non-violence.

So far from being a de-mythologiser (some of the Indian Renaissance figures could be described as that, for example, Raja Rammohan Roy) Gandhi drew on mythology fully in his religious thinking, enlisting an imagination that was singularly in tune with the ethos of the masses whose spokesman he was. This brings out something further. Gandhi was able not so much to remythologise, as one could say Bankim Chandra Chatterjee did, as to find in the mythical world of the common man a storehouse of symbols to which *new* meaning could be given. This ties in, it will immediately be seen, with his unorthodox interpretation of the *Gītā*. It is, I would suggest, not too far-fetched, for example, to glimpse somewhere at the back of his mind the idea of the many-armed deities of popular iconography brought down to earth, transformed into the many human arms needed in the vast task of transforming society. The new look he gives modern Hinduism, unlike the new look given by some theologians to Christian belief, was not a new look which looked askance at popular imagination and observance. Although he was not a temple-goer himself, he saw in the simple worship of the ordinary villager, whether it be the pouring of water on a tree, or an obeisance to the sun, not things which needed to be corrected in the light of superior insight, but acts of recognition of the mystery of the universe with all its indwelling sacred powers and with which man needs to be in tune if his life is to be touched by the healing influence of grace.

A misunderstanding of this side of Gandhi's nature leads some to associate him with the civilisation of the bullock-cart, to dub him an anti-intellectual, someone who wilfully disregarded the call of reason. It is a misunderstanding, for the claim of reason, the need for reason, was always there in Gandhi's own mind. Each tenet, if one can use such a word about Gandhi's thinking, was examined in the light of reason and if found wanting, was rejected. He was by no means unaware of the tussle between reason and unexamined belief, or still more, ritual practice. But he often found that there were very good reasons for what simple people did by instinct, and in such cases he acted as a mediator in the task of persuading others, critics especially, of the sound sense behind popular belief or practice. Where a practice was found to be both against reason and in defiance of man's moral sense, he had no hesitation in denouncing it. The clearest case of this is his denunciation of untouchability. Not only in the case of myths and practices, but concepts too, it is worth noting the extent to which Gandhi salvaged notions from the arcanas of ancient Indian thought, gave them a good dusting, sometimes enough to knock off a few of their corners, and remoulded them into an almost unrecognisable shape. The detective's eye is sometimes called for in investigating Gandhi's religious thought, for it is not always easy to realise that what he puts forward from time to time is an old idea, but burnished in such a way that it can shine forth in the light of twentieth century challenges.

Religious pluralism does not pose for him philosophical problems about rival truth claims, because of his adherence to the ancient Hindu and Jain belief in the fragmentariness of all men's visions of the truth. Religious pluralism is considered by Gandhi in connection with the practical exigencies of living together peacefully. His own experience of living in a multi-religious society, something he shares in common with all who live on the Indian sub-continent, provides a constant reminder that the discussion of religious truth is not a mere theoretical matter but has a direct bearing on how men behave towards each other, *bearing with* each other's credal and 'observational' differences, and that the whole question is in fact intimately related to whether men of different persuasions can *live* together in harmony or not. All this strikes a familiar note in every society today where friction sometimes leads to explosive situations between different communities. Gandhi reminds us here too of another important thing, that behind apparently credal boundaries lies a territory of a very different kind, the territory of economic inequality, racial prejudice, even such simple matters as what a man eats or is forbidden to eat, whether his skin may be white, black or brown. One of the first things Gandhi did when he went to Noakhali in November 1946, to investigate the unhappy communal situation there, was to send his volunteers to make an economic survey of the area. It was found that this district in Bengal (now in Bangladesh) had a population which was 18 per cent Hindu and 82 per cent Muslim. The landed proprietors were mostly Hindu and collectively owned about three fourths of the land. He said to some of his volunteers on this occasion, 'This is not a communal problem; it is an economic one.'

Gandhi's insight into the complexities, social, political and economic, of the multi-religious society which was his own, reveals a quality which is poorly described by the word eclecticism. It is a term which has often been used with reference to the Hindu mind and not only by outsiders. Brajendranath Seal, one of the most outstanding savants of Bengal, wrote of the synthetic spirit of the ancient Hindus. He did not use the word with the pejorative Kraemerian overtones that the word 'syncretism' has come to have. Indian culture *has* shown extraordinary assimilative powers. The product that has resulted is many-textured, and as in other societies in many parts of the world today, it has sensitive places where the weave may be wearing thin, or where it seems to be stretched beyond bearing. But Gandhi was no eclectic, if by eclecticism we mean a patchwork of ideas culled from here and there, guided by the whim of the moment and the chance influences that may come one's way. His long cavalcade of encounters with all sorts and conditions of men ranging from English vegetarians, nature cure faddists, theosophists, fundamentalist Christians, Muslim merchants, political leaders like Gokhale, his close friends C. F. Andrews and Rabindranath Tagore, to the village folk he understood so well, left an imprint on his mind. It would have been extraordinary had it been otherwise. But the man and his thought reveal far more than eclecticism. What emerges is a personal testament which is strangely moving. Let me put it another way. In an age when consistency may often seem to demand things which we *know* are at variance with the needs of man's psyche, Gandhi's at times maddening inconsistencies and contradictions show something which might be described if not as concordant discord (within the scope of his own person) then as contrapuntal in a way which challenges new listening.

Gandhi's religious thinking has both the stamp of his own personal pilgrimage, that is to say a confessional character, and at the same time is shot through with a vision splendid which he believed could be a beacon light (the word 'pole star' comes to mind) for all men everywhere. His personal experience of living in a society where the distinction between sacred and profane was a somewhat unnatural one, and where people of very different ethnic types and ways of life were actually living side by side, gave him a unique advantage in thinking out what the shape of a future community might be like. His own 'experiments with truth', as he called them, are on record as evidence of both the difficulties and the potentialities of such a quest. In this respect Gandhi's passionate concern with the building of a new society which would be free of exploitation, and in which the lowliest of the low would have their minimum needs satisfied, was the concern of an outstanding Indian with a conscience. He was not a theoriser indulging in the formulation of blueprints of a Utopia for tomorrow. He was concerned about the India of today. But does this have anything to do with religious thought? For Gandhi it most certainly did. Religion for him was not in a watertight compartment, sealed off from the agony of living in conditions of scarcity. In this he has much in common with the religious thinkers of Latin America who see the struggle for human liberation as part and parcel of the quest for salvation, or with Dietrich Bonhoeffer's relating of *kerygma* (proclamation) to the condition of persecuted humanity.

To get this in proper perspective and to see Gandhi as a man who was very much engaged with life in this world, and with its quality, sets the record straight for those who associate 'eastern thought' with techniques of meditation, retreats from the world, yogic exercises and the like. He was a passionate believer in spiritual power, and whatever this may mean will have to be gone into later. But meditation, the life of contemplation as such, smacked of spiritual luxury, as much out of tune with reality as the palaces of marble and concrete that stand cheek by jowl alongside the hovels of the poor. This is not to say that Gandhi did not have an inner life of his own. There is ample evidence that he did. But the saga of man's search for truth was not for him an isolated saga. If the unfurled wings of faith strove towards the beyond, we were no less sustained by the bonds which link man and man, for it was these that constituted the very dimension of that striving. If it be granted that spiritual matters concern truths we cannot fully understand with our minds then Gandhi has something novel to suggest in this regard. He was a great believer in the wisdom of the heart. But he saw spiritual growth not in terms of a still point within the soul but in the form of widening sympathies and their natural expression in service. For Gandhi the cognitive content of faith is as much directed to the widening of human perceptiveness as it is directed to a closer relation to God. He was not one of those who saw the mystical as in any sense a way out of the spiritual dilemma of modern man. He sees this dilemma much as men of faith and conscience in other parts of the world see it today – how to be of service in the world while at the same time sensitive to those outreachings of the spirit which seem to beckon us further still. From Gandhi's point of view the contemplative who turns his back on *work* could not be an exemplar for every man. The Trappist monks he admired in South Africa also engaged in agricultural work, a combination of silence and practical activity he found very appealing. He once said that meditation and worship were not exclusive things to be kept locked up in a strong box. They must be seen in every act of ours.[2] The current fads and fancies of those who go in for meditative techniques in some of the new cults in the west are unGandhian in a variety of ways. He would perhaps comment, with his unfailing sense of humour, that it was not surprising that those who overeat should have to adopt painful measures to remedy the situation; that it was not surprising that many of the young should want to run away from the heartless thing that industrial civilisation has become; that men will always seek new ways of reaching out in community towards each other because no man can live alone. It was, however, his strong conviction that society cannot be reformed by running away from it. One must try and show that better ways of life are possible, that simplicity is best. This is after all what is contained in the ancient ashram idea. Retreat for Gandhi, if indeed retreat it was, was always retreat into what he called constructive work, trying to improve the life of the villagers, trying to bring about Hindu–Muslim unity, working towards the betterment of the condition of women and children. What is more, he had a poor opinion of those who were easy converts to a religion different from their own. Our prayer for others should be that each be granted the light he needed, and this light may not be the light one needed oneself. The Hindu should be a better Hindu, the Muslim a better Muslim, the Christian a better Christian.

Gandhi always regarded time as precious. Life was all too short for the many activities that had to be packed into it. The life of meditation may attract men of a different stamp. But Gandhi does not belong to the contemplative tradition which, it might be necessary to stress, is itself only one of the traditions in Indian thought. He was far too involved in political affairs in South Africa and then in India to be other than a karmayogi, a man of action. His own spiritual exercises are a strange medley of practices which include cleaning of latrines, giving enemas to sick children, listening to the woes of endless streams of visitors, spending time on a voluminous correspondence with all manner of people, quacks, genuine seekers, indignant objectors, friends on the same wavelength as himself, and those whom he described as 'the tallest in the land'. The nearest he gets to meditation is perhaps his frequent repetition of Rāmnām, the name of God. This for him, has a mantric power. But it is not a mantra given by a guru. It is something which can be repeated by an illiterate villager as well as by a pandit well-versed in Sanskrit. It is, if you like, the epitome of democratic prayer. But he was happiest repeating this prayer along with others. In 1927 he wrote that when he was alone he certainly did pray but he felt very lonely without a congregation to share the prayer with him.[3] This is not the language of the traditional seeker of the cave of the heart, of one who pursues the path of meditation. Prayer, as Gandhi understood it and practised it, was a means of training in the use of soul-force, a turning of the searchlight inwards, a yearning of the heart. We constantly return to this stress on the heart, for it was a most vital one for Gandhi. Pedagogue as he was he was convinced that the heart of modern man had become a barren thing. The Vaishnava tradition of Gujarat and Maharashtra praises the man who is not a pastmaster of learning, or who can contemplate in an undistracted manner, but the man whose heart melts at another's woe and who presumably goes on to do something about it. It was necessary to say all this, in introducing Gandhi's thought, in view of contemporary interest in techniques of meditation. Gandhi does have his own techniques of discipline, of self-purification as he calls it, but these should not be conflated with the techniques which have been used by contemplatives of various traditions for centuries, or with fashionable cultic practices which attract some people today. Gandhi was not in search of new experiences. His aim was to become a fitter instrument of service.

There is another clue which may be of use before we go any further. In the twentieth century there has been much re-thinking of the problematic of the concept of God. The very word 'God' is a stumbling block to many. Besides, there are traditions, such as the Buddhist, where the concept seems to be absent. In Gandhi's religious thought there are traces of a way out of the impasse. At one stage in his spiritual growth he hit on the idea of Truth as more fundamental than that of God, and to elucidate what he means by this is a very formidable task indeed.

Yet if we are on the look out for a new theological breakthrough in Gandhi we may be disappointed. Gandhi had no great opinion of theologians, and mainly for the good reason that he did not think that religion was a matter to be *talked* about. In the idiom of another tradition, religion was concerned with going about doing good. Gandhi's own 'religious language' is fed from many sources, and for someone who was as down to earth as he was, his discourse was amazingly full of rich metaphors and parables which had deep resonances for those who heard him and which had roots not only in scripture but in the folk tradition transmitted by the saint-bards of mediaeval India. Seeing how these homely metaphors enter into his elucidation of Truth and lead us into greener pastures than the circumnavigations of those who confine themselves to God-talk will be another of the themes to be pursued along the way.

2 Gandhi's Religious Thought and Indian Traditions

Strictly speaking, Indian traditional thought, diversified as it is, contains neither philosophy of religion nor theology as these are commonly understood. Some Indian thinkers, S. Radhakrishnan for one, make much of the view that Hinduism is, above all, a way of life. Those who belong to other traditions have justly pointed out that the same can be said of other faiths as well. What Hindus mean when they talk of a way of life, however, is that Hinduism is not credal in form but concerns patterns of living, including rituals and other practices, for example those involved in certain seasonal festivals, which are not wholly ritualistic. At the same time a man can be a Hindu, that is to say regard himself as one and be regarded as one by others, even if he does not follow any particular one of the practices that other Hindus may follow. So 'religious thought' is a phrase that has some justification in the Indian context, for it can cover both the complex structures of consciousness and their behavioural manifestations which are what we seek to probe in understanding Gandhi's complex response to India's multi-dimensional religious traditions. Philosophers have by no means been the most reliable guides to what these structures are, and we shall find, in Gandhi especially, a man whose own religious life was not mainly shaped by philosophical texts, even by scriptural authorities, but by a host of factors, the chief of which will occupy us in this chapter.

In the Indian context the core concept in religion is not necessarily the concept of God, and there are several important streams of thought in which the concept is absent. Indian religious life has always set great store by the verdict of individual experience, and experience is, as we would expect, given shape by the tradition in which it takes place. Where the tradition is not one where intellectual constructs provide stumbling blocks, the way is clear for the religious aspirant to seek his own path. This combination of rootedness and spiritual quest is symbolised no less in the holy man dwelling in a cave in the Himalayas than in the sadhu type who goes from place to place, not only visiting places of pilgrimage, but exploring the rich tapestry of the Indian sub-continent, its mountains, valleys and rivers, moving amidst the teeming millions with their multiform ways of day to day living. What, to the Christian, may smack of spiritual nomadism, the Hindu does not see in this way at all. The pilgrims on their way to Canterbury had their faces set towards a fixed goal. The Indian *parivrājaka* (wanderer) is a man who explores the horizontal diversity of the world and is wrongly understood as a man who has turned his back on it. Visitors to India notice the extent to which people seem to be constantly on the move. No doubt a lot of this is taken up with ritual occasions to do with special events in the family. But the Hindu is as much taken up with everyday living as anyone else and in this living he is constantly made aware that there are others who live differently from the way he does.

Gandhi's family background provides a good illustration of what has been indicated so far. Gandhi was born on 2 October 1869, on the west coast of India, into a Vaishnava family of the Vallabhacharya tradition. His mother, Putali Bai, belonged to the Pranāmi sect founded by Mehraj Thakore, born in Saurashtra, later called 'Prānanāth' (Lord of Life) by his followers. Gujarat, with its many religions, was a likely place for this attempt to synthesise Hinduism, Islam and other faiths. Gandhi, later on accompanied by his young wife, used to be taken not only to the Vaishnava temple to seek a blessing, but also to those of the Pranamis. His mother hailed from a village near Junagadh where Narsinh Mehta lived during the fifteenth century. This saint–poet, specially beloved of Gandhi throughout his life, was a Brahmin, but he used to visit the quarters of untouchable friends and sing bhajans (hymns) in praise of Vishnu. Jains and Muslims were frequent visitors to the household and it came naturally to young Mohan to accept the fact that the supreme could be sought in a great variety of ways. The only jarring note at this stage was provided by the fundamentalist Christian missionaries who went in for street-corner preaching and who not only denounced those who believed anything other what they themselves believed, but were associated in the popular imagination not only with the foreign imperial power but also with alien customs like beef-eating and the drinking of liquor. Gandhi's first encounter with Christians was certainly most unfortunate. The glaring gulf between profession and practice, the way in which converts were made and the fact that the latter seemed to look upon aping their foreign mentors in matters of dress and food as part and parcel of their conversion, all grated on a sensibility which had already been schooled in a discipline of a very different mould. The spirit of gentleness, allowing a man to pursue his *swadharma*, his own faith, respecting the faiths of others, was ingrained in young Gandhi and the militancy of the missionaries with their talk of 'saving souls', as if everyone else lived in darkness, created an impression in Gandhi's mind which only years spent in London and South Africa were able to modify.

Gandhi adopted during this early stage of his life a devotional practice which was to remain with him all throughout his life, the repetition of 'Rāmnām', the name of God. 'Japa' or repetition of a holy word, or sometimes *shloka* (verse), is a familiar religious practice in India, extending into a relatively modern outgrowth such as Sikhism. During his father's illness, the days in the year 1885 which Gandhi's biographers have described in detail and which occasioned a major traumatic experience in his life, a friend of his father's, Ladha Maharaj, used to visit the house and recite the *Rāmāyana* to him in Tulsidas' version. The epic is a story about a vow made by Rāma's father as a result of which Rāma is banished. Gandhi was present during these recitations and was to describe the *Rāmāyana* later as 'the greatest book in all devotional literature'. He sees it as embodying the idea that 'truth is the foundation of all merit and virtue', a fable of perfect fidelity to vows. Choosing a theme for a talk to school children in Bhithiharva in 1918, he quoted certain couplets from Tulsidas' *Rāmāyana*,[1] how Bharata . . .

Strictly observed the vows of Yama,
Niyama, Shama, Dama;
And made it easy for our race
To see Rām face to face.

Speaking in Patna in 1925[2] he quoted Tulsidas' saying: 'The root of religion is pity', and added 'It is necessary to revive this religion of pity or compassion in India.' That he was not moved by the mere *concept* of God is made clear here: 'To think of God as "God" does not fire me as the name Rāma does. . . . Therefore my whole soul rejects the teaching that Rāma is not my God.'[3] By 'my God' he is referring to the 'Iṣṭadevatā' idea, the notion of 'chosen deity'. Epic literature has the status of scripture to the ordinary man in India. Rāmnām provides an avenue of devotion for all castes alike, even for those whom a hierarchical social system had relegated to the lowliest position of all. He wrote: '*Rāmnām* is a door of purification even for the illiterate.'⁴ Rāma as an ideal man, with heroic qualities, is regarded as God-like. To the devotee Rāma *is* God. This to my mind, points up the role of religious imagination in filling out conceptions of divinity. A conception is not a mere concept. Again we come across the idea of religious thought as concerned with structures of consciousness where thinking, feeling and imagining are deeply interfused. Tulsidas is himself a focus of adoration as 'the great spirit that gave to an aching world the all-healing mantra of Rāmanāma.'⁵ A mantra need not be given by a guru, nor need it be a sentence. 'Rāmnām' and the mystic syllable 'Om' are cases in point. A mantra serves as a focus for concentration, that is to say, it helps the aspirant to avoid distraction; it invokes forces, e.g. calling upon Rāma invokes the aid of Rāma; and builds up a reservoir of spiritual power. The mantra is what is described in *The Cloud of Unknowing* as 'a naked intent direct unto God without any other cause than Himself . . .' . . . 'fasten this word to thine heart, so that it never go thence for thing that befalleth. . . . With this word, thou shalt beat on this cloud (the cloud of unknowing) and this darkness above thee.'⁶ But there is another dimension to Gandhi's interpretation of Rāmnām. A rather longer quotation is needed at this point:⁷

Hanuman tore open his heart and showed that there was nothing there but Rāmanāma. I have none of the power of Hanuman to tear open my heart, but if any of you feel inclined to do it, I assure you you will find nothing there but love for Rāma whom I see face to face in the starving millions of India.

When he explained what the India of his dreams would be like, he often used the image of Rāma Rājya, where there would be 'rights alike of prince and pauper', 'sovereignty of the people based on pure moral authority', 'rule over self', 'the kingdom of Righteousness on earth'. The last of these phrases is significant, for heaven does not stand for the highest stage of man's ascent in Indian traditions. For righteousness to prevail, for *dharma* to prevail, is the highest we can envisage as a goal of human endeavour as long as man is in the flesh.

Gandhi has written a lot about *dharma* and his conception of it underwent considerable modification as the years went by. In the strict sense there is no word for 'religion' in Indian languages. The word *dharma* serves where in other languages the word religion would be used. It is basically an ethico-religious concept, and if to say this does not seem to throw much light, one can liken it to the Judaic idea of righteousness which is perhaps the nearest one can get to the feel of the idea. Concept-wise 'natural law' has some of its overtones, in the Stoic rather than in the Christian sense. Etymologically, *dharma* is that which holds, a sustaining order which upholds the individual and society and in turn has to be upheld by them. It is a binding factor and to this extent overlaps in meaning with at least one of the many-textured meanings of 'religion'. Indian thought traditionally regards the moral law in the universe as part of *ṛta*, cosmic law, something which mere conceptual clarification (about is and ought) in the contemporary manner will fail to fathom. An analogue which brings us closer to the sense of *dharma* is the Platonic Form of the Good which is both ground and goal of endeavour. The universe, in Hindu thought, is a universe of gods and men environed not by alien but by supportive powers in nature. The idea of a gulf between man and nature, which certain other thought systems focus on, is absent in the Indian tradition. *Dharma* is a concept which evolved over the centuries, ossifying in certain periods, but renewing its dynamism time and time again. *Dharma* is one of the four values or *puruṣārthas*, the others being *ārtha* (wealth), *kāma* (happiness), and *mokṣa* (liberation). As far as we can make out, there was no inhibition about the first two of these in the minds of the ancient Hindus. Statecraft, the acquisition of wealth, the pursuit of happiness, were all activities which were not seen as in principle conflicting with *dharma*. But the Hindu mind, to the extent it is proper to speak of such a thing, tended to veer between the notions of enjoyment and renunciation, and the philosophically inclined began to look on *dharma* as a means to something further, that is, to liberation seen in a metaphysical manner. At its worst, some historians these days may like to suggest, certain classes might have found it convenient to stress the idea of *mokṣa*. But there are other considerations which must be taken into account too if we are to do justice to the idea of *dharma* as a key notion in Indian religious thought.

To stress *dharma* was always to stress the importance of the *stability* of society. Man had before him a model of equilibrium in nature itself, an idea found also in the astronomy of the ancient Greeks.

Dharma stood for an ideal of society which should be non-competitive, each man doing his proper work. The idea, moreover, focusses on duties not on rights. If this sounds out of date to modern ears it must also be noted that the defence of *dharma* involved the righting of injustices, the restoring of the balance which men in their ignorance or out of selfish passions had disturbed. Even to make of *dharma* the route to *mokṣa* was after all to stress the indispensability of social values to the seeker after the metaphysical ultimate. There is an interesting, but perhaps, non vicious circularity built into the idea. Only the *dhārmik* man is able to understand what *dharma* is about. In the pursuit of *dharma* he becomes more *dhārmik*. Even in ordinary parlance it is customary to refer approvingly to so and so as *dhārmik*. This may in any particular case refer to piety in ritual observances, goodness of character, being charitable etc.

In addition to the concept of *dharma* in the singular, *dharmas* in the plural were traditionally *classified* in various ways. Briefly there was *varṇadharma* (the duties relating to the four castes, Brāhmana, Kṣatriya, Vaiśya and Śūdra); *āśramadharma* (duties to do with the four stages of life i.e. *brahmacarya*, garhasthya, vānaprastha and sannyāsa; *naimittikadharmas* (obligatory on special occasions), and finally *guṇadharma* (for example, the duty of a king to protect his subjects). It is perhaps necessary to add a footnote here and point out that caste was a later development, which came about for historical reasons, and which, as a series of reformist thinkers over the centuries have taken pains to emphasise, was a departure from the original ideal of *varṇa* or division of duties according to personal qualities.

One of the main things Gandhi emphasised was that caste had nothing to do with religion. It was a later excrescence on what had originally been basically the principle of division of labour and of duties. What remained was an outstanding feature of the Hindu *social system*, but this should in no way be confused with religion, with *dharma*, with the life it was good and reasonable for men to lead.

The idea of *swadharma*, of doing what it was one's proper business to do, set limits to ambition and enabled a man to develop his potentialities. But it requires discrimination and intelligence to discover what one's *swadharma* is. In his early years in India, after the South Africa experience, Gandhi spoke in favour of following one's hereditary occupation. What was behind it, I believe, was his perception of the undoubted fact that industrialisation would gradually erode the network of traditional occupations that had provided a livelihood for villagers for centuries. Indeed, in advanced industrial societies today, where is the blacksmith, the maker of handmade shoes and all those engaged in the supporting crafts that go along with an agricultural economy? Industrial civilisation would never be able to provide a livelihood for the teeming millions of India, to whom, in Gandhi's own words, God could only appear in the form of work.

Gandhi turned the tables on Swami Vivekananda's formula that all men should be brahmins, by saying that all should become *śūdras*. *Śūdras* are those who *serve*, and what was more needed than service whether in Indian society or elsewhere? There were two practical ways in which Gandhi thought a more egalitarian society could be brought about. The duties of scavenging and bread labour should be part of the *dharma*, the duty, of each and every Indian. He was working out his ideas in a society where dirty work was the lot of the untouchables, the outcastes of Hindu society, and where manual work was considered inferior to the work of the scholar, lawyer and teacher. The concept of bread labour, which he adopted from Bondareff, advocated that each man should engage in some productive activity, such as spinning or agriculture, every day, in addition to the work he ordinarily did. Belief in the therapeutic value of manual work was a belief he shared with his brother in the spirit, Tolstoy. It was a salutary prescription in a culture where all too many associated religion with the man with the begging bowl (allegedly the occasion of merit in those who gave him alms), with conspicuous expenditure on elaborate rituals, or with those who opted out of society through the institution of *sannyāsa* and became in fact parasites on that society.

Ruskin's views on the equal value of different kinds of work to society and the parable of the talents in the New Testament confirmed him in his belief that all hold their talents in trust for the good of society. In this way, as was laid down in the *Gītā*, he linked the *dharma* of the individual with *lokasaṃgraha*, the welfare of all. *Dharma* then, could be appealed to in the cause of transforming society. Gandhi saw it not as something to be preserved as a museum piece but a powerful lever of social change, if only men would see it that way. At the time of the mill workers' struggle against their employers in Ahmedabad in 1918 he said that if the employers had any regard for *dharma* they would think twice about opposing the workers, and that in ancient times a situation where workers were starving had not been looked on as an opportunity for employers to exploit them.

Gandhi's understanding of *dharma* is writ large in his life work. There is a near-Kantian element about his belief that a man must 'inevitably know' how to discriminate between *dharma* and its antithesis.[8] To the ashram sisters who looked to him for guidance he wrote that *dharma* meant selfless service of others, mastery over passions, fearlessness, and most important of all, devotion. But there is clearly a contextual element in *dharma*. It is not a formalistic principle. It is shaped by one's own special gifts, the discipline a man voluntarily undertakes (for without discipline there can be no question of *dharma*), and requires a moral insight which leads a man beyond the performance of his customary duties. This is the Gandhian counterpart of the second mile. In his own personal experience, Gandhi felt himself to be *addressed* by events, so that an active response was called forth from him by things which made others pass by on the other side. In this respect his understanding of *dharma* went far beyond the maxim 'My station and its duties'. Indian folklore is full of cautionary tales about what befalls those who meddle in matters which do not concern them. The monkey who, out of curiosity, tries to remove an axe wedged in a fallen tree is rewarded by getting his tail jammed in the cleft as the axe comes free. The animal who masquerades as what he is not, is eventually exposed and humiliated by the rest of the animal kingdom. There are plenty of tales whose chief moral is to warn the reader or listener to mind his own business. But how is one to gauge what is one's business and what is not? The range of acts of omission is dauntingly large and there is always more we might have done, had we been adventurous or large-hearted enough. Here Gandhi's advice is to look to the needs of our neighbour. This apparently well-worn maxim has special overtones in the Hindu context. My neighbour is not a member of my family (i.e. one to whom I have special obligations) and he may have a different caste or religion from mine. But my *dharma* extends to a response to his need in so far as my limited capacities can satisfy it.

Gandhi himself had two talismen in this connection *ahimsa* and *satya* which he speaks of as 'the royal road of *dharma* that leads both to earthly and spiritual bliss'.[9] The traditional idea of holding fast comes out again in the following:[10]

Thus Dharma is a difficult and complex thing. The faithful may believe that there does exist some power. Call it God, or give it any other name, but recognise It and be firmly set in Its recognition.

Our heart and mind must be fixed upon one thing only – truth and *ahimsa*.

In each generation what *dharma* involves has to be rethought. So in his opinion spinning is *yuga-dharma* (*dharma* for the present era). In conditions of acute poverty *khādi* (handspun cloth) is Annapurna (the Goddess that gives food). He goes so far as to call it the universal *dharma* of all, and the *highest dharma*. Examples of *adharma* (irreligion is about the nearest in meaning one can get to this) include condemning a man to untouchability, and failing to wear *khādi*. But how is one to correlate inner discipline and the new observances which for Gandhi do acquire a near-ritual, and certainly a symbolic character? At a women's meeting in Bengal in May 1925, Mahadev Desai, his secretary, and a man who was one of the closest to him spiritually, records that Gandhi said that the *dharma*s of pity, truth and preservation of high character constituted internal purity, while spinning and wearing *khādi* were the outer.[11] There is an echo from Tulsidas at this point for it was he who said that 'Pity (the word used is *dayā*) is the road of *dharma*'.[12] There are many other interesting overtones from the Indian classics in Gandhi's successive elucid-ations of what *dharma* means today. He writes:[13] 'It is my *dharma* to suppress emotional surges. I would, therefore, always attempt to resist the ripples of the mind.' This recalls Patañjali's aphorism on yoga, that yoga means subsidence of the 'wavelets' of the mind. Gandhi is referring here to disturbing elements in the mind. Otherwise he was a great believer in what he called heart-churning, the stirrings of the heart which are evidence of an awakened conscience and which for him (this is my own way of seeing it) are the inner counterpart of the classic churning of the ocean in which both gods and demons took part. In both cases what resulted was something creative. For to Gandhi our deepest aspirations are in tune with the ground plan of the universe and in our striving there is a mysterious connivance of powers at work in spite of man's inhumanity to man.

As religious thought and religious practice are inextricably connected, it is interesting to see what Gandhi's attitude to temple-going was like. The extent and character of temple-going varies in different parts of India and with various sections and classes of the population. A survey, if one were made, would not provide the kind of evidence of religious affiliation that a survey of church-going would in a western country. Whereas church-going would be regarded as involved in being a practising Christian, temple-going is not a *sine qua non* for being a practising Hindu. But Gandhi's own behavioural patterns in this regard do tell us something further about his relation to mainstream Hinduism (if this question-begging phrase can be allowed) and also his departures from it. As a child, we learn from his *Autobiography*,[14] he often went to the Haveli, the Vaishnava temple, with his mother, who was very devout. But he confesses, 'it never appealed to me. I did not like its glitter and pomp'. He was also taken along to Shiva's and Rāma's temples. In his adult life, both in the ashrams he founded in South Africa and in India, no temples were built. His puritan cast of mind was repelled by the tinsel effect of many Hindu temples and as a lover of quietness he found the noise 'suffocating'. His deep devotion to his mother, however, made him see that what for himself personally was a dispensable adjunct to worship may, for others, be necessary. Romain Rolland, in his Diary, recalls a discussion which took place between Gandhi and Tagore, where Gandhi defended idols, 'believing the masses incapable of raising themselves immediately to abstract ideas'. It was part of the famous discussion in which Tagore protested against the 'symbolic' burning of foreign cloth and the way in which Gandhi looked upon the latter as 'impure'.

When Gandhi visited the temple of Kanya-Kumari, a famous place of pilgrimage in South India, he recognised that the ordinary man 'requires some concrete object to help him on concentration'. Bishop Heber notwithstanding, the Hindu does not worship stocks and stones, but the 'man who makes a stone or gold image, invokes the presence of God into it, gets absorbed in it and thus purifies himself . . .'.[15] In fanaticism, however, Gandhi found a form of idolatry that must be grown out of. Since God appears to us in the form in which we worship, we must allow that he appears in other forms to others also. Idol worship is not a sin, but inability to see any virtue in any other form of worshipping the Deity save one's own, is a form of irreligion or untruth. He puckishly speaks of himself as both an idolator and an iconoclast, valuing 'the spirit behind idol worship'. Did he not, moreover, idolise the masses seeing in them the symbol of the face of God Himself? Inquirers asked him whether, since he was not a temple-goer himself (but claiming, however, no special virtue on that account), was it not inconsistent on his part to spend so much time advocating temple-entry for the Harijans. He was quite clear in his mind that though places of worship 'are but a shadow of the Reality', to 'reject the necessity of temples is to reject the necessity of God, religion and earthly existence'. Harijans, as part of the Hindu community, ill-treated though they had been for centuries by high-caste Hindus, must not be deprived of their heritage. Small wonder that Kasturba, his wife, was once severely taken to task by her husband for visiting a temple where Harijans were not allowed.

Gandhi referred to Yeravda Jail, where he was imprisoned in 1930, as Yeravda Mandir (temple) and gave this as his address when he wrote every week to the ashramites in Sabarmati. This finds sanction, one could say, in the *Bhagavat*, for there it is said that: 'wherever people meet and utter His name from their hearts, there God dwells, there is His temple'.[16] The refrain of one of the bhajans sung at Gandhi's prayer meetings likens 'the mind of a devotee to a temple of worship wherein pure love resided permanently and illumined the heart'.[17] It was almost as if in his spiritual growth Gandhi had outgrown the needs which, especially the unlettered villagers he loved, still had. But this is not to say that he had not found out for himself other symbols, both of observance and inner quest, which took their place and which give us important clues to his religious life.

Acceptance of the concepts of *karma* and rebirth are rightly considered to be essential constituents of the Hindu world-view. The various philosophical schools vary among themselves as to the open-endedness or otherwise of the former and along with this variation, there are important differences in the attendant concept of self/soul/person as the case may be. Gandhi's thinking on these matters, it must be emphasised, does not spring from *intellectual* wrestling with the issues involved. He has, almost unconsciously, been nourished by his own heritage, and the flowering of ideas which results in this particular matter takes a recognisable and familiar shape.

If *karma* could traditionally be sometimes seen as providing a warrant for not interfering in the course of others' lives (cf. say the reactions of some early nineteenth century diehards in Europe who thought the poverty of the poor was their own fault), Gandhi sets the record straight in the following way. The *karma* theory and serving the lowly are perfectly compatible because, 'hereditary traits, whether physical or moral, can be and should be removed and changed'.[18] As was remarked earlier, Gandhi's attitude to those close to him was strongly pedagogical and the natural pedagogue is able both to draw out the qualities inherent in the pupil and encourage possibilities of growth. The doctrine of *karma*, in any case,

Gandhi warned, was not to be appealed to in defence of evils such as untouchability. A further departure from the strict causal line analysis built into the *karma* concept is his assumption of responsibility for acts which the observer would scarcely trace back to his direct agency. His five day fast in penance for the outbreak of violence in February 1922 in Chauri Chaura and his reaction to the Bihar earthquake in 1934 are cases in point.

His comments on reincarnation follow rather more orthodox lines. An early comment, made in May 1918, and recorded by Mahadev Desai, runs as follows:[19]

> I, for one, would not call a man a Hindu, if he does not believe in reincarnation. . . . Don't you see that every moment millions of beings are born and millions die? That itself suggests that there must be reincarnation? . . . He who does not believe in it cannot have any real faith in the regeneration of fallen souls.

The philosopher will find in this two non sequiturs. At least one other alternative (barring the possibility of extinction at death) is that beings proceed from stage to stage without return to the world that we commonly inhabit. It is also conceivable that the 'regeneration of fallen souls' could take place in other realms (other than this world of space and time) where there would be no question of return to this world either in a human or non-human form. But Gandhi's thinking here follows well-worn tracks. In 1926 he puts it this way[20]: 'It is not possible in one birth entirely to undo the results of our past doings . . .'. Conversing with C. F. Andrews he said that human life in this present birth is one of a series. In this present existence a certain discipline has to be gone through, but there were further experiences which would have to be gone through in future births. The matter had exercised his imagination even in his youth and he had written to his Jain mentor, Raychandbhai, asking whether anyone could remember his past lives or have any idea of his future lives. Of the husband and wife relationship he wrote:[21] 'they become friends in a special sense, never to be parted in this life or in the lives to come'.

Gandhi's correspondence with Tolstoy[22] includes an interesting reference to reincarnation. This arose in the context of Tolstoy's famous *A letter to a Hindu* (written in reply to a letter from C. R. Das, who was the editor of *Free Hindustan*) dated 14 December 1908, and in it Tolstoy writes of 'the indubitable, eternal truth inherent in man, which is one and the same in all the great religions of the world'. Gandhi had read this letter with the sense that he had found a kindred spirit in Tolstoy and while he was in London he followed it up with a letter to Tolstoy about the situation in the Transvaal. The letter is dated 1 October 1909, and in it he asked Tolstoy to 'please remove the word "reincarnation" from the other things you have dissuaded your reader from', on the grounds that it is a cherished belief of millions, and it 'explains reasonably the many mysteries of life', and had been a solace to the passive resisters in the jails of the Transvaal. Tolstoy's reply, dated 7 October 1909, runs like this:

> as it appears to me, the belief in a re-birth will never be able to strike such deep roots in and restrain mankind as the belief in the immortality of the soul and the faith in divine truth and love.

There was deep agreement between both great men on 'the infinite possibilities of universal love', in Gandhi's own words. But Gandhi, following the Jain tradition, saw this not as confined to mankind but embracing all living beings. Tolstoy's mention of the extent to which a belief in re-birth may or may not 'restrain mankind', brings in a new consideration, and here one can but feel one's way. The notion of re-birth could, if uncharitably interpreted, be made an excuse for injustices committed in the present birth, on the ground that matters should be evened out in lives to come. The stress, for Tolstoy, was on the law of love. Writing to Gandhi on 7 September 1910, he pleas for:

> the discipline of love undeformed by false interpretation. Love is the aspiration for communion and solidarity with other souls, and that aspiration always liberates the source of noble activities.

There is none the less an intriguing contrapuntal relation between the two themes, what might provide 'solace' to some and what would be a restraining influence for all. The prospect of successive births had been traditionally regarded as a daunting one, and *moksa* was seen in terms of liberation from the cycle of births and deaths. As human existence inevitably involves some suffering (the philosophers had stressed the suffering aspect and the artists the blissful aspect) and traditionally suffering was regarded as something all men would naturally like to be rid of, it would seem to follow logically that the prospect of further births was weighted more in the direction of an increase in suffering rather than otherwise. One of the prayers[23] included in the *Ashram Bhajanāvalī* throws some light on Gandhi's thinking on these matters. It includes the following lines: 'I desire neither earthly kingdom nor paradise, no, not even release from birth and death. I desire only the release of afflicted life from misery.' The prayer no doubt seems to have Buddhist overtones. The goal of the devotee is seen as the relief of suffering humanity, not as personal release from bondage. The mood expressed is much closer to the *Bodhisattva* than to the *arhat* idea. Moreover Gandhi said, on more than one occasion, that he would like to be reborn as an untouchable so as to be completely identified with them and serve them. Such an expression of a *desire* for rebirth is quite innovative as far as Hindu tradition goes.

Gandhi is one of those men for whom death presented no fears. C. F. Andrews recorded[24] his giving of 'intellectual assent to the proposition that death is only a big change in life and nothing more and should be welcomed as such whenever it arrives'. In a letter to Tagore's one time secretary, Amiya Chakravarty, he wrote[25]: 'When the isolated drops melt, they share the majesty of the ocean to which they belong. In isolation they die but to meet the ocean again.' Putting these various perspectives together the picture we get is that of a man who thought of action not as a way of undoing past *karma*s, of accumulating merit (according to only the simplest balance and account version of the karma concept) which would serve him well in a future life, but as a matter of pressing concern in *this* life, a life in which our main duty was to alleviate the miseries of others so that they could fulfil their own destiny.

When Gandhi tried to explain to inquirers what the essence of the Hindu tradition was, it was to the hymns of the mediaeval saints that he appealed most often. For example, addressing missionaries in Calcutta on 18 August 1925 he quoted a line from Surdas, the blind mediaeval saint-bard, saying that 'the essence of our religious books can be boiled down into the simple adage: 'Nirbala ka bala Rām, (God is the strength of the helpless and weak)'. No doubt Gandhi had a strange gift for choosing language which his audience would immediately grasp. His favourite hymn was Narsinh Mehta's 'The True Vaishnava' which begins: 'He is a real Vaishnava, who feels the suffering of others as his own suffering.' His frequent references to the writings of the saints fits in with his conviction that 'religious subjects must be viewed and discussed from the light that our heart throws on them, not our intellect'.[26] The folk tradition often challenged scriptural authority and the priests, and proclaimed that templegoing was not the heart of religion. Gandhi seems to have regarded the hymn or bhajan as a means of remaining 'constantly attuned with truth'. In the same year that he used this expression he said,[27] in one of his prayer discourses, that: ' . . . in various ways that please the mind, different hymns speak of only one thing – the vision of God – in order to make our centrifugal mind pin-pointed in Him'. A similar idea, that of the role of the bhajan in focussing the mind on God, is contained in another image: 'These hymns are like an army that stops the mind from going out to eat grass (food of an army) and makes it drink only nectar (the drink of gods).'[28] These three images together do not pull in different directions. To one who plays a musical instrument, especially a stringed instrument, (and Gandhi often refers to the strings of the heart), tuning is essential if one is to keep in pitch, clarity of vision, not wandering away – all contain the idea of concentration about a central point. The nectar image brings in a further note – that of bliss. To drink nectar is to share what is familiar to the Gods. But the bhajan singer is still an *abhyāsi*, an imperfect being, training in yoga. A suggestive conflation of the mythical and the philosophical speaks of 'Thy Word' (as revealed in the bhajan written by a poet-saint) protecting the devotee from the demon of fog (which is ignorance). Another hymn prays for the removal of the veil which obscures the soul. Gandhi follows the same tradition. We would not be justified, I think, in *contrasting* this with the idea of the singing of hymns as a part of *worship*. The two need not be polarised or felt to be distinct. We shall return to this theme again when we consider Gandhi's response to Christianity.

Gandhi's respect for popular religion makes him rather different from some of the reformers of the Indian Renaissance, such as Raja Rammohan Roy, who saw religion in more intellectual a manner than Gandhi did. But wherever popular religion was on the wrong track in his opinion, Gandhi did not hesitate to speak out boldly. On the occasion of the Calcutta session of the Congress in 1901 he visited the Kali temple and was repelled by the sight of goats being slaughtered, saying that he considered this to be 'positive irreligion', and that he did 'not consider it to be a part of Hinduism'. On a visit to Hrishikesh he discussed the significance of the sacred thread and the *shikhā* (tuft of hair which orthodox brahmins have) and said that the right to wear the sacred thread could only come after Hinduism had purged itself of untouchability. If symbols were made into fetishes, then they were fit only to be discarded. He had himself got rid of the *shikhā* on the eve of going to England, but when he later realised that 'cowardice had been the reason for discarding it' he let it grow again. The legendary accounts of creation given in *Manusmṛti* did not impress him, nor did he think much of the habit of 'frequenting places of pilgrimage in search of piety'. The *Bhagavata Purāṇa*, which inspires a great deal of popular religion, was not something he came to in his early study of religious literature but much later.

At the back of this discussion lies the critical issue of the place of reason in religious thinking. There are two misrepresentations which can easily trap the unwary. One is that Gandhi was an anti-intellectual. This point is often made by Marxist critics who like to fit facts into an avowedly intellectual model, that of a dialectical process. Gandhi's respect for facts does not make him thereby an anti-intellectual. Another misrepresentation (it is sometimes combined with the former one) is that Gandhi's thinking is full of inconsistencies and that this is typical of Hindu thinking as such, so it is no great surprise that a modern Hindu, even a reformist one like Gandhi, should seem to be contradicting himself at every turn. My own approach goes something like this. Searching for the '*logic* of religious language' may be an interesting intellectual exercise, but it can be a very unreliable guide to the structures of religious experience. Our present treasure hunt is focussed on Gandhi's religious thought, and religious thought in India, especially in the Hindu tradition and those traditions which developed out of it, has always had a strongly intuitive strain. But this is by no means to say that not much is thought of the intellect in the Hindu tradition. A great deal of intellectual skill went in defence of positions held not so much on the basis of instinct as on the basis of the verdict of the experiences had by a succession of religious men who came for the most part from very lowly walks of life. It is on this part of the Hindu tradition that Gandhi largely drew.

This, however, did not prevent him from having a sensitive ear for the demands of reason. He spoke of 'the acid test of reason', and added that:[29]

> Error, no matter however immemorial it may be, cannot derive sanctity, and even a Vedic text if it is inconsistent with morality, with injustice, will have to go by the board.

His conception of error is idiosyncratic, as will be seen later in discussing truth. Error, for Gandhi, ranges from all the matters classifiable under *adharma* or irreligion, to what is perhaps the crowning error for him, that is, regarding Infinite Spirit as the same as the body of flesh and blood. That the test of reason is equivalent to the test of conscience for Gandhi is suggested by his own contribution to the volume of tributes edited by Radhakrishnan in which he wrote that he declined to be bound by any interpretation, however learned it may be, if it were repugnant to reason or moral sense.[30] Gandhi felt himself to be *addressed* by events and he responded in tune with the dictates of an inner voice; but it was a voice fully informed by his rational assessment of the situation. Or, using another metaphor, reason was for him a finely honed instrument purified in the course of vigorous discipline. When it led him to act, his actions were there for all to see and he welcomed any criticism which would open his eyes to any departure from truth on his part. Gandhi was singularly free from doubts and scepticism, the usual accompaniments of a rational outlook. This stemmed I think from two major sources, his faith in God and his faith in the infinite potentialities that dwell in man, especially man in association with his fellows. Likewise his recognition of the need for the secular (for example, for a just distribution of *artha*, wealth) did not make him deaf to the call of the holy. Such a man can neither be dubbed an anti-intellectual, nor a defender of inconsistencies.

It is very pertinent in this connection to look at some examples of the way in which he restated some old myths and doctrines in the light of the challenges of the twentieth century and India's needs during his own lifetime. In the famous *The Great Sentinel* article in 1921 he refers to India's poverty thus: 'The circulation about her feet and legs has almost stopped'.[31] How can the 'health' of Indian improve if the lower castes are in an impoverished condition? In a prayer discourse of Vishnu five years later (Vishnu, in the familiar iconography carries a conch, mace, disc and lotus) he said:[32]

> The symbol of the lotus suggests how soft the Lord is towards His devotees. But there is the mace for those who are not His devotees and have their faces turned away from Him. It seems as if the Government has partly imitated this in Lahore. In Lord Lawrence's status there is a pen in one hand and a sword in the other.

At one go we have a picture of Gandhi the man who had at his finger tips and in his heart the idiom of the masses, the educator, the man who makes no distinction between religion and politics, and above all we have a delightful thumbnail sketch of Gandhi the humourist. He made constant references to the penances of legendary kings, saints and rishis whose penances brought about results, not only the result of inner purification, but visible benefits in the form of *lokasaṁgraha*, the welfare of all. The identification of Rāmarājya and Swaraj (which stands for self-rule both at the individual and national level) has many rich connotations which cannot be gone into here. But it may be worth noting that, according to Valmiki, Rāma Rājya was not conceived of in wholly rural terms. Ayodhya was hardly a village. The India of Gandhi's dreams would have contained villages in a transformed sense, not the dung-heaps that they were in his own time.

His knowledge of Hindu traditions also shows itself in his reference to philosophical matters:[33]

> You Hindus, are believers in *abheda* (absence of essential difference between one creature and another). How can you regard a human being an untouchable? Are you not ashamed of this ostracism?

He was bold enough to hit out at high caste members of his audiences, who sometimes hid behind an alleged scriptural warrant to justify inhuman practices, warning them that 'Even about our Shastras (scriptures) we should have *neerksheer viveka*[34]. The idea of *seva* or service, traditionally applied in many contexts – service to the land, cattle, family (especially elders) clans, gurus, gods – is restated by Gandhi with a focus on serving the untouchables, the lowliest of the low.[35] There is an echo here, no doubt, of Swami Vivekananda's concept of Daridranārāyan, or 'My God the Poor'. The whole idea of *prasād*, moreover, it seems to me, takes a new turn in Gandhi's religious thinking. *Prasād* is the material form of the 'grace' of a deity or a holy man. But is it necessary to go to a temple to receive *prasād*? Food is blessed when it is shared. No ceremony, whether in temple or church, can endow food with a quality it does not already possess, *provided*, and this is the major proviso, we share it with the hungry.

I have devoted the major part of this chapter to the Hindu tradition, and that too, largely to matters not usually deemed to be

particularly philosophical. I have done so deliberately. Gandhi was
never guilty of academic verbiage. He was a man of the people, not a
professional philosopher. It would be a mockery if we were to induce
any kind of philosophical system or theology from what he said and
did, even more so, in the fashionable analytic manner, to pick away
at the alleged 'logic' or otherwise of his 'religious language'. The
man and his thinking are all of a piece. He was canny enough to steer
completely clear of the artificial distinctions philosophers make
between one concept and another, and still more, the distinctions
made between the rational and allegedly irrational parts of the
human psyche.[36] We have to see the man as he is.

I have so far stressed Gandhi's 'Hinduness', and we shall return to
this. But it is also very necessary to be aware of the Jain elements in
his mental make-up. These were pronounced enough for even Bal
Gangadhar Tilak to have taken it for granted at one time that
Gandhi was a Jain rather than a Hindu. Only the limitations
imposed by the size this book has to conform to constrain me to
mention very briefly and sketchily what these elements were. Jain
influences in the Gujarat of Gandhi's time were very strong indeed.
Raychandbhai, the saintly Jain jeweller, was the nearest to a guru
that Gandhi ever had. He dealt patiently with a long series of
questions posed to him by Gandhi while he was in South Africa. The
questions reflect Gandhi's search for enlightenment on a variety of
themes including the soul, God, *moksa*, whether any particular
religion can be said to be 'best', and the incarnation idea. The help
he received on these thorny matters led Gandhi to say that
Raychandbhai 'had reached the very outskirts of the land of mukti'.
An interesting comment is attached to this, that Raychandbhai was
in reality neither a Jain nor a Vaishnava. 'He was one who had gone
beyond all such limitations and had succeeded in completely
identifying himself with every living creature. . . . He was free from
contradiction between speech and behaviour.'[37] To go beyond the
labels which mark off one religious tradition from another is not to
see everything as one in any simplistic metaphysical manner but to
be able to identify oneself with all that lives. To do this converges
with the Vaishnava injunction to share in others' woes. The
contraditions that are to be worried about are not about the relation
between one statement and another, but between profession and
practice.

Gandhi found the Jain theory of *anekāntavāda*, the many-sidedness of reality, very appealing, and derived from it one of his most foundational beliefs, that of the fragmentariness of our understanding of truth. It provides the metaphysical basis both of his conception of ahimsa and of democracy, including that of a democracy of religions. If all we have is but a fragmentary view, we have no right to impose our fragment on others. Each view has its own validity, and to say this should not be confused with what philosophers dub 'relativism'. From Jainism he derives also the notion of a 'discipline of spiritual self-perfection', which, inter alia, involves vows and fasts. The Jains believe that every soul has a vast reservoir of energy which is increased and released in those who follow the path of discipline laid down by Mahavir. Jainism has a pluralistic metaphysic and takes to an extreme position the line of thinking expressed in Albert Schweitzer's well known phrase 'reverence for life'. One can extract an ecological message out of this, and yet at the same time an attitude to insects that would veto any attempt at modern methods of agriculture and pest control. So, not surprisingly, the Jains turned to business rather than agriculture. 'Nāstik' (unorthodox) though Jainism be, Gandhi was right in seeing it as an outgrowth of Hindu tradition. There is the same kind of this-worldly/other-worldly mix. But whereas Jain asceticism was directed to the goal of spiritual perfection for the *individual*, Gandhi's view was somewhat different, and he found non-Jain reasons for his asceticism. In a country (or world) where others are poor, one should live as they do. Frugality and temperance are healthy, i.e. they work. Devotion to a great cause requires careful use of time and energy. He must set an example to those who set store by externals (e.g. he must dress and eat simply). His conception of ahimsa, moreover, was more positive and less extreme than the Jain version. As we 'breathe or blink or till the land' we can't help killing a number of living beings. Jain ethics sees the ideal state as that of *samyaktva*, abstaining from causing suffering to others and answering evil by good or love. Gandhi thinks of purification not merely in terms of releasing the soul from karmic defilement but of making oneself a fitter instrument for serving one's fellowmen. The Jain has the goal of *kevalajñāna* (perfect knowledge) before him. But Gandhi does not see the goal in terms of personal attainment but in terms of the liberation of all.

He seems to have acquired a near-Pauline attitude towards the flesh from the Jains. He also was confirmed in his enjoyment of silence by his knowledge of Jain practices (a _muni_ is a man observing silence). But he frankly states that his version of _syādvāda_ is not that of the learned, but peculiarly his own:[38]

> It is this doctrine that has taught me to judge a Mussalman from his own standpoint and a Christian from his. . . . I am gifted with the eye to see myself as others see me and _vice versa_.

Moreover an access of spiritual power comes about not only through personal ascesis but through _collective action_; the non-violent strength of the many. So all in all, Tagore was right in feeling that Gandhi's asceticism was not to be compared to that of 'spiritual athletes' a term which could not unjustly be applied to Jain monks, but was something peculiarly his own.

While Gandhi was in London as a young student of law he read Edwin Arnold's _The Light of Asia_ and found in the spirit of renunciation and compassion of the Buddha, the advocacy of curbing of needs and rejection of animal sacrifice, things which found an answering echo in his own heart. As was his custom, he understood religious teachings from various sources according to his own light. In the conception of _nirvāṇa_ he saw another way of recognising 'the need to extinguish the base in us', to reduce oneself to zero. The Mahayana 'all or none' principle chimed in with his own conviction that if all living creatures are bound together in one great chain of existence the liberation of each is tied up with the liberation of all. In both Buddha and Christ he found exemplars of an active spirituality that avoids 'idle meditation'[39] and showed the dynamism of gentleness and love.

As far as the various traditions and religious literatures of Indian origin are concerned perhaps in no other case was his own light _as_ unorthodox and new as in his understanding of the _Bhagavad Gītā_. Rather surprisingly Gandhi did not familiarise himself with this most loved scriptural text in the Hindu tradition until he read Sir Edwin Arnold's _The Song Celestial_ during his student days in London. It became his favourite devotional literature for a lifetime and he gradually worked out an interpretation of it that was so unusual that his associates suggested he make his own translation of the text. This translation, he said, was not designed primarily for scholars but for women, business men, _śūdras_ and others who have little or no literary equipment. In other words, it was a translation for everyman. The Gujarati text was published on 12 March 1930, a very significant date, the day on which he marched to Dandi from Sabarmati. Gandhi was particularly fond of the first verse of the *Īśopaniṣad* which tells of the all-pervading nature of God, creator and master of the universe, which preaches renunciation, and promises that God will supply all the devotee's needs. In 1946 Gandhi learnt that this verse had been an inspiration and turning point in the life of Maharshi Devendranath (Tagore's father). In any case he always felt that the *Gītā* provided a commentary on this verse. That Gandhi ascribes to the *Gītā* 'a totally new meaning from that ordinarily given'[40] is fully recognised by himself. He does not claim for his new interpretation, to which he gives the name *anasakti yoga*, the innovativeness of new theologising (i.e. an attempt to construct a new framework), but that it is the result of 'prayerful study and experience'.[41]

Now the reader who approaches the *Gītā* in a more philosophical manner, but still with the attitude of the seeker, an attitude always advised by Gandhi, finds certain problems arising in his or her mind, and I only have the space, and the competence, to pinpoint a few. Is the performance of specific duties sufficient to promote *lokasaṃgraha*, the welfare of all, and is it in fact damaging to the fabric of society if a man undertakes another's duties (see III. 35)? Is love for all creatures, compassion for the distressed and forgiveness of the guilty (v. 25; XVI. 2–4), compatible with detachment? Can there be such a thing as a righteous war? How is *niṣkāmkarma* related to devotion to the Lord? If either is made a means to the other we seem to be landed with a means/end tangle. In any case something more dynamic than *sthitaprajña* seems to be called for, and freedom from egoity seems too negative an idea to provide a leverage of concern for *lokasaṃgraha* and the warmth of heart that the devotee presumably needs.

There are a series of reformist thinkers who have highlighted the activist strain in the *Gītā*, a strain which the text certainly contains. It has also generally been agreed that the *Gītā* carries forward Hindu thinking on religion in important ways, for example, seeing liberation in an integrated way so as to enlist knowledge, devotion and action, pointing out that devotion succeeds awe and submission and that *sakāma-karma* is preferable to inertness or indifference.

The new things claimed by Gandhi are these: that the *Mahābhārata* and *Gītā* are allegorical; that the *Gītā* teaches ahimsa (for renunciation is impossible without observance of ahimsa) and so the attitude of *anasakti* (the spirit of renunciation or selflessness) is the basis of *karma* (duty; action). The *avatar* idea indicates man's wish to become like God rather than indicates God's descent to man. It is possible for every human being to become perfect, as God is, and it is necessary for us to aspire towards it. As for the 'gospel' element in the *Gītā* it is this:[42] 'The *Gita* contains the gospel of work, the gospel of *Bhakti* or devotion, the gospel of *Jñāna* or knowledge. Life should be a harmonious whole of these three.' But the key to all of these is 'the doctrine of *anaśakti*' (selflessness).

Now it is clear that if all action involves attachment and, what is more, 'drags from birth to death and death to birth the soul', the action that leads to liberation will have to be of a special kind, otherwise it will only lead to further bondage. Gandhi understands very well the bondage of action and that we cannot fully control the consequences of our acts. So he is, it would seem, in favour of a *Gesinnungsethik*. His own personal insight tells him that the message of renunciation that the *Gītā* contains indicates 'perfect observance of *ahimsa* in every shape and form'. He goes so far as to say that ahimsa is a much earlier doctrine and that the *Gītā* takes it for granted. Gandhi's own experience finds an echo in the fact that there is no 'line of demarcation between salvation and worldly pursuits' in the *Gītā*. For Gandhi, salvation is as much to do with politics and economics and the health of society as it is to do with the health of the soul. Gandhi reads his own meaning into the connotation of sacrifice as service (See *Gītā*, III). For him sacrifice means bread labour, which we came across earlier. To be detached from the fruits of action is not to abandon them. Simply *because* the contemplated action may go awry and unintended consequences follow, we need to be constantly on the alert. His conduct of successive satyagraha campaigns gives ample illustration of this.

In human life the quest of perfection is an endless process. Not only Gandhi but everyone else would agree. The discussion of what perfection involves (going beyond the three guṇas and reaching the state of a *guṇatīla*) leads him to a curious line of reasoning to the effect that for us Krishna is not an exemplar:[43]

> If we believe Krishna to be God, we must impute to him omniscience and omnipotence. Such an one can surely destroy. But we are puny mortals ever erring and ever revising our views and opinions. We may not, without coming to grief, ape Krishna, the inspirer of the *Gītā*.

This is a point to be remembered later when we look at Gandhi's theological differences with Christians for whom Christ *is* an exemplar.

The elucidation of the internalisation of the battle between good and evil which goes on in the human heart, a non-violent battle, 'non-cooperation between the forces of darkness and those of light', and which Gandhi sees allegorically portrayed in the battle-field of Kurukshetra, calls for some mention of how good and evil are seen in the Hindu tradition. It is not evil, but suffering, which poses a metaphysical problem in Hindu philosophy. Since man is an imperfect being he bears within himself the seeds of weakness as well as of greatness. Gandhi uses several terms for evil – what is *adharma*, the Satanic, and sometimes the work *nāpāk* or unholy. Then there are tricky passages like the following:[44]

> If anyone has been able to overcome Satan it is God. It is He who created Satan and He who can overcome him. Satan cannot be defeated by human power. It is God alone who brings about his defeat, through a person who follows God's dictates like a bonded slave.

Rethought, this is not as startling as it at first sight appears. Satan is not a mythical being but a name for some of the powers which dwell within man himself. An evil like untouchability can only be overcome through human effort, by spiritual heroes (satyagrahis) who follow God's commands and are thus strengthened by his grace. He used a delightful homely analogy which was fully intelligible to his listeners in Chhinwada on 1 January 1921: 'Satan always creeps into us through the holes of our own weaknesses. It is our business to fill up these holes'. The traditional Indian house has at least one hole in each ground floor room to facilitate washing of the floor. These have to be stopped up in seasons when snakes are around. At one go Gandhi cleverly combines the language of the book of Genesis and common Indian experience. But C. F. Andrews records that Gandhi fails to find any rational *explanation* of why evil should exist at all, speaking rather appealingly of God as 'long-suffering and patient precisely because he permits evil in the world'. Wrestling with evil, that is both the evil systems man has created such as exploitative economies and iniquitous social practices, and the traditional enemies within the gate such as anger, lust etc., brings a man closer to God.

In his own conduct of public affairs Gandhi was particularly sensitive to the polarity of creation and destruction. Lord Krishna is[45] 'the Lord of the Universe, the creator, preserver and destroyer of us all. He may destroy because he creates'. We cannot compare ourselves with the Lord, because man is but a *saṁsārin*, destined to many births. Moreover, God's destructive power (cf. the capacity mythically personified in Shiva) is matched by his creative agency. Man only too often is sheerly destructive. For this reason even non-cooperation, most surely a non-violent strategy, needed to be matched by something *positive*, Gandhi called it constructive work (it involved causes like Hindu-Muslim unity, working with the untouchables, and various programmes of rural uplift), so that man's creative energies could have full play and be embodied in new social structures that could serve as a model for the future.

Gandhi's interpretation of the *Gītā* is certainly characteristically his own and it can be seen in contrast to those of earlier commentators. Śaṁkara saw the *Gītā* as a work on the spiritual attainment of the *sannyāsī*. Rāmānuja and Vallabha found in it the glorification of *bhakti* and *saguṇa upāsanā*. Tilak stressed *karma-yoga* and Aurobindo the cultivation of divine consciousness (whatever this might mean). What is no less interesting is the way in which he drew on it in his public discourses, especially on caste duties, and in contexts which one would normally take as falling outside 'religious thought'. Kālidāsa had defined a *kṣatriya* as 'one who saves others from wounds, not one who inflicts them'. To citizens at Sojitra, Gandhi said, regarding their ill treatment of Harijans:[46] 'If you regard yourselves as *kṣatriyas*, you cannot belabour them, cannot follow the diabolical practice of exacting too much work for too little payment.' He also reminded others of the *kṣatriya* virtues of *apalāyan* (not fleeing from the battlefield), protection of women and the poor, and observance of a pledge once taken. And to an audience in Maharashtra his teaching of *abhedbuddhi* (a sense of no distinction between oneself and others) takes form in an appeal that they should feel the indignities of Jallianwalabagh (the shooting of Indian civilians by the British army at Amritsar in 1919) as their own. Gandhi extracted out of the *Gītā* not only the message of non-violence (which for him was an implicate of the whole concept of renunciation when thought through) but an ethos of *work*. The ideal man that is projected in this new interpretation is a yogi in a very different sense from the traditional one. He is a man whose battles with selfhood result in practical benefit to all, especially those outside the four *varnas*, who are also our kith and kin; whose imperturbability is no bar to his deep involvement in the pressing issues of the day. *Jñāna* is to be used to understand *situations* and gain insight into possibilities for action; *bhakti* speaks of the law of love which enables us to respond to those in need; *karma* is the path not just of action but of *service*, of constructive work, not for the maintenance of the stability of society as it is, with all its injustices, but in order to *transform* it in accordance with the vision of a new society, call it the Kingdom of Heaven on earth or Rāma Rājya if you will. None of this is possible, Gandhi thought, without both human effort and divine grace.

Gandhi's answers to the questions posed earlier run something like this. The performance of specific duties is not enough; however it is a starting point. But each is called upon to have the questing spirit of the *brahmin* (typified in love of learning), the courage of the *kṣatriya*, the ability to husband resources carefully (Gandhi so often referred laughingly to the virtues of the banias, the caste to which he himself belonged) and the life of service which was traditionally expected of the *śūdras* but which should now be embraced by all. With the duties of scavenging and bread labour seen as incumbent on every man a new outlook could develop and the barriers between castes disappear. The idea of each following his *swadharma* (his inner destiny) was a good idea, Gandhi thought, in so far as it recognised the need for each man to make a voyage of self-discovery and pursue his chosen path. All economic barriers which obstructed such a voyage and all inner constraints which shackled man's spirit must be tackled boldly. Only in this sense can there be a righteous war. And, for Gandhi, it will be a non-violent one, but revolutionary nonetheless, as it will bring about at the same time a revolution in men's own hearts and in society as a whole. The whole idea of *anaśakti yoga* suggests a non-Freudian, non-violent reservoir of power which can be channelised for the good of all. *Lokasaṁgraha* cannot come about if the poorest of the poor are exploited, or, to extend the idea to today, if there is poverty and misery anywhere in the world.

The detachment that is required is none other than the spirit of self-renunciation which enables one to leave self-interest out of account. It does not mean that we should not follow up our actions carefully or shirk the responsibility for the consequences of our acts. Love of all creatures is itself service of the Lord, for selflessness is the mark of the devotee. What moves contemporary man to alleviate the condition of his fellows is not the mere sense of duty, but the warmth of heart which is itself an expression of man's devotion to God. The 'and' in the pregnant phrase 'Love God, and thy neighbour as thyself' in another tradition, disappears. To love one's neighbour *is* to love God. Such a man is steadfast as a rock, he is a *sthitaprajña*. His faith will not be shaken by adverse events. The message of the *Gītā* is not the call to become God, but to become *godlike*. To see at the heart of the *Gītā* the message of ahimsa startled Gandhi's contemporaries much in the same sort of way that some people in the west have been startled by talk of the 'myth of the incarnation'. The cases are of course not quite parallel, as the discussion of the latter has been closely tied up with historical considerations and a whole tradition of critical scholarship which has no precise counterpart in the history of Hinduism. But the great scriptures of the world are hospitable in the sense that each generation finds new meanings, discards some, and challenges men to new avenues of service. Gandhi is certainly a man who rethought his tradition in the light of his own experience. His venture witnesses not only to scholarship but to a remarkable ability to combine rootedness with openness of heart.

3 The Impact of Christianity on Gandhi

It has already been noted that Gandhi's first impressions of Christianity were shaped by the aggressive evangelical style of missionaries of a bygone era in his home town. Several decades were to pass before this style was replaced by something more kindly, less arrogantly self-righteous. During his student days in London, Gandhi studied the New Testament and met a number of fine people among Quakers and others and began to make a distinction in his mind between Christianity, Christians and Christ. The impact of the Sermon on the Mount on his mind was to remain with him all his life. The extent to which Hindus and Muslims of Gandhi's generation associated Christianity with the imperial connection and an alien pattern of life (including food and dress) in pre-Independence days needs to be appreciated by the sympathetic reader today. First impressions take some getting over. In London, Gandhi was exposed to many influences which left their mark on him in later life, vegetarianism, free-thinking (the two were often conjoined), and a homespun brand of genuine piety which was less aggressive than what he had previously encountered simply because it was on home ground and dissociated from the flag. The friends he made in London were fired with a moral earnestness which he could understand and appreciate. About the same time, he encountered the teaching of Lord Buddha and found much in common between the spirit of renunciation and compassion expressed in the lives of both Lord Buddha and Christ. His questing spirit was awakened on religious matters and, student as he was, new ideas fell on fertile ground. He was not greatly troubled by theological problems at this stage in his career.

His experience in South Africa brought him into close touch with, once more, the evangelical brands of Christianity and there were plenty of friends to take him along to prayer meetings, and, from the best of motives no doubt, try to 'save' his soul. His correspondence from South Africa with Raychandbhai, his Jain mentor, includes questions about the nature of God which are rather strange questions to put to a Jain. The questions seem to reflect thinking on some of the matters he would have heard his friends speak about at their services and prayer meetings. While he could respect their sincerity of belief and was a close friend of men like the Rev. Joseph Doke who showed him great personal kindness, he was put off by dogmatic theological stances and confirmed in his earlier conviction that each man must work out his own salvation in the tradition in which he was rooted. Hinduism is non-credal in character and Gandhi failed to see why a man's salvation should depend on 'accepting Christ as one's "personal Saviour",' formal 'communicant' membership of a Christian church and so forth. His mind and heart could not be contained in any kind of formal straight-jacket, and as has been noticed, his attitude to his own tradition also bears the stamp of a man whose dwelling place has all its windows and doors open. In a tropical climate, to press the metaphor, in a multi-religious society, this makes good sense. Gandhi had not been a member of a family where men of many faiths were frequent visitors, for nothing.

It may be useful now to see what Gandhi's theological difficulties were, for some of these are not unlike the difficulties which many who live in the west have today. These stumbling blocks did not arise in his mind all at once, but over a period of time, and there is evidence of them in conversations recorded by others and in printed statements. To take them all together will give us a picture of a man who has reflected in depth on religious matters and adopts a very definitely rational approach in spite of being alive to the fact that religious stances in the last analysis depend on faith. I shall present the difficulties in the form in which they appeared to Gandhi and, as it were, from his point of view.

Christians (the evangelical ones he came across) speak of 'being saved' as if this is a once for all event, as if it were something highly personal. Now liberation for the Hindu is not from sin, but from the cycle of births and deaths. Gandhi's position was not identical with the orthodox one, but it was certainly a matter of continual *striving*, not a 'crisis' experience of a Kierkegaardian kind, still less an emotional conversion at the penitential bench. Just as the Christian awareness of the sinfulness of man goes beyond an insight into the contingency of reason, Gandhi's understanding of human imperfection goes beyond an insight into the extent of human ignorance. For him it is the Buddhist and Jain list of human weaknesses, hatred, anger, cowardice and the rest that are to be brought under control by the twin agencies of inner disicipline and Divine grace. Moreover, for Gandhi as for the Mahayana Buddhist, there can be no individual liberation without liberation for all. Gandhi's own personal religious style seems to have been devoid of the kind of ecstasies experienced by some of his friends, and who thought he was missing a great deal by not having such experiences. He was also 'put off' by the haranguing style of non-conformist sermonising (in which the call to 'being saved' was the focus) since for him religion was not a matter of talking but of doing. The petitionary type of prayer, moreover, which predominated in Christian services, was not something which was echoed in his own experience. Petitionary prayer for Gandhi was, if one could put it in this way, in the language of a different tradition, at the lowest rung of spiritual ascent.

Next comes the problem about the Divine sonship of Jesus Christ. The notion of *avatār* in Hinduism is not the same as the concept of the incarnation in Christianity. There can be any number of *avatār*s, for God reveals Himself in many ways according to man's needs, and especially in times of crisis on a world-scale, when He may appear as Lord to his devotees. (That I am not sure if I should use the upper case 'H' here is perhaps significant). In addition to going along with this ingrained Hindu acceptance of the plurality of revelations, Gandhi also held the Jain position that any particular view of the truth we may have is necessarily partial and incomplete. It is *false* only if taken to be exclusively true. Added to this, in connection with Gandhi's own interpretation of the *Gītā*, we have already noticed Gandhi's personal opinion that the *avatār* idea witnesses to the *human* desire to be godlike. With such a background a man is not in a position to accept any extraordinary uniqueness about the person of Christ. The Indian tradition (which includes the Jain and the Buddhist) accommodates a plurality of great souls, just as it has room for a plurality of holy men.

The idea of the vicarious suffering of a single being who atones for the sins of all, including those born before his time and those of generations to come, does not make sense on the Hindu view. If we are on separate karmic tracks, so to say, no man can relieve another of the burden of his own particular karmic defilements. This is a strict view, belonging to the Jain stream of thought rather than, say, to the Vaishnava. The task of penance is an endless one. No other man can undertake on my behalf the working out of my own path of self-purification. When Gandhi undertakes a penitential fast, he does so not to atone vicariously for what others have done but because he believes there has been some *failing in himself* which has brought about an untoward event (e.g. a breach of ashram discipline, an outbreak of violence, a communal disturbance). If we are all sons of God, no special case can be made out for a particular man being a son in some supervenient sense. The Hindu sees the barrier to a liberated life not in sin, (which he conceives in a particularistic manner rather than as a generalised condition to which all men are heir) but in *bondage*, a bondage from which men can gain release through a large variety of ways including *japa* (repetition of the divine name), pilgrimages, the singing of bhajans, vows, ritual practices, fasts, discriminatory knowledge (being able to distinguish the Self from the empirical self) and so forth. According to some schools of thought divine grace is essential in all this. But in any case the idea that salvation can be brought about at one go through confession of belief in a personal saviour strikes an alien note.

A comment on the connotation of sonship and other associated concepts may be pertinent at this stage. Although there are references to a primal progenitor in the Hindu scriptures, e.g. in the *Gītā*, the concept of the Fatherhood of God cannot be said to be by any means a central one in Hinduism. Sonship, of course, could be derived, logically, from the concept of a mother goddess, a concept which is present in folk traditions in several parts of the country. In fact, however, this derivation has not been made. When Gandhi speaks, as he often does, of all men as brothers, the implication which comes naturally in Judaeo–Semitic traditions that God is the divine Father cannot be taken as read. The image of brotherhood itself is not free of overtones if one thinks of Cain and Abel. We need to look elsewhere for the source of the brotherhood idea. The words for 'brother' and 'sister' are added as a matter of course to the names of those who are addressed in Gujarati conversation, and all over India there are parallel honorific terms indicating relationship which enter into ordinary usage without any theological resonance coming in. That God can appear in various forms is something that the Hindu takes in in his stride. The question that the Hindu asks is 'What is special about *this* particular man?' If we drop the word 'sonship' and retain the notion of 'divinity' this will be an attribute that, potentially, cannot be denied of *any* man. Hindus will say, and

Gandhi speaks for them, that we all share a common humanity and as such share a divinity which is yet to be 'realised' or brought to full consciousness. This can only be done through a process of self-purification. It is easier, that is to say, for Gandhi to see Christ as the Son of Man than as the Son of God. It is Christ the Son of Man that he meets in the Beatitudes and before whom he bows his head. Throughout his long pilgrimage Gandhi draws a distinction between Christ and what theologians have made of Christianity, a distinction which is a very valid one in the opinion of the present author.

Let us continue with some more of Gandhi's theological difficulties. His reaction to the 'exemplar' concept has already been touched on in the discussion of the *Gītā*. A divine Being cannot be an exemplar for man. Man progresses towards perfection essentially through a *mārga*, a path, and not through imitation of God or the gods. This ties is oddly with certain strands in early Greek thought, but for different reasons. The dwellers on Mount Olympus mirror the follies of men in their own behaviour. Epic figures are often warnings rather than exemplars. In the Hindu tradition both gods and men are subject to a cosmic law which transcends both. The question for Gandhi turns on the idea of the most perfect man. That God or the Ultimate (Gandhi wisely does not attach great importance to which word may be used) is all perfect is taken for granted. There is even an Anselmian element in his thinking, as we shall discover in discussing Truth, which identifies supreme existence with the very nature of the Ultimate. But what of the notion of a 'perfect man'? Such a phrase is for Gandhi self-contradictory. To speak of 'the most perfect man ever born' not only raises invidious comparisons – and in any case, who is in a position to compare any one man with all the rest who have ever existed or might exist in the future? –, but ignores what for Gandhi is a fundamental truth, that it is in the nature of man to *pursue* perfection. No single being can claim to be the way, the truth and the life. The Truth is the life and since we all have fragmentary views of Truth, there can be no *one* life which is superior in a paradigmatic form. The following quotation is revealing:[1]

> To say that he was perfect is to deny God's superiority to man. . . . Being necessarily limited by the bonds of flesh, we can attain perfection only after the dissolution of the body. Therefore God alone is absolutely perfect. When he descends to earth, He of His own accord limits Himself.

Now in the Hindu and Jain tradition it is more common to speak of certain outstanding individuals in terms of 'God-realisation' or sometimes 'self-realisation', than of perfection. Perhaps there was a rationale behind this. The language of attributes (which includes the attribute perfection) can be extended ad infinitum. Spinoza wisely pointed out that our knowledge of attributes was strictly limited and that there can be an infinite proliferation of attributes in the case of the Supreme Being. (Leibniz would add, positive compossible attributes). Unlike the Muslim, the Hindu does not make a big thing of the 'names' of God. God is, par excellence, what is nameless, formless, what is, if you like, beyond our conceptual nets. The 'realised' man (he who has reached a certain state of awareness, and perhaps a state of goodness, beyond the ordinary) is spoken of as *guṇātīla*. Here one is 'freed from pairs of opposites'. Gandhi's comments on Discourse XIV of the *Gītā* which deals with the three *guṇas* are illuminating in this connection. We are, in the pilgrim's progress of the soul, to rise to a state where we are governed predominantly by the *sattva* principle. The mark of the *sattvika* is to be able to see unity in diversity. To rise beyond the three *guṇas* is to become the 'perfect man'. He brings in an analogy:[2]

> Take water, which in its solid state remains on the earth; it cannot ascend until it is rarefied into steam. But once it is rarefied it rises up in the sky where at last it is transformed into clouds which drop down in the form of rain and fructify and bless the earth. We are all like water, we have to strive so to rarefy ourselves that all the ego in us perishes and we may merge in the infinite to the eternal good of all.

Gandhi's religious life was not as Pelagian or as Advaitic (a peculiar and doubtless incompatible combination!) as this quotation would suggest. Self-realisation is becoming 'like unto God'.[3] To be Godlike is not to *be* God.

There is also another clue in the Indian tradition. The great soul is not seen as an incarnated divine being, or a mediator, but often as *bandhu* or friend. Krishna comes to Arjuna's aid in his time of distress, as a friend. The Vaishnava tradition describes in great detail the gradations of friendship or love which become more powerful symbols, for those in this tradition, than the symbols of sonship, brotherhood etc. The Christian will not find it difficult to find a parallel.

Although some enthusiasts speak of Gandhi as if he had attained the *Brāhmi* State, Gandhi's own assessment of himself was as a seeker after *sthitaprajña*, a humble seeker after truth. The thing to fasten on to in this context is Gandhi's conviction that to be human is to be imperfect. To stress the humanness of Christ, therefore, brings him down to our level, not as Canon Quick once put it, by 'a mysterious self-limitation' on the part of the Creator, but four-squarely on the ground, in the world of human finitude. Gandhi was not well enough versed in the Old Testament to be able to grapple with the idea of Messiahship. He seems to have again been 'put off' Judaism, almost Zaehner-fashion, by hitting upon only the earliest conception of Yahweh, associating the Old Testament with the doctrine of an eye for an eye and a tooth for a tooth, which he thought the Boers followed scrupulously, and missing the beauty of the Psalms, their at times Vedic lyricism, and the infinite compassion of a Hosea.

It has already been maintained that Gandhi, in line with the religious thinking of his countrymen, does not set much store on historicity. Whether Krishna or Ram actually lived is not a matter which has bearing on the verdict of a religious imagination which could project figures of such sublime proportions. Whether brahmins had in ancient times actually done X, Y or Z, whether or not it was recorded in the Shastras, was subordinate to the question of what they should be doing *now*. As for historical Hinduism it contained 'untouchability, superstitious worship of stocks and stones, animal sacrifice and so on'. This he would say to a Hindu audience which he was lovingly chastising, because *their* need was to recognise the necessity of a thorough reformation of the tradition.

To a missionary audience in Bangalore he used different language:[4]

> I may suggest that God did not bear the Cross only 1900 years ago, but He bears it today. . . . Do not then preach the God of history, but show Him as He lives today through you. . . . It is better to allow our lives to speak for us than our words.

A Christian today, whether in India or anywhere else, could echo the same sentiment. But the following would give him pause:[5] Even if 'the man called Jesus never lived . . . the Sermon on the Mount would still be true for me'. To Gandhi God appeared in *action*, not as a person. This was what was at the core of his own experience. How else, he once said to Dr. Mott, the missionary, could a man account for deliverance in his darkest hour? The inner voice which addressed him in the thick of his non-violent battles, and when the world was too much with him, was an indwelling spirit and not a person (or Person) encountered.

His dislike of the whole idea of conversion, as stressed by missionaries seeking to augment their flock, can be seen both in his personal letters, for example to Mirabehn, and in his addresses. To a Baptist congregation in Cuttack he said the following:[6]

> if a person discards his country, his customs and his old connections and manners when he changes his religion, he becomes all the more unfit to gain a knowledge of God. For a change of religion means really a conversion of the heart. When there is a real conversion, the man's heart grows. . . . In my view your object in changing your religion should be to bring about the prosperity of your country.

The turning point experience in Gandhi's life was not a religious experience as such but the traumatic occasion in Maritzburg, the capital of Natal, when he was pushed out of the train at night in the severe cold of a South African winter. Throughout his life he was to look upon South Africa as 'that God-forsaken Continent where I found my God'. If conversion made a man's heart narrow, that is, if it made him believe that those who were not of his persuasion were 'unsaved', or worse, cast into outer darkness, this was no conversion at all. The *metabasis eis allo genos* needed (I am recasting Gandhi's thought in more philosophical language) was the turning away from selfishness and self-righteousness to 'the spirit of service'. This introduces one of Gandhi's most seminal contributions to the understanding of spiritual growth – the sense of expansion it is characterised by. It was an idea he thought out for himself. It is also linked, it seems to me, with the oceanic circle idea he uses in his social thinking, and about which more will be said later, a gradually expanding area of participation, with the individual at the centre. The Jains spoke in terms of spiritual progress, and the Hindus in terms of the removal of the *Kośas* (sheaths) of egoity which veil the soul. The image of growth would have found an answering echo in a philosopher, much neglected these days, H. W. B. Joseph, who never tired of stressing the helpfulness of biological analogies to the metaphysician.

Hindu tradition witnesses to a strange tandem of nostalgia for the infinite and a domesticating of the gods. Gandhi was a man of the soil. It came naturally to him to think of conversion not in terms of credal allegiance but of putting down roots, reaching out, providing shade to the weary, and shedding a fragrance which, to continue the metaphor, is recognised by the observer, but of which the tree is itself unaware. Gandhi had no patience with self-conscious piety and his breath was sometimes almost taken away (but not quite, for his large heartedness and sense of humour would come to his rescue) by the arrogance of the evangelically twice-born. Here was the same kind of brahminical stiff-necked attitutde that he found in the upper castes of his own community. In short Gandhi was all for a change of heart, in fact the whole technique of satyagraha was based on this, and he believed the humblest peasant to be perhaps more capable of it than the intellectual or any other member of what he called 'the classes'. For Gandhi, a change of heart is seen in changed relationships, for example between employer and employed, between Hindu and Muslim, between caste Hindus and the so-called untouchables. But this was a very different matter from changing one's label, turning one's back on the traditions of one's forefathers and giving intellectual assent to a set of alien concepts which could find no answering chord in the hearts of those whose traditional symbols were of a very different kind. It is a token of Gandhi's sympathetic response to the New Testament and to its central figure that he did not dwell on the things in it which strike an alien note to anyone steeped in the Indian tradition, including in this the Jain and the Buddhist streams (for example, the Gadarene swine episode). He singles out the inacceptability of once for all atonement, of vicarious suffering, of conversion (in the light of following one's own *swadharma*), of a single God-man, and the belief that there is 'none other name' through whom man can be saved. He had a soft corner for Christian friends with theological difficulties, for C. F. Andrews, his brother in the spirit who had misgivings over some of the Thirty-Nine Articles, and for Verrier Elwin who at one time fell foul of ecclesiastical authority and to whom he wrote comfortingly: 'Your church is in your heart. Your pulpit is the whole earth. The blue sky is the roof of your church.' Could it be that in answer to the thundering evangelical battering which he patiently endured on many a day in South Africa, 'There is power in the Blood!' – something which is quite offensive to anyone with imagination, let alone to a man with Jain roots and who was to react with

revulsion to Kali worship – he thought out his own rejoinder, the
power of soul-force, an inward strength which would grow through
discipline, be fed through fellowship and fortified by grace? His last
word to the theologians is epitomised in his advice to a correspondent, that God is not 'encased in a safe to be approached only
through a little hole bored in it', but that He can be approached
'through billions of openings by those who are humble and pure of
heart'. God is not to be captured in theological nets. Those who
come nearest to Him are indeed, for Gandhi, those of whom it is
written in the Sermon on the Mount. This brings us to the positive
part of Gandhi's response to the New Testament.

Gandhi records in his *Autobiography* that the understanding of
Christianity 'in its proper perspective' would not be possible for him
unless he knew his own religion thoroughly. His study of the New
Testament and of the *Gītā* went on simultaneously, not only in
London, but in South Africa and throughout his life. He seems to
have started reading the Old Testament and got as far as the Book of
Exodus! He listened to famous preachers in London and attended
Dr. Parker's Thursday midday talks in the City Temple. Joseph
Doke, who wrote the first biography of Gandhi[7] (their number is
now legion), and knew his friend well, notes that, in his reading of
the Bible, when Gandhi came to the Sermon on the Mount, his
reaction was not that this was something new but that surely there
was no distinction between Hinduism as represented in the *Bhagavad
Gītā* and 'this revelation of Christ', concluding that 'both must come
from the same source'. He found the message of renunciation and
living service in both. A Gujarati poem he had learned in school
went something like this:[8] 'If a man gives you a drink of water and
you give him a drink in return, that is nothing; Real beauty consists
in doing good against evil.' It is Doke too who makes one of the most
perceptive remarks about Gandhi's response to Christianity:[9]

> I question whether any system of religion can absolutely hold
> him. His views are too closely allied to Christianity to be entirely
> Hindu; and too deeply saturated with Hinduism to be called
> Christian, while his sympathies are so wide and catholic that one
> would imagine he has reached a point where the formulae of sects
> are meaningless.

The years 1909–10 were memorable for Gandhi's correspondence with Tolstoy. His understanding of the New Testament

deepened through reading Tolstoy's *The Kingdom of God is within you* and Tolstoy's interpreting of this Kingdom as the reign of 'inward perfection, truth and love'. Both Tolstoy and Gandhi looked forward to a new order where a transformed inner life would find natural expression in a transformed community. Both great men found in the message of 'Resist not evil' not a passive principle but the positive power of soul-force, 'the infinite possibilities of universal love'. He was to meet another great-souled and kindred spirit a few years later.

Gandhi first met C. F. Andrews on the quay at Durban on 1 January 1914 and the latter bent to touch his feet. The influence that started then was to work both ways. The basis for friendship was their mutual faith in the power of love and their concern for the dispossessed of the earth. In early March, C. F. Andrews wrote to Rabindranath Tagore a letter in which he confessed that:

> We might see in the world's higher religions a branching family tree. . . . It will mean a lonely pilgrimage for me, for it means giving up claims for the Christian position which everyone in the West whom I know and love could not conceive of doing.

Not only C. F. Andrews and Romain Rolland, but Sir George Rainy, a member of the commission of inquiry in Champaran, compared Gandhi with St. Paul because of his passion for self-discipline. (Andrews also compared him with St. Francis of Assisi). There is something ironic about the Pauline comparison because Gandhi was not particularly attracted to St. Paul. He wrote in 1928:[10] 'I draw a great distinction between The Sermon on the Mount and the Letters of Paul. They are a graft on Christ's teaching, his own gloss apart from Christ's own experience.' And yet when he was in Motihari in connection with the Champaran campaign he wrote to his nephew Maganlalbhai, sending him as a 'gift', Paul's famous passage in I Corinthians, Ch.13: 'Though I speak with the tongues of men and of angels. . . . But the greatest of these is charity.'

At his prayer meetings Gandhi sometimes gave discourses on the Bible and there were often people who voiced objection to this practice. In November 1926 he ran a series of articles in *Young India* on the Sermon on the Mount, concluding 'Thus Jesus has given a definition of perfect *dharma* in those verses.' But he was worried over Matt. Ch.5, v. 22, 'Whosoever is angry with his brother without a cause shall be in danger of judgement', and he comments: 'These words are inconsistent with the *ahimsa* of Jesus'.[11] All this, the reader may note, was interspersed in the same article, with discussions on the practical problem of dealing with mad and stray dogs about which Jains were exercised. 1926 was a year of retirement from public life for Gandhi and withdrawal to the ashram in Sabarmati. It was during the same year that he gave special discourses on the Bible. But he left for Wardha on 3 December 1926 and the discourses were incomplete. He had, however, already made clear that the Sermon on the Mount contained *yamas* (cardinal spiritual exercises) and that the Lord's Prayer 'contains everything that the few letters of the Gayatri Mantra mean . . . one whose ideas can be repro-duced in the language of every religion'.[12] In this way he turns the tables neatly on those who later were to speak of the unknown Christ of Hinduism. In a significant statement made towards the end of his life he is reported to have said the following:[13] 'He added that Jesus Christ might be looked upon as belonging to Christians only, but he did not belong to any community, inasmuch as the lessons that Jesus Christ gave belonged to the whole world.' This echoes what he had said to Mrs. Polak decades earlier, that to be a good Hindu was to be a good Christian and that there was no need to 'become' a Christian in order to be 'a believer in the beauty of the teachings of Jesus or to try to follow his example'. Orthodox Christianity, he wrote to a Swiss friend in 1936, had distorted the message of Jesus. As was stressed by some of the leaders of the Bengal Renaissance, Gandhi too saw in Jesus an Asiatic. A series of empires, beginning with the Roman and ending with the British, had so overlaid his message, to say nothing of superstructures created by theologians, that it had become almost unrecognisable. Gandhi here shows a trait common to twentieth century interpreters of their own respecting traditions, a desire to get back to an *Ur*-message and a claim that it is this *Ur*-message which is most relevant to man's present condition.

But perhaps the most interesting question of all still remains. What did Gandhi think of the person of Christ? At first sight, and from what has already been referred to under 'theological dif-ficulties', the answer may seem to be inevitably negative. But the position is not so simple. Romain Rolland writes in his *Diary*[14] that on his way back from the Round Table Conference in 1931, when he visited the Vatican Museum: ' . . . he sees on the altar a fourteenth – or fifteenth – century crucifix, very stiff and harsh; this is the one thing which moves him'. The documentary film on the whole tour has recorded this moment, and Gandhi is seen as deeply moved by the sight of Christ crucified. On the way home, as S. S. Pilsna neared Bombay, Gandhi was asked to give a Christmas message. It was 4 a.m. on Christmas morning and dawn was yet to break. A group of Catholics, Protestants, and Gandhi's own Hindu entourage sat on the floor round Gandhi's shawled figure. It was his customary prayer hour. The message was this. When peace shone in individual and collective life then only could we say that Christ is born. Christ's birth would then be a perennial happening, illuminating the life of each man. Christianity had not yet been achieved. When we could love each other completely, and harboured no thought of retribution, only then would our life be Christian. Had not Gandhi, a man of peace, of reconciliation, seen into the heart of the teaching of the Prince of Peace?

But there is also evidence of a different kind. Commenting on a letter of Raj Kumari Kaur's published in *Harijan* in 1937, Gandhi says:[15] 'There is in Hinduism room enough for Jesus as there is for Muhammed, Zoroaster and Moses. For me the different religions are beautiful flowers from the same garden, or they are branches of the same majestic tree.' This can be interpreted in more than one way. Hinduism is infinitely hospitable. Another way is to find in the quotation a sense that Jesus is *different* from Muhammed etc. But then, different in what way? We have to approach this in a roundabout manner, as Gandhi gives no straight answer. To missionaries in Calcutta he says in 1925[16]:

> I do not experience spiritual consciousness in my life through that Jesus (the historical Jesus). But if by Jesus you mean the eternal Jesus, if by Jesus you understand the religion of universal love that dwells in the heart, then that Jesus lives in my heart – to the same extent that Krishna lives, that Rama lives. If I did not feel the presence of that living God, at the painful sights I see in the world,' I would be a raving maniac and my destination would be the Hooghli (river). As, however, that Indweller shines in the heart, I have not been a pessimist now or ever before.

The Christian theologian finds this promising at one point, and then in the next breath what seems to have been conceded is taken away. But let us take another look.

Gandhi makes a distinction between the historical Jesus and the eternal Jesus. The historical Jesus was born and died on a cross. I have not been able to trace any explicit opinion on the resurrection in Gandhi's writings. But the material is so prolix that this is not to say that a reference may not be there. The one reference I have located is rather a funny one. Arguing with Christian vegetarians who claimed that Jesus was also a vegetarian, he reminded them that there is a reference to his having eaten broiled fish after the Resurrection! The Hindu in any case does not 'require' a special 'event' to convince him that death is not the end. There is a cycle of births and deaths. How, and if, there is an eschaton on such a model we shall consider in the treatment of *mokṣa*. Does Gandhi mean, by the next point (it is not a stage in an argument, but a phase in his confessional statement) that the eternal Jesus *is* the eternal Krishna or the eternal Rāma? Or does he mean that *each* lives in his heart, each with his own savour, so to say? One cannot push Gandhi into a corner in this way. What Gandhi finds in Jesus is the embodiment of universal love. He is ready to speak of eternal events and includes among these 'the miraculous birth' and 'the Cross' as such.

Gandhi has commented on many of the leading events in Christ's life to a far greater extent than has any other modern Hindu. In fact he brings to the understanding of these events a Hindu insight which adds a new dimension to the interpretation of the relevant passages in the New Testament even for a Christian. On the temptations of Christ he writes:[17]

> When he (a man) conquers the first temptation (of hunger), he gains mastery over his senses. That endows him with strength. That strength itself is the second temptation. . . . When a man thus gains mastery over strength, he becomes a master of *siddhis* (miracle-working powers). These *siddhis* are his third temptation.

His Hindu insight again makes him regard Christ's baptism by John as initiation by a guru[18] and say that he 'received baptism purposely from one who could be no more than his servant in spiritual standing'.[19] The guru idea has been explored in recent years by Christian theologians in India, but not too successfully, for the guru in Hindu tradition is preceptor, but not mediator. The tables can even be turned and guru and disciple reverse their roles. Gandhi goes on to speak of Jesus as 'a servant of the people or a spiritual aspirant'. If one takes up the initiation by a guru idea then the notion of being a spiritual aspirant naturally follows. Christ he sees as entering on a life, a new life, which the Christian does speak of as 'ministry'. The passage is so illuminating for its picture of Christ through Gandhi's eyes that I quote it in full:[20]

> He was a servant of the people or a spiritual aspirant. The first lesson He took through baptism at the hands of John, was that of humility and self-purification. He thought of aligning himself with the millions by taking baptism and a bath in the Jordan.

To equate being a servant of the people and being a spiritual aspirant came naturally to Gandhi since for him the spiritual quest is equated with greater and greater identification with the suffering masses. The sequence of baptism, fasting and then temptations is readily intelligible to Gandhi. He sees it as a successive discipline, a progressive process of self-purification, the testing to which every man must submit. The reader must be told, however, that all this discussion (which no doubt can provide cues for further theological probing) was interspersed with talk about *khādi*, the homespun cloth which for Gandhi was *his* own particular symbol for identification with the poor.

Gandhi, then, does think in terms of the 'universality' of Christ. But this can mean different things. What Gandhi means by it is formulated by him thus:[21]

> Jesus expressed, as no other could, the spirit and will of God, It is in this sense that I see Him as the Son of God. And because the life of Jesus has the significance and the transcendency to which I have alluded, I believe that He belongs not solely to Christianity, but to the entire world, to all races and people.

But this is not to say that those who have not heard the name of Christ Jesus cannot do the will of the Lord.[22] The following year (1936) he refers to Jesus as 'a great world teacher among others', saying that 'He affects my life no less because I regard him as one among the many begotten sons of God',[23] and the year after that, states that 'Jesus preached not a new religion but a new life.'[24]

Writing to his Christian friend J. C. Kumarappa, he says that[25] 'For me Jesus was preeminently a man of unshakeable resolution, i.e. vows. His yea was yea forever'. That Jesus by his death and by his blood redeemed the sins of the world was not something his reason could accept. His death on the cross was an example to the world, but that there was some mysterious or miraculous virtue in it his 'heart' could not accept. Christ was 'the prince of satyagrahis' because his only weapon was the weapon of love. Was it not ironical that the man who swept away the distinction between Jew and Gentile should become a cult figure for a community who regarded themselves as being the privileged recipients of a special revelation?

Even so, the example of Christ's suffering was throughout his life, as Gandhi put it, 'a factor in the composition of my undying faith in non-violence', and it was this faith which ruled all his actions. It was our duty to multiply the bonds of love between man and man. Jesus was prepared to die on the cross and every man should be so prepared. The goal of Gandhi's life was the founding of a non-violent society. This is far closer to the Christian idea of the Kingdom of God than it is to the *mokṣa* concept of the Hindu tradition. But each community must put its own house in order. Nothing is to be gained by changing labels. The divine powers within us all are infinite. In some these are seen in a paradigmatic form, as in the case of Christ and the Buddha. But the new Jerusalem must be built brick by brick from below. It would not descend from Heaven. The city of God for Gandhi was no doubt the village of God. Gandhi's lifework consisted in wrestling with principalities and powers. But he had a very special sense of kinship with the Son of Man who collected dust on his feet on the rocky path to the Mount of Olivet, who went about doing good, and who fell foul of the authorities, including the leaders of his own community. It was Jesus the Son of Man that Gandhi could greet as a brother. In reminding his friends and associates that Christ was not the exclusive possession of Christendom, but belonged to all men, Gandhi reminded the world of something that had been forgotten and, as Romain Rolland never tired of pointing out, he quickened the conscience of men of goodwill professing a variety of traditions and faiths, reminding them of the path of self-sacrifice and love.

As a footnote I may add the following. In 1932 Rabindranath Tagore sent C. F. Andrews a letter[26] which was very appreciative of the latter's *What I owe to Christ*. The friendship between Gandhi, Tagore and Andrews was like a brotherhood of kindred souls in spite of the differences of temperament between them. In that letter Tagore wrote:

> The mode of self-expression in a Christian life is in love which works. In that of a Hindu it is in love with contemplates, enjoys the spiritual emotion as an end in itself. . . . My idea of the divine

has concentrated in Man The Eternal, and I find that in your own religious experience. You have the same idea centred in a concrete historic personality.

How does Gandhi stand in relation to Tagore's characterisation of the Christian and Hindu ways of life? Gandhi discovered in the Hindu tradition, if we have been on the right track so far, a *non-contemplative* activist strand which he strengthened till it was capable of being a lifeline for the toiling millions of his country. Tagore, an artist in life, witnessed to his own artist's vision of a world to be exulted in, an infinity which beckons unfurled wings. Tagore and Gandhi were one in their confidence in Man The Eternal, man who is endowed with potential divinity. If the phrase 'love which works' is a singularly happy one for describing the mode of self-expression in a Christian life, it is no less a singularly appropriate description of what Gandhi believed *being human* involves.

But Gandhi could see that as yet we were mere beginners in the working of love. Towards the end of his life he wrote that 'Spiritual force is like any other force at the service of man'.[27] In a sense this is true and in a sense untrue. Although the power of love has been wellknown to man perhaps ever since his first appearance on the earth, its full potential as a force which can transform both the individual and society has scarcely begun to be explored. To Gandhi it was a power which could be best set to work in voluntary organisations, in groups where two or three are gathered together. Hinduism is not an institutionalised religion. Christendom as a blanket term had also accommodated humbug, hypocrisy and exploitative structures such as colonialism, against all of which he had set his face. But what could be a finer vision for man to have before him than that of a life in which love is an operative force? Through Tagore's insightful comment we come a little closer to what for Gandhi was his heart's desire.

4 Experiments with Truth

If we take our clue from Gandhi's relation to Christian thought (begging the distinction between Christ, Christianity and Christians which he thought it proper to make) then it would not be far wrong to say that the way, the truth and the life are not incarnated in a person or Person for Gandhi, and that, of the three, what he understands by truth is the key to the rest. Begging the question has some excuse, although not warrant, in that 'religious thought' itself, the theme of this whole study, is a phrase about which Gandhi himself would have been rather unhappy. However we must proceed.

Experimenting with truth is not something new in the Indian tradition, continuing to use this as a blanket term to cover Hindu as well as Jain and Buddhist streams. Yogic practices and meditative techniques all come into this category. In fact, it is quite useful to see Gandhi's own experiments against such a backdrop because this brings home how distinctive they were. Gandhi's experiments were integral to his own personal *ascesis*. But unlike, say, Sri Ramakrishna's 'exercises', they were not mainly focussed on inwardness, but were tied up with something not unlike what the Marxists call *praxis*. They were conducted very much in the public eye and Gandhi himself succeeding, sometimes failing, and yet believing that the experiments had a *value*, and witnessed to something that others too could find out for themselves if they so willed. It was for this reason, among others, that his experiments often found natural expression and embodiment in ashram living, a shared way of life. But, even apart from the ashrams, many of his 'experiments' *involved* other people.

It is known to all researchers into Gandhi's thought that a stage came in his life when he found the formulation 'Truth is God' preferable to 'God is Truth'. The word Truth is not *substituted* for God, but serves to elucidate what 'God' means for Gandhi. The new formulation came out of his encounter with atheist conscientious objectors in Lausanne in 1931 for whom no doubt the very concept

58

of God was a stumbling block. As a student in London, it will be remembered, Gandhi had come across a kind of free-thinking which he could have encountered in certain circles in the Calcutta of his day, but which for a youth from Porbandar, came as startlingly new. For Gandhi himself atheism was nothing other than 'a Sahara'. But he saw a moral earnestness in people like Charles Bradlaugh, whose funeral he attended, which he could not help admiring. Could it not be that other seekers, including those who professed no religious belief, were actually on the track of truth, and that this was a term which best expressed the central thrust of man's striving for better things, whether this be a new social order or a new personal style of life? The company of truth seekers included scientists exploring the world of nature, artists creating works of beauty, and villagers pursuing their traditional way of life with humility and infinite patience. It was a bold idea, to identify at one go all that could be contained under what was for Gandhi one of his central insights about man, that man is a creature who has aspirations. Gandhi speaks for all those who find the concept of God puzzling. In a sense he sees that the very word 'God' provides the biggest stumbling block of all. For Gandhi the focus is certainly not on God-talk. We have already mentioned that he was rather impatient with those who wanted merely 'to talk about religion'. Those who were interested in 'religious language' were on the wrong track. He has much in common with the One who answered questioners with the brief advice 'Feed my sheep'. Gandhi's truth was a unique combination of a personal style of life and a technique for tackling injustices, truth that is, no doubt, in a sense other than as philosophers commonly understand it.

And yet there are strong metaphysical resonances in the word truth as it has been used in the Hindu tradition, so that when Gandhi speaks of truth the attentive listener needs to become aware of tones which reverberate, much as in Indian music a recurrent motif makes itself heard in the midst of an arabesque of sound. My metaphor is used advisedly. Gandhi often spoken of being attuned with truth. Of all the arts, Gandhi was perhaps fondest of music, and bhajans (hymns) were a regular feature of his prayer-meetings. He once mentioned to Dilip Kumar Roy, the singer and musicologist, that he could not 'even conceive of the evolution of India's religious life without her music'. Repetition is built into Indian music, whether it be the classical music beloved of connoisseurs, or the devotional songs sung by the populace. What then is the ground theme? To answer this leads us back not to a single pedal note, but to a raga on which variations are possible, but within the framework of a certain pattern. The pattern is there in Gandhi's thinking, and the variations are the work of a master.

Gandhi writes in his *Autobiography* of the deep inpression made on him in his youth by the play *Harishchandra*. King Harishchandra is a kind of Hindu counterpart of Job in respect of the testing that he undergoes. The ascetic Viswamitra makes a bet that he can make King Harishchandra tell a lie. Trapping him into making a promise, the King loses everything he has, but Viswamitra offers to restore everything if Harishchandra is willing to pretend the promise was never made. When the King refuses, a series of disasters befalls him. The tragic story unfolds and eventually Viswamitra admits his defeat and the gods restore Harishchandra and his Queen to their former state. Job is called upon to curse God and Harishchandra to tell an untruth. Harischandra, for Gandhi, is an ideal truth-speaker, a man who keeps his vows, and undergoes all manner of ordeals. Like Rāma, he is an ideal king and cares for his people. He 'follows truth', as Gandhi puts it in his *Autobiography*.

In the Upanishads the references to truth lie thick as leaves in the forests of Aryavarta. The Taittirīya Upanishad says 'Brahma is Truth eternal, intelligence immeasurable'. Untruth is to be conquered with truth, as light overcomes darkness. Truth as *sat* exists beyond, unconditioned by space and time. The morning prayer in the ashram at Wardha included the famous lines: 'From untruth lead me to truth, from darkness lead me unto light, from death lead me unto life everlasting.' The *Ashram Bhajanāvalī* (hymn book) also includes this: 'Early in the morning I call to mind that Being which is felt in the heart, which is *sat* (the eternal), *chit* (knowledge), and *sukham*, which is the state reached by perfect men and which is the superstate.' In 1925, during the Vykom campaign for Harijan entry into the temples, Gandhi quoted a line from the *Mahābhārata*: 'There is no *dharma* other (or higher) than Truth'. It is also said in the Mahābhārata:[1] 'Put a thousand *yajñas* (sacrifices) in one pan of a balance and truth in the other. Truth will be found to weigh heavier.' Rāma Rājya is often referred to as *Satyayuga*, the golden age of truth. Truth is also mentioned by Manu as being 'the common duty of all the four divisions'. To truth is attributed power and victory. The rishis, the sages, proclaim *satyameva jayat nanṛtam* (truth alone is victorious, never falsehood). Gandhi sees the whole Hindu tradition as a 'relentless pursuit after truth'.

All this time we have been speaking of truth as *sat*, as ontological absolute, or in the western tradition, as Being. What is characteristic of the Hindu approach is to see the quest of *sat*, of *Being*, as not a mainly cognitive affair (which inevitably runs into the classical impasse, the transcendence of the cognisandum and the finitude of the cogniser), but as the goal of *all* human endeavour, enlisting man's total energies. Man is in quest of *sat* as the hart pants after the water-brooks. The resemblance between the language of the Psalms and that of India's devotional literatures is so striking that I cannot help drawing attention to this much-neglected chiming in of insights of very diverse traditions. Gandhi was not a professional philosopher. But he embodies his own heritage to such an extent that to think of man as rooted in the ontological comes naturally to him. It is something which he finds deeply confirmed in the devotional literature of the country folk, especially of his own Gujarat. It also comes out in his occasional use of the word 'truly' as an epithet for a person, or a mode of action which shines with the clear light of *sat*, what exists paradigmatically. A favourite Gujarati stanza written by Shamal Bhatt, which was often quoted by him, runs like this:

But the truly noble know all men as one,
And return with gladness good for evil done.

'Really' and 'truly' in ordinary language have lost their ontological overtones. One has to go back through many centuries of British history to find the phrase 'good men and true' used naturally. Gandhi, one might go so far as to say, recovers the ontological root out of which our common use of 'true', 'truly', 'true to', have grown. So far, then, the strong warrant for regarding Truth as ontological ground, *sat* as primal existence, as *Being*, is supported by a long history in India's tradition.

But, apart from the ontological, there is also the ontic, truth as concerned with fact. Gandhi's training as a lawyer made him especially alert to facts. In April 1894, a fledgling lawyer on his first big assignment, he set to work to dig out the facts connected with Dada Abdulla's case in South Africa. At every stage, in every campaign he conducted throughout his long life of political involvement, scrupulous records were kept, and fact-finding was an indispensable preliminary to embarking on any action. Any volunteer who distorted the facts was severely taken to task. Volunteers who returned with the report that the houses in Beliaghata (a district in Calcutta) during riot-stricken days had been 'razed to the ground' were made to look very foolish. Gandhi suspected that in that particular area things could not have taken so extreme a turn. So, taking some volunteers along, he went to investigate for himself. True enough, windows and doors, sometimes roofs, had been damaged. There were blood stains on the walls. But the walls were standing. To say that the district had been 'razed to the ground' was an 'untruth'.

But for Gandhi facts were not just facts and nothing more. I suggested earlier that he felt himself to be *addressed by events*. We distort fact by speaking of it as brute fact. A fact provides opportunities for action. Possibilities for action lie betwixt 'the facts' and the human factor, the men and women involved in the situation. The people involved, the mill-workers in Ahmedabad, the brahmins of Vykom, the Hindus and Muslims of Patuakhali, are part of 'the given', to shift to philosophical language for the moment. A respect for the facts, therefore, includes an understanding of what makes people tick, why they behave as they do, a willingness to see, behind the prejudices, even the hatreds, the human face, and behind that face a reservoir of powers for good or ill. Gandhi was humanist enough ('humanist' is far too small and hackneyed a word) to believe that the powers for good outweighed those on the other side.

The way in which truth concerns fact, and fact in turn concerns the human component in situations, is closely connected, I believe, with how Gandhi sees the relation between man and nature. It also ties in with how the natural world is linked to that ontological level of which we spoke earlier. There is a line in Hindi which Gandhi often quoted and which says that everything 'belongs' to God. As late as February, 1947,[2] a little less than a year before his death, he reiterated his position that since everything belonged to God it was for His [sic] people as a whole and not for a particular individual. The main discussion on that occasion was taken up with his theory of trusteeship. Gandhi seems to have arrived by a route of his own to the two views of 'nature' familiar in the western tradition, nature as red in tooth and claw, and nature as ideal. He speaks of the 'forces of nature' and also of soul-force. Talking about village republics and modern civilisation he said[3] ' . . . that is real civilisation in my view, in which the forces of nature are used with restraint'. Not only man, but nature too, is not to be exploited. The language of many traditions converges in the following:[4] 'I can see distinctly that there is none so merciful as Nature. And Nature is God. God is Love. And who has not suffered from the lash of love'. Gandhi does not see in 'nature's everyday performances' something indifferent to man, or in text-book fashion, 'natural evil'. He is out of step with one strong strain in Hindu thought which sets store by the *alaukik*, the supernatural, and which regards extraordinary powers as the mark of spiritual strength. When some questioners asked about miracles he quipped[5] 'What's the good of overturning Nature?' He was a firm believer in a link between the life of the spirit and the laws of health. His dietetic experiments are a whole story in themselves, and Gandhi certainly counted them among his experiments with truth. One can see how vegetarianism fits in with using the forces of nature with restraint. Although the statistics were not available in Gandhi's time, it is common knowledge today that maintenance of a cattle population sufficient to sustain a non-vegetarian diet requires a far larger supply of cereals than does the amount needed to sustain a vegetarian diet.

When he was invited to address Rotarians in Calcutta his choice of a subject had an element of mischief about it, 'the economic and spiritual importance of the spinning wheel'. The audience of prosperous businessmen must have been disconcerted. His speech, however, brings out very clearly the links between economics and so-called spiritual matters, in traditional terms, the link between *artha* (wealth) and *dharma* (righteousness). This is what he said:

> The spiritual aspect flows from it (the economic). I read with avid interest Drummond's 'Natural Law in the Spiritual World'. If I had his facile pen, I would demonstrate it better that there is a spiritual law in the natural world.

Gandhi's inversion of Drummond's formulation echoes the ancient equilibrium principle of Greek and Indo-Aryan thought, a principle which has reappeared as conscious policy in contemporary eco-logical and environmentalist thinking. If there is a spiritual law at work in nature, it makes sense to go in for nature cures when one is ill, for disease is 'a breach of Nature's laws'; it makes sense to eat as much uncooked food as possible (whatever Lévi-Strauss may have said about the advance of civilisation). Gandhi no doubt picked up many of his dietary fads from his vegetarian friends in England. Outside the Punjab the eating of raw things is not a common practice in India. Food tends to be over-cooked. What was Gandhi after? Economising, living close to nature, showing what he could do without, keeping down his blood-pressure by avoiding salt? Probably all of these. And what was religious about it? If man's nature is 'not Himsa but Ahimsa' this has to be shown in every aspect of life. Vegetarianism follows. Those who have altered their diet on learning how battery hens are treated, or pâté de foie gras is made, are on the same wavelength as Gandhi.

But there is more to come. How are the forces of nature to be used with restraint? This includes both the forces without and within man. It includes not wasting water in a country where in some areas to this day drinking water has to be fetched by the womenfolk on foot from miles away. It includes minimising wants so that there is enough to go round. It includes a selective development of the powers within man himself. And here comes a hard saying:[6] 'It is not man's duty to develop all his faculties to perfection; his duty is to develop all his God-ward faculties to perfection and suppress completely those of a contrary tendency.' Man's distinction is his capacity for moral progress. Gandhi thought of this capacity in terms of self-purification. We have noticed before two major motifs in Indian culture, the spirit of renunciation and the spirit which reaches out to expression and gives birth to art. Gandhi embodies in himself the first of these. But his outstanding innovation was to make of renunciation itself an avenue of creative fulfilment for men in their collective existence. If one looks for a criterion of what God-ward tendencies are, Gandhi will refer us back to truth and non-violence. If the objector points out that some of the experiments, for example, *brahmacharya*, surely involve doing violence to oneself, Gandhi's answer in effect takes us back to a hoary Hindu belief in the value of conservation of energy, a kind of pre-Freudian libido theory, a reservoir of powers which, through being dammed up, are thereby set free for channelisation in other directions.

From all that is known about his personal life it does seem as if his fund of compassion and tenderness were at the disposal of the multitude instead of being confined within the limits of the family. Just as he had stepped beyond the boundaries of creeds his personal energies and allegiances exceeded familial ties and were available to those with whom he came into contract, a kind of sublimation maybe, but all in all a path which he believed would take him God-ward, that is, away from narrow selfhood and the tiny horizons of personal satisfaction. Man has to understand 'his position among other creatures' and find his most fulfilling work in life. The civilised man is the one who has an insight into the network of relations which are involved in nature, who utilises this knowledge to build up relationships, and who recognises the ultimate binding force to be the force of love.

Gandhi often speaks of different kinds of forces, divisive and unitive. Twentieth century physics has made men aware of the energy released through fission, a cataclysmic power which can be used for good or ill. The counterpart in the human world involves just the opposite process, the coming together of men of goodwill and the winning over of the rest through the vital energy of what he called soul-force. But if within the given, what is available for utilisation, we recognise these human resources that man bears within himself, especially when he is in association with his fellows, and if we regard human destiny as being specifically dedicated to the building of a new and more just order than what hitherto 'man has made of man' it is not difficult to see that truth for Gandhi is no less concerned with 'fact' than with *sat*, the ontic and ontological. It also shows how he was able to be on terms of intimacy with professional scientists whose lifework was dedicated to the pursuit of truth about the universe. It was the very same dedication with which he endowed his own striving after a vision of a new society, a free society, a kingdom of transformed relationships.

Nature, for Gandhi, was not only facticity, a reservoir of forces to be respected and also to be used with restraint for the benefit of man, but a source of inspiration. This aspect of his personal life has been largely neglected by those who have written on Gandhi. To Dilip Kumar Roy he wrote:[7] 'Nature suffices for my inspiration. Have I not gazed and gazed at the marvellous mystery of the starry vault, hardly ever tiring of that great panorama? . . . .Beside God's handiwork does not man's fade into insignificance?' He said something similar to Nandalal Bose, the artist, on his visit to Santiniketan in 1945. As they were walking through one of the buildings, the sunlight fell on a pattern of cracks in the stone floor. Gandhi stopped and gazed at it and people wondered, not without apprehension, what he was looking at. They knew he was a stickler for cleanliness. Was the floor perhaps not sufficiently clean? But he turned and asked Nandalal, partly in wonder, and no doubt partly with his inimitable sense of mischief, 'Nandalal, can you make anything as beautiful as that?' In a place famous for its batik prints, Gandhi the tireless and down to earth teacher, was at it again. Mahadev Desai reports in a Gujarati article[8] that Gandhi told an inquirer that:

the man, who can lose himself in ecstasy at the thought of the marvellous creation of God, at the sight of the heavenly dome lighted by the moon and countless stars, will not need to cast a glance at the pictures of such sights drawn by the most skilful painter.

To the same inquirer Gandhi spoke of 'the spiritual joy in the way-farer's or beggar's song, the natural beauty of the sky.' Small wonder that at the Faizpur session of the Congress, where the venue of the meeting was near the locality where Harijans lived, Gandhi's request to those in charge of the arrangements was that the sweepers themselves decorate the place with marigolds and the brooms and baskets of their traditional vocation. To celebrate is to involve the poorest of the poor; there is beauty in the objects of everyday use, even in the tools used by those assigned the dirtiest of jobs by an unjust society, for to work is to pray.

God's *līlā* (His divine play or handiwork) is also in operation in the human heart. This is why Gandhi reminded the inquirer that:

> one who can ever and always perceive in his own heart the play of the Divine that is visible also in the sky outside, will not be much concerned about looking even at the beautiful natural scenery of the moon and the brilliant clusters of stars.

It is necessary to note that Gandhi does not arrive at this conclusion via the Advaitin's doctrine of *māyā*. His own insight is rather confirmed through Kabir, the weaver-poet and saint who sees in the fabric of the universe a superb work by the Divine Dyer and of whom Gandhi says:[9] ' For him the whole creation conjured up from the objects of the senses cognised by sound, touch, form, taste, and smell had arisen within the space of his heart.' We shall return later to this idea of the space of the heart, microcosm of the universe, but a small space, almost Belloc-fashion, whose area needs expanding. Just to get the record straight, and also to appreciate how Gandhi invokes both Plato and the New Testament, wresting from them a message which was his own, this short mention of Gandhi's response to nature as a source of inspiration can be capped with something he said to Ramachandran, one of his faithful ashramites:[10] ' . . . Truth is the first thing to be sought for, and Beauty and Goodness will be added unto you.' The same year, in conversation with Dilip Kumar Roy, for he enjoyed tilting with artists on their own territory, he had insisted that asceticism is the greatest of all arts. The ascetic tendency in Gandhi is seen very clearly in his recourse to vows and fasts, in the Jain manner. Vows and fasts were among his major experiments with truth and many a time, it must be admitted, they occasioned sincere misgivings among some of his closest friends. It is to this controversial area in Gandhi's religious thought that attention must be directed next.

We need to return again and again to Gandhi's insistence on the fragmentariness of our respective visions of the truth, and on the *validity* of each. In order to gain even this partial vision, a *mārga*, a path or series of disciplines, is necessary. Gandhi's working out of his own *mārga* overlaps very considerably with the Jain list of *vratas* (resolutions); non-violence, fearlessness, chastity, non-stealing and non-possession are some of the points where he is at one with the Jains. Another clue to help us in uncovering the lineaments of his thought is his belief in the continuity of means and ends, and his conviction that the end never justifies the means. Let us link this with a famous line in the *Īśopaniṣad*, an untranslatable line, to the effect that what veils truth *itself* possesses a lustre; it shines out. The devotee prays that he may be able to penetrate the veil and see the even greater glory that is visible to the eye of him who loves truth. A vow, then, is more than a *rule*. It has far more in common with an existential pledge, a self-committal. So although we need vows because of the 'tempest raging in us' (here Gandhi is surely brother to St. Paul and St. Augustine), to take a vow is a 'sign' of strength, and becomes 'a bulwark of strength'. Gandhi finds in God 'the very image of the vow' (in another idiom, the God who neither slumbers nor sleeps). He draws on his bania family tradition, writing to the ashramites at Sabarmati from Yeravda Central Prison in 1930, and saying that all business depends upon men fulfilling their promises. The vow is part of the strict preliminary discipline needed if a man is to 'qualify', 'make experiments in the spiritual realm'. He compares this discipline with the preliminary instruction needed before a scientific experiment is conducted, and this becomes intelligible if we recall his stress on both the spiritual law in the natural world and the natural law in the spiritual world. The *Gītā* enjoins steadfastness. The very sequence of day and night, the cycle of the seasons, speaks of an order, a *dependability* in which Gandhi sees nothing mechanical, but almost finds a model for human activity. We should, he wrote to J. C. Kumarappa be 'at least as true and faithful as the sun, if not truer and more faithful.'[11]

But whereas a scientific experiment or hypothesis is applied to what is outside oneself, an experiment with truth is carried out first of all on oneself. I say first of all because many of Gandhi's experiments enlisted others, for example, diets for the ashramites, the spinning wheel, chastity, Hindu-Muslim unity, satyagraha etc. In this respect, the vow is a paradigm experiment with truth because no one can make a vow on behalf of another person. The notion that the study of *religion* requires preliminary observations, that insight is preceded by training, is built into Hindu tradition. What is special about Gandhi's development of the tradition is the utilisation of recognised pathways to individual liberation for the wider purpose of the transformation of society. The idea that one should take on only as much as one can in the shape of self-commital is built into Patañjali's distinction between *yamas* (cardinal spiritual exercises) and *niyamas* (ancillary exercises, cf. Jain *aṇuvratas*). So when Gandhi visited the Trappist monastery in South Africa and observed the routine there, the self-imposed discipline of daily work including silence (which he much appreciated), he found something which was very familiar and congenial. Whereas the once for all commital enjoined by his Christian non-conformist friends found no answering echo in his own experience, the Catholic practice of 'exercises', the little of it that he had some across, aroused his admiration.

Gandhi's undertaking of vows was a lifelong business, beginning with the vows he made to his mother before leaving the country. The vows were actually made before Becharji Swami, a family friend who had become a Jain monk. This in itself is interesting. Becharji Swami, like the Gandhi family, was a Modh bania, but who had voluntarily embraced the rigorous discipline of Jain monkhood. Such a course of action was not as uncommon in Gujarat as it might have been elsewhere. Gandhi, I believe, from this time onwards began to attach special importance to the vow, not as a formalistic framework to keep one on the rails so to say, but as a way of entering more deeply into the truth, of being *in* the truth, of belonging to it, or being rooted in it. I am putting it this way because I think it is necessary to stress the threefold connotation of truth that Gandhi seems to invoke, truth as *sat* or Being, truth as what is the case (which shows itself in his respect for fact, interpreted in the way I have suggested) and truth as that to which a man holds fast, that is, existentially. The vow then has a crucial role in enabling one to witness to the truth, to be *in* it existentially.

Two of his close friends, however, were most unhappy about

Gandhi's stress on vows. In the first ashram Gandhi set up in India, in Ahmedabad, the inmates had to take the vows of truth, non-violence, celibacy, control of the palate (i.e. abstemiousness in diet), non-stealing, non-possession, swadeshi (a complex concept that included self-sufficiency in respect of the use of indigenous products) fearlessness, and the elimination of untouchability. The list was added to, rather than subtracted from, in that the constructive programme which Gandhi believed must go parallel with the non-violent campaigns against exploitation, involved major policies, such as Hindu–Muslim unity, to which his associates were committed in a whole-hearted way and with the force of a pledge. About some of these vows, however, there are curious variants which Gandhi permitted, whenever he was convinced that the step was made in good faith. When a child was born to a married couple in the ashram, and the news was conveyed to him, he asked to see the baby and enjoyed playing with it. Dietary rules were flexible in the interest of health and in the exploration of possible simplified diets which would be within the reach of the poor. In spite of his vegetarianism, when he found that the health of some of his Bengali volunteers in Noakhali was suffering because of a fishless diet, he laughingly advised that they should go back to their natural food. After all, since the fish flourished in the water of the flooded paddy fields there could be no great harm in eating them! There would be greater harm in lowering one's efficiency through an unaccustomed diet and jeopardising the campaign thereby. As for non-stealing and non-possession, Gandhi believed that to possess more than the minimum was equivalent to theft, and blessed is he that has little as long as his brother has even less. The examples I have given are intended to show that Gandhi was not as inflexible as some of his critics thought he was. He believed that a great cause demanded self-sacrifice and that ashram living in a mixed community needed a certain discipline regarding sleeping arrangements and so forth if the community were to serve as a model for the rest of society.

C. F. Andrew's objection, born of his own experience with vows, having taken orders, was that 'life is always a growth into something new and unexpected and original'.[12] A vow, therefore, had a cramping effect. J. C. Kumarappa's reservations were based on the consideration that people were made differently, and had different needs; no one could legislate for all men. A vow was at most 'a helpful crutch', 'a protective hedge', 'The vow-maker is on a moral plane, not on the spiritual.'[13] But the distinction between moral and

spiritual planes is not one which really obtains for Gandhi any more
than it obtained for Moses. The tempest raging within, referred to
earlier by Gandhi, was not a Kantian conflict between duty and
inclination but a battle between Rāma and Rāvaṇa. The Ṛgvedic
meaning of *vrata* (vow) is 'divine will or command', so our
comparison with Moses is not too far-fetched. Moral growth,
making oneself a fit instrument of service, is not to be contrasted with
spiritual life, but is part and parcel of it. Hindu mythology is replete
with stories of ordeals undergone by gods and men. Gandhi himself
was to undergo, during his life, ordeals as great as the ancient ordeals
by fire. Vows were not for every man. They were not Pelagian
exercises to be embarked on out of a confidence in one's own powers.
Without Rāma, without God on his side, a man's vow will in fact be
ineffective. Gandhi had himself found vows of help as spiritual
exercises. But again, the end product was not to be an arrogant
athleticism, but an influx of power, an internal accretion which
would bear fruit. But only through God's grace. It was his belief,
fortified by his favourite Upanishad, the *Īśopaniṣad*, that after the
act of renunciation God supplies all one's needs. A vow is both an act
of renunciation and an act of resolution. In his *Autobiography*, Gandhi
wrote that he had found in his experiments a source of power for
work in the political field. The method caught on. In the Transvaal
and in Ahmedabad, the vow became part of the satyagraha
technique.

The vow in these various ways throws light on Gandhi's
understanding of 'the truth that is in you' (a phrase he used in a
letter to C. F. Andrews) and his pragmatic insistence that truth
could be *applied*. Although as a good student of the *Gita* he knew one
should not be attached to the fruits of action, the fact was that the
new style *tapasya* worked out in the ashrams, and which strikes the
observer as very rigorous, *did* bear unusual fruit. Volunteers from
Gujarat went as far afield as distant Bihar to lend a hand in the
Champaran campaign in 1917, and at the time of the Salt
Satyagraha, on 12 March 1930, seventy eight trained members of
the Sabarmati ashram accompanied Gandhi, walking a distance of
about 385 kms to Dandi on the sea-coast. They were joined by
thousands as they went on their way from village to village, singing
devotional music as they went. It was early on the morning of 6 April
that the historic procession reached the shore. Gandhi bent down
and picked up a lump of salt in defiance of the Salt Tax and held it
up for everyone to see. The salt had not lost its savour nor vows their
efficacy.

Should we include fasting among Gandhi's experiments with truth? There is warrant for doing so if we see the fast both as a means of self-purification and a method of persuasion. From Gandhi's point of view a fast was not a means of political blackmail but a penitential act, embarked on, not as a flexing of spiritual muscles, but as a necessary part of the discipline which makes one a fitter instrument of service. Gandhi had seen his mother fast when he was a young boy and observed *Ekādashī* (the eleventh day) fast with her. Regular fasts for various purposes (e.g. the welfare of a husband, to obtain a boon etc.) are part of the Hindu calendar of observances. The belief that austerities release inner powers is common to the many branches of the tree of Indian tradition. Gandhi was familiar with the discipline of doing without, something not merely appropriate, but obligatory in his view, if one is living in the midst of those who do not possess even the minimum necessities. A fast is an extreme form of doing without. Fasting is a potent way of purifying the inner voice. As he said once, what eyes are for the outer world, fasts are for the inner. There is no doubt that Gandhi regarded fasting as a form of *tapasya* which influenced others and which therefore illustrated very well his seeing of religion and politics as part of the same continuum – search for the truth, both at the individual and collective levels. If removal of injustice is a part of religious duty, methods used for removal of injustice, provided they are non-violent, ipso facto become religious duties. During the Ahmedabad campaign highlighted by Erik H. Erikson, he wrote[14] to a Danish missionary friend that the four days of his fast 'were to me days of peace, blessing and spiritual uplifting'. In 1931 he undertook a fast against untouchability which Pyarelal refers to as 'a Himalayan penance'[15]. This particular fast again, like his vows, occasioned grave misgivings in his friend Charlie Andrews. The latter wrote[16] to Gandhi that the weapon of fasting: ' . . . if it is not uniquely used for a God-given opportunity will certainly be used by fanatics to force an issue which may be reactionary instead of progressive . . .'.

Gandhi's clarification is clearest in his letter written from Yeravda Central Prison to Madeleine Rolland about the contemplated second fast. He speaks of the fast as 'the logical outcome of a prayerful search after truth', 'an intense spiritual effort, a spiritual striving'. He continues:[17] 'It is a penance and a process of self-purification. Such a fast generates a silent unseen force which may, if it is of requisite strength and purity, pervade all mankind.' Gandhi's own interpretation of his survival of the twenty one day fast, begun on 8 May 1933, was that God still needed him to fight and that he would return to the fight 'with renewed ardour'.

After he was released from Yeravda Prison, Andrews commented that Gandhi as a Hindu had a 'different idea of the spiritual effect of suffering' from that of the Christian, and Gandhi agreed that this was the case. Behind Gandhi's resort to fasting no doubt lies a different view of the body too. Jains believe that it is desirable to eradicate as far as possible *dehātmabhāva* (man's consciousness of the oneness of the body and the soul). In an address at the Guildhouse Church, London, on 23 September 1931 under the auspices of the Franciscan Society, with Dr Maude Royden in the chair, he said that one's body was not one's own and it was his constant desire that this body (referring to himself) 'may also be surrendered at the will of God'. This shows a conflation of Jain and Vaishnava sentiments which is very characteristic of Gandhi's religious thought. It is not that the body is of little account. All his experiments with diet, with nature cures, his prescribing for the ailments of friends and countless visitors, his concern for the eradication of poverty, show Gandhi's respect for the body, the place where we are. But one should be prepared to die, to surrender the body, for what one believes. The readiness to fast unto death provides the test case of this. In this connection it may be mentioned that on the evening of 1 September 1947, before embarking on his fast for communal harmony in Calcutta, an interesting sidelight was thrown on Gandhi's understanding of truth. As was customary, Gandhi prepared a statement to be released to the press. The original draft included the line:[18] 'I shall, as usual, permit myself to add salt and soda bicarb and sour limes to the water I may wish to drink during the fast.' Rajagopalachari, who was standing by, noticed the mention of sour limes and asked why this item was to be added to the water if Gandhi's intention was to fast unto death in order to move the hearts of the people. Gandhi immediately crossed out the words, and later commented to Nirmal Kumar Bose that he evidently harboured a desire to survive the fast, and that Rajaji had known him for many years 'and the departure from truth did not escape him'.[19] One of Gandhi's striking images for utmost self-giving runs like this:[20] 'It is the characteristic of the candle to consume itself and give light to others. Never, therefore, avoid serving people as best as you can.' Whatever may have been the political impact of Gandhi's fasts, for Gandhi they formed an integral part of his marshalling of his own inner forces, his calling upon God in time of need, his belief that the voluntary assumption of suffering moved the hearts of others and that this in turn released the untapped energies for good that were vested in ordinary men and women. Gandhi was ready to be consumed if thereby light could be given to others.

Mention has just been made of one occasion when Gandhi used the word 'untruth'. If we gather together some more examples, they enable us to see a little more clearly what Gandhi understands by irreligion. The list includes untouchability, sham and humbug of every kind (including pretending to be a *brahmachari* but actually not being one), anger, malice and jealousy. The use of goat's milk at a time of illness (Gandhi had vowed not to drink milk when he found out how cows were being treated) Gandhi regarded as a break of a pledge and therefore classified it as untruth. Lack of courage appears as untruth to one who regards fearlessness as one of the essential laws of self-purification. Theologians may be somewhat dismayed to learn that Gandhi regarded theology too as a source of untruth.[21] He was a believer in actions rather than words. As he once put it, spiritual truth 'transmits itself'. There was already so much that set up a barrier between us and the supreme–injustice, human ignorance and weakness, the inhumanity of man to man. To erect a barrier of words was only further to veil the face of God from man. It was during his oration on C. R. Das' death that he said 'The act will speak unerringly'.[22] So when Gandhi insisted that falsehood is never victorious he is referring to all the many kinds of untruth which he was convinced will not prevail against *sat*, reverting here to our starting point, the ontological meaning of truth. Truth-telling in the everyday sense of course comes into this (it may be recalled that in 1905 Gandhi wrote an article on George Washington) and Gandhi liked to quote a verse by the poet Shamaldas to the effect that the true bania does not tell a lie; moreover he does not give short weight or have anything to do with theft, slander, untruth, and pride. Anger, malice and jealousy are as much lies as is false speech. In short, it is proper to stress that far more than one of W. D Ross' prima facie duties is built into Gandhi's truth.

The words that Gandhi uses interchangeably with 'untruth' include *nāpāk* (unholy), Satanism, evil, *adharma*, irreligion, deadly sin. Small wonder that the fight against untruth must be relentless and that the seeker after truth needs a heart as hard as granite. Tagore, writing on Gandhi, said that he had 'given us a vision of the *śakti* of truth'.[23] *Śakti* is a powerful word. It does not have the cognitive connotations of the word 'truth'. Tagore's way of putting it has the poet's sure touch. To tap this source of energy is to be 'saturated with the spirit of *sat*'.[24] But there is a gentler aspect too. The seeker after truth has a heart 'tender as the lotus'. Are these two faces of the seeker after Truth not matched by Truth itself, the *tremendum* and the *fascinosum* spoken of in the *Gītā*? Gandhi had an amazing gift for conveying his ideas in the idiom which would be most familiar to his listeners. To the ashram inmates with whom he was always in close touch when he travelled the length and breadth of India he wrote that truth was a 'synonym for final beatitude',[25] and to his friend and fellow-worker, Jamnalal Bajaj he wrote that 'out of truth emerges love and tenderness.'[26] Truth so envisaged is surely a fount of joy.

Gandhi does often speak of truths in the plural. Of these there are two which, so to say, provide the axes for all the rest: that man is a moral being who must ceaselessly strive for perfection, and that, since our views of truth are but fragmentary, no man must impose his own partial vision on others. This is the foundation for Gandhi's belief in non-violence. Being true to the light as we see it necessarily means being non-violent. The extensive literature on Gandhi's thought treats truth and non-violence as tandem terms, and rightly so. It is an ontological conception of Truth, rooted in the Indian tradition which provides the ground for Gandhi's non-violent theory of action. Small wonder that when Lord Curzon delivered his convocation address as Chancellor of Calcutta University in 1905, claiming that 'the highest ideal of truth is to a large extent a Western opinion' Gandhi reacted at once with a long rejoinder in *Indian Opinion*.[27] The rejoinder consists of pages of quotations from Hindu sources and calls upon Lord Curzon to apologise. The interpretation of truth we have been trying to elucidate in this chapter is perhaps not a western interpretation, or rather it sets out a perspective which is not confined to any particular spot on the compass. It has a global character, and, in a way which would delight any Platonist, fuses the goal of metaphysical and ethical endeavour. The next step in exploring Gandhi's religious thought is to see in what way non-violence is an implicate in his allegiance to Truth.

5 The Non-Violent Weapon of Suffering

Indian metaphysical and religious thinking sees not so much evil, as *suffering*, as the chief problem. To go into why this is so would take us further afield than space allows. The theist of the Judaeo-Semitic tradition with his insight into God as the embodiment of goodness in His Divine Person grapples with the undoubted presence of evil in the world. A very different cosmology makes room for evil among the dramatis personae of the cosmic drama, seeing in this drama a whole hierarchy of beings ranging from demons to gods, a many-levelled stage, where man is an actor – sometimes a victim and sometimes a hero. The forces within and without involve him in this cosmic drama, and that suffering is part of his lot is accepted as a fact of his existence. It is no less a fact that he is capable of reaching peaks of joy, in human relationships and in the creative work of art and craft, and these give a foretaste of a bliss which is beyond imagining and yet which is mirrored in the mood of celebration which dominates most forms of Indian art. A cyclical view of time reconciles man to the repetitive phases of his destiny, bearing within it, if not an *eschaton* as conceived on a linear model, then, at least the promise of a chance to try again. The cycle of births and deaths strikes a man in a fearsome way if he sees it as the prospect of further chains of suffering. Even outside the Indian tradition, who has not at some time felt himself to be in a cosmic trap, a treadmill from which there seems no escape? Suffering then, in the Indian mind, has always posed itself, to the philosophers and sages, as something to be got rid of, that is, as a *practical* problem.

Bondage, however, is not the last word. The different systems along with their analysis of the causes of bondage, or to change the idiom, in their probing of the depths of human finitude, also set out a way or *mārga*, a path which, if followed, can take man out of the maze. Divine grace may, or may not, feature in the system, depending on whether the theistic hypothesis is present or not, and, as in theologies of other traditions, on the extent to which man is conceived to be imperfect. It is striking that all Indian systems, barring the Cārvāka, take it for granted that the central target of ethico-religious endeavour is the removal of suffering. In working out how this was to be done, Indian thinkers were in a bit of a quandary. The activist alternative, presented inter alia quite unmistakably in the *Gītā*, carried along with it a danger. To act is to accumulate further *karma*s and thus to add to one's bondage. Even though the possibility of evening up the account through further births might be consolatory, the very opposite effect might be brought about. We might go down rather than up.

Reformist Hindu thought from the nineteenth century onwards was bold enough to attempt to cut through this problem. But it was not until Gandhi that we find the innovatory idea of suffering ('the richest treasure of life') itself being regarded as a way of dealing with suffering. This paradox will have to be elucidated. Gandhi is traditional in seeing the central human task as that of getting rid of suffering and in seeing this as a *practical* matter. But he sees the sufferings of men in a particularistic way, rather than, as the philosophers had seen it, as a general cosmic condition. Secondly, he centres on the sufferings of *others* as the focus of our meliorist efforts, not the shuffling off of the chains of bondage for our own personal liberation. The sufferings to be got rid of stem from the injustices that beset the poor; they derive from wickedness in high places as well as from wickedness within the human heart (the traditional vices of anger, greed, lust and so forth). Gandhi is not concerned with finding a metaphysical justification for suffering or with speculating about its cause. His scientific eye diagnoses the diseases of society, his heart responds to those in distress, and he works out a new *tapasya*, a new *mārga* for *tackling* human miseries.

In a manner which is strikingly contemporary, Gandhi pinpoints violence as the chief malady of our times. If anyone asks Gandhi what is wrong with violence he has his answers ready. One violent action leads to another; for example, violent speech provokes angry retorts from the other side. Secondly, violence concentrates power in the hands of a few. He is thinking here of the violence typified in colonialism and the economic systems which deprive the poor by concentrating wealth in feudal and capitalist structures. Thirdly, violence leads to suffering and degradation. His Ambulance Corps work in the Boer and Zulu wars brought him face to face with the misery caused by war. Warfare is the externalisation of violence in the human heart. Violence *is* evil. This is why the words 'ahimsa

paramo dharma' (the prime duty is non-violence) possess for
Gandhi near-mantric power. Gandhi we saw earlier, sees man as a
reservoir of powers for good and ill. The task set us is to channelise
man's energies in such a way that good predominates. It is not
enough to say, as had been said by generations of sages, that good
actions promote *lokasaṁgraha*, the welfare of all. Time was running
out, and human misery was on the increase. It was not enough to
search among metaphysical systems for a remedy for suffering. We
need to revolutionise our social environment, and this can come
about only through a revolution in the human heart. A method is
needed which not only the spiritually strong can use, which those
who have adopted *sannyāsa*, or those who are pursuing cloistered
virtues can employ. A method is needed for every man, a moral
equivalent of warfare which will release the constructive energies
that all men possess and which will enable man to build up a good
life for all. Gandhi believed this method to be the method of non-
violence, the voluntary assumption of suffering by an individual and
by a group as a self-purificatory act, an example to others, and as a
way of converting the heart of the oppressor. The expression 'moral
equivalent of warfare' is significant, for if there were anything worse
than violence, it was cowardice, especially the cowardice born of
selfishness and fear, or the cowardice born of inertia, the feeling that
nothing can be done.

The difference between voluntary suffering and involuntary
suffering was a very basic one for Gandhi. The sufferings of the poor
were not of their own choosing. Gandhi makes short shrift of the
classic excuse that one's condition in this life is the result of bad deeds
in previous lives. Social injustice is a challenge to be faced here and
now. Reality has to be changed. Here he is in agreement with Marx.
The two big differences are Gandhi's belief that reality must be
changed non-violently lest we add to the total burden of suffering in
the world, and that in so doing we chime in with reality at a deeper
level since we are thereby operating according to the law of love.
Voluntary suffering or self-sacrifice is what Gandhi puts in place of
the ancient *yagña* or sacrifice. The reign of love is to be brought about
not through the sacrificial love of God's Son on the Cross, but
through every man's acts of self-sacrifice. Gandhi often uses
the image of the cross to drive his message home. In 1927 he
wrote:[1]

God did not bear the Cross only 1900 years ago, but He bears it
today, and He dies and is resurrected from day to day. It would be

poor comfort to the world if it had to depend upon a historical God who died 2000 years ago. Do not then preach the God of history, but show Him as He lives today through you.

These words were addressed to a Christian audience. Gandhi very evidently believed in the *power* of suffering, for some years later he wrote:[2] 'I saw that nations like individuals could only be made through the agony of the Cross and in no other way.' But if the power of suffering is not to be seen paradigmatically in a redemptive act, how then is it to be seen? To answer this we need to return to his South African experience out of which the whole gospel of non-violence was born.

It *was* a gospel in the sense that it amounted to the good news that the poorest of the poor were shown a way of using their non-violent strength; that out of man's very weakness he could accomplish mightily. For Gandhi himself this was by no means as Pelagian a strategy as it sounds. His own life was conducted, one could truly say, in the presence of God and it was his own experience that God came to the help of the helpless. Gandhi himself recalled how he came to forge the weapon of satyagraha in South Africa when mere talk, petitions, negotiations had failed:[3]

It came to me that we should refuse to obey legislation that was degrading and let them put us in jail if they liked. Thus came into being the moral equivalent of war. . . . Since then the conviction has been growing upon me, that things of fundamental import-ance to the people are not secured by reason alone but have to be purchased with their suffering. Suffering is the law of human beings; war is the law of the jungle. But suffering is infinitely more powerful than the law of the jungle for converting the opponent and opening his ears, which are otherwise shut, to the voice of reason. . . . The appeal of reason is more to the head but the penetration of the heart comes from suffering. It opens up the inner understanding in man. Suffering is the badge of the human race, not the sword.

It is a long quotation but rich in content. It may seem paradoxical that the man who speaks of satyagraha as a science in the making should confess the limits of reason. It can be looked upon in this way. How can one persuade the fanatic, the man who through stubborn-ness, vested interest, ingrained orthodoxy or whatever, is not to be persuaded in favour of what we believe to be right and just. The method of reason, as shown in reasoning, comes up against 'stoppers', and perhaps everyone who has argued about the role of reasoning in ethics has granted that this is so. To think of man as a rational animal scarcely cuts ice, and the Greeks were perhaps in the best position of all (one has only to look at their dramas, their mystery cults) to appreciate that man's psyche cannot be confined within the straightjacket of reason. Those who thought in terms of rule and those who thought in terms of *telos* might have wished it were otherwise. But the nature of man has its shallow pools and swamps, its depths and heights, and what is religious life but a coming to terms with all these many territories, a strengthening of man's noblest instincts, a conviction that his highest aspirations echo an order which *is* paradigmatically and which sustains him in all his endeavours?.

Gandhi's was not the method of injunction, of preaching, because he believed that the ears of those who are determined not to hear are unlikely to be unstopped through mere talk. One can of course, through reason, established theories, found systems and so forth. But what was at stake was not systems but 'things of fundamental importance to the people'. This includes the securing of civic rights, the gaining of national independence, the ending of the exploitation of the poor by the rich. Discussion and negotiation may take us part of the way but they will not take us to the end of the road. Self-suffering is more than a tool of conflict resolution, it is a way of 'changing reality'. That suffering is the badge of the human race had been the belief of generations of people living in India reflected in the philosophers' obsession with *dukha*. Christianity made the Cross and the Resurrection the central events in the redemption of man by God in the form of the one who was both Son of Man and Son of God. The fact remains that the revolutionary potential both of the Mahāvākyam of the Upanishads (Thou art that) and the message of 'Love God and thy neighbour as thyself' had some how got lost along the way. Institutionalised structures, whether of caste, priesthood, or church; the spirit of exclusiveness which was in each case foreign to the *Ur*-message—all had in practice made of religion a very un-revolutionary thing, a bastion of the status quo, of a self-congratulatory sense that we are not as other men.

Gandhi found that what is most inescapable about human life, the fact that man must suffer, can be turned to good account. Gone was the traditional belief that suffering was at all costs to be got rid of.

Gone too was the idea of individual suffering of an isolationist kind, undertaken through austerities, in quest of self-perfection. In place of the Jain concept of the spiritual hero who recovers the pristine purity of a soul which has become tainted through karmic defilement, Gandhi puts the heroism of the group of satyagrahis who undertake a movement to redress economic, civic, social or political grievances. The 'conversion' aimed at is not a conversion of belief externalised in a formal changing of religious labels. Gandhi does use the word conversion, and he is very well aware of its religious overtones. The opponent is to be converted, to undergo a change of heart, when he sees that the satyagrahis are willing to stake their all for what they believe to be true.

Why should anyone voluntarily add to his sufferings when, as it is, suffering is the common lot of men? Many elements enter into Gandhi's thinking at this point. As a Vaishnava, he has faith that man is a being who is capable of being touched by another's woe. The reverse is also the case. Man can harden his heart and refuse to regard another's suffering as any business of his own. But Gandhi believed that, since men share a common humanity, sooner or later the 'opponent' will be won over. This apparent 'conquest' by the satyagrahis was, however, not a defeat for the other side, but a conquest for them too, in that they had been able to rise above the factors which had previously stood in the way of understanding. But there are several conditions which had to be fulfilled first on the part of the satyagrahis. We have seen that Gandhi was a great believer in the importance of discipline for spiritual growth, and with the wisdom of a spiritual director he had his finger on the pulse of those he led, sensing their readiness or otherwise for embarking on a particular campaign. Here again there are overtones from the past. In both the Hindu and Jain modes of *ascesis*, a distinction is drawn between the discipline (including the vows) proper to a householder and what is proper for the *sannyāsi* or the monk. Gandhi's reaction to this traditional distinction is complex. While on the one hand he stresses the importance of stages – a major example is found in the stages of the national movement which he led over a period of decades – he is no less insistent that the techniques of self-suffering, sacrifice for a cause, is something which the humblest man, including the householder, can use, provided, of course, he under-goes the necessary preliminary training. This discipline included what Gandhi called non-violence in thought. But ideas have a natural outcome in action and non-violent actions have a persuasive power greater than that of words. This was not a *theory* but what Gandhi had found to be the case.

It may be useful to mention an example of non-violent action in a context which involved an apparently religious matter, to get the feel of how the principle worked. Vykom in Kerala enters modern Indian history as the place where in 1925 an important satyagraha movement took place to vindicate the civic rights of the untouchables to pass down a particular road, and eventually opened up the whole question of the right of *any* Hindu, whether caste Hindu or otherwise, to enter a temple. There are interesting features about this particular campaign. First of all, it illustrates Gandhi's insistence that each religious community must put its own house in order. Untouchability was a blot on the name of Hinduism, a canker, a disease – he seeks for words that are as strong as possible. Since it is a matter which concerns the Hindu community it is no solution if the untouchables run away and became Buddhists as Dr Ambedkar advised. Each must find his salvation within his own community. But this required non-violent defiance of the brahmins' edict not to use a certain road, a willingness of the untouchables to undergo hardship in so doing, and a parallel constructive effort on their part to improve their own life by observing cleanliness, improving their crops through the use of compost, spinning, and a host of other things involved in Gandhi's conception of rural reconstruction. It is those who bear the brunt of a particular injustice who must learn to mobilise their non-violent strength in order to improve their condition. This was why he did not allow the Sikhs to open charitable kitchens in Vykom (this is a characteristically Sikh way of dispensing charity to those in distress), commented discouragingly on Christian efforts to eradicate untouchability, and spoke against the dole system.

What then becomes of the principle of bearing one another's burdens? Straight off it must be said in answering this question that Gandhi is not at all hamstrung by any philosophical allegiance to separate karmic lines. It is a principle that must be carried out first. and foremost with those with whom we are immediately associated. Here Gandhi has something very significant to say in the light of the caste allegiances of Hindu society. When he went to Noakhali on his historic peace-making tour in 1946, he urged the riot-stricken people to organise themselves as fisherfolk, as weavers, as peasants; let the unit for collective action be the immediate associates in daily work. Here was a new teaching regarding identification of one's neighbour. Later, when Gandhian workers tried to organise peace brigades in other parts of the country, it was on a neighbourhood basis. So it happened that even in the midst of terrible communal conflagration the import of 'who is my neighbour' was not totally lost and there were heroic cases, both in Bengal and the Punjab, of Muslims sheltering Hindus and Hindus sheltering Muslims, often at the cost of their own lives.

The independent observer may have some difficulties over Gandhi's embracing of suffering as an operative principle. In pre-Independence days the satyagraha weapon, for weapon it was, seemed to be nothing less than a form of political blackmail. But a generation familiar with Martin Luther King and Danilo Dolci, with French worker-priests, and the politically involved clergy of many countries in Latin America, and familiar moreover with the catastrophic effects of violence (including assassinations, the taking of hostages, urban guerilla strategies, and isolated acts of terrorism which wipe out innocent civilians) is in a better position to appreciate what Gandhi was about. The mighty weaponry of powerful states has not proved itself able to control violence, still less to neutralise it. In so many parts of the globe today there are stalemate situations where the man in the street suffers, entire governments are held to ransom and the future spells not hope but panic as to where terror will strike next. That we are in dire need of a method of de-fusing the loci of violence in our society would be readily conceded today.

But will the method of self-suffering work in dealing with every kind of situation? The method presupposes a certain gallantry in the adversary. It is easy to think of cases in the past and present where that gallantry was, and is, conspicuously absent. Here Gandhi would say that such considerations did not show up the method as ineffective. It rather showed that our preparation had been wanting. The supporting constructive work which was an indispensable parallel activity to the voluntary assumption of suffering in order to right injustices, had been absent or inadequate, or our timing had been wrong (a factor to which Gandhi was extraordinarily sensitive). If a situation were allowed to deteriorate beyond a certain point, it is this deterioration, rather than failure of the method of self-suffering, which was to blame. Gandhi did provide a criterion which is sometimes forgotten, and it is this. In conditions where cowardice and violence are the only alternatives then violence is the lesser evil. In spite of giving the impression at times of seeing things in black and white, Gandhi had in fact his own way of assessing the imponderables of a situation, and no decision was taken without as thorough an inquiry into the factors concerned, especially the human element, as was possible in the circumstances. That self-suffering will eventually move the heart of the opponent was an article of faith with him. But even if it did not, he believed it was better to be killed than to kill, apparently to fail, than to give in to tyranny. Gandhi was a pragmatist as well as an idealist. He used the weapon of self-suffering over a period of many decades, beginning with the South African period of his life. He showed it could be used to alter economic, social and political situations, and the very movements he led brought out the extent to which the three were inextricably related. But to the end of his days he confessed that the weapon was a new one, yet to be perfected, a technique which was still in an experimental form. Without the preliminary self-purification on which he laid such stress the method could degenerate into a form of blackmail or sheer coercion. Whatever methods we use, they are, after all, carried out by men, and men are fallible beings.

A further difficulty confronts the contemporary thinking man brought up to regard secularism as a desiratum and who finds in Gandhi's approach a disconcerting conflation of the religious and the political. Is not the fact that we are discussing the satyagraha movements under the rubric of his religious thought direct evidence of this? The *Autobiography* once more provides a clue:[4]

> To see the universal and all-pervading spirit of Truth face to face one must be able to love the meanest of creation as oneself. And a man who aspires after that cannot afford to keep out of any field of life. That is why my devotion to Truth has drawn me into the field of politics; and I can say without the slightest hesitation and yet in all humility that those who say that religion has nothing to do with politics do not know what religion means.

It is worth marking the difference between this approach and two others. The Jain reverence for life which is taken to an extreme point in customs like covering the mouth and nose, feeding ants with sugar, and which led to the avoidance of agriculture for it cannot be carried out without the destruction of life, resulted in directing the Jain community into business. The Islamic belief in theocracy has amounted to a refusal to distinguish religion from politics and an attempt to shape every aspect of life strictly according to theological tenets derived from the Koran. Gandhi's attitude appears in a very different light from both of these. He had no patience with the ant-feeding type of Jain, who, following the insect theme, strained at a gnat but swallowed a camel, for example, who adulterated ghee. Gandhi's approach to scriptures was always very liberal. If there was anything in scripture which offended against reason or conscience, so much the worse for scripture. In any case man's God-given powers of scrutiny and criticism should be turned on the written word no less than on institutions – all were man-made.

We have already seen that Gandhi did not believe that the human mind or human society could be divided into watertight compartments, social, political and religious. One has only to observe any big rally today in India to see how all three are inter-connected. Since the spiritual law does not work in a field of its own but through the ordinary activities of life, it works in the political sphere also, even though at times, and these are the words Gandhi himself uses, politics may encircle us like the coils of a snake. The symbol is significant. The snake is a symbol of power in Indian mythology and no one appreciated better than Gandhi that politics is to do with power. How can this power be humanised? This was the crux for Gandhi. And the answer – only through the counter power of soul-force. In spite of Gandhi's passionate adoption of a life-style of self-purification for himself he was not one with Tolstoy in relying on this alone. Time was running out and the people perish. New institutions must be built up in a progressive manner; social structures must be transformed, and political instruments forged which could be responsive to the will of an enlightened people.

I have said nothing so far of the history of the Indian National Congress and its part in the Indian struggle for independence. This story falls outside the limits of the current study. But anyone who cares to read through the proceedings of the successive sessions of the Congress cannot fail to be struck by the extent to which ethical and religious language enters into the discussions. To what extent was it *possible* to be non-violent? Did non-violence actually work? Such questions entered into what were on the surface purely political debates. The concept of *dharma* itself united the individual, the political and the cosmic. The language of duties, and of *seva* or service, was the language in which, traditionally, a man defined his place in society. What Gandhi tried to show, in a very practical fashion, was that Acton's famous dictum can be countered. If power is genuinely shared, if the new Jerusalem is built up from below, we would find therein a political purification analogous to the individual self-purification to which Gandhi and his satyagrahis were committed. To go along this line of thinking is to tend to the conclusion that for Gandhi democracy was far more basic a concept than secularism. *Pravṛtti* or involvement, did not, for Gandhi, mean an abandonment of individualism, although it did mean that the solitary pursuit of enlightenment in the midst of human misery was the height of luxury, and all luxuries for Gandhi were a form of theft. Just because Gandhi enters the history books as an innovator of a form of collective action we must not forget that at the root of it all is his profound belief in the value of the individual and his faith in his powers. At the centre of the oceanic circle, his famous model of transformed society, stands the individual. This is what I mean by saying that for him democracy is more vital a concept than that of secularism. The secularist, in different ages and contexts, carried on a broadside against clericalism, against principalities and powers in religious places. When free India adopted secularism as a state policy she did so in no small part thanks to the training in *satya* and ahimsa that the old guard of political workers had received. Secularism as a militant principle in opposition to religious authority is uneasily grafted on to the Hindu frame of thought. But as practical state policy in a multi-religious community it could easily be assimilated by Hindu society although not so easily by the Muslims.

Secularism in recent years has tended to become a blanket term which covers a hotch-potch of ideas. Compared to the militant Hindu nationalist revivalists of the nineteenth century Gandhi seems almost a secularist. And yet, if we take his handling of Hindu-Muslim relations, it is clear that his policy was not secularist, if by this we mean an attempt to prune away all religious considerations from political matters. To encourage the Hindu to be a better Hindu and the Muslim a better Muslim is not to advocate secularism. Religion had become politicised as far as some of the nineteenth century revivalists were concerned. What happens if one tries to *moralise* politics in a society where the concept of *dharma* is as much religious as ethical? Is it possible to invoke a particular element or even cluster of elements in a religious matrix without opening a Pandora's box? To open Pandora's box can be to unleash forces which go against the ultimate objective, the alleviation of the miseries of the poor. And yet the attempt to mobilise the social energies of the ordinary man *is* in tune with what these days passes under the umbrella of secularism. But the secularist per se wants to attain social justice, keeping in a separate compartment those aspects of life which derive from religious authority, be it the authority of scripture or that of an institution. Gandhi differs in certain important ways from this sort of secularism. For one thing the whole technique of the voluntary assumption of suffering in order to rectify injustice is not directed solely to this end but to winning over the heart of the opponent, that is to say, to the establishing of a new human relationship. Secondly, Gandhi, speaking from the vantage point of experience in India, did not believe that it was in fact *possible* to keep various aspects of life in watertight compartments. Take matters as simple as food or dress. In India, barring the westernised elite, both of these reflect a man's social, economic, and often religious identity. Thirdly, and this is perhaps the most vital of all, the secularist forms his policies keeping in view the needs of *l'homme moyen sensuel*. Gandhi, however, firmly believed that the saint and the ordinary man were on the same wavelength. The vows taken by the monk and the satyagrahi are not so very different in kind. The satyagrahi needs to forego the pleasures of the *grhastha* stage of life. The *core* disciplines are the same for all. Gandhi, however, believed in moderation. Moreover the strength needed by *muni* (monk), satyagrahi and ordinary man alike was nourished by divine grace. Bearing this last point in mind, and for Gandhi it was a crucial one, the powers within man, if fully tapped, are stronger than any of the state powers behind which the secularist is likely to take refuge. We come back then to Gandhi the democrat rather than Gandhi the secularist, the democrat for whom each single individual has value and whose fragmentary view of truth has its own validity.

We have yet to elucidate two very important facets of Gandhi's teaching on self-suffering, that ahimsa is the farthest limit of humility,[5] and that there is such a thing as the law of love. The importance of humility among the fruits of the spirit, to borrow a phrase, is an implicate of the fragmentariness of our visions of the truth. There is no room for being puffed up about our own particular view when other views are possible and are actually held by our fellow human beings. This is why Gandhi says:[6] 'Out of truth emanate love, tenderness, humility. A votary of truth has to be humble as the dust. His humility increases with his observance of truth.' Humility is the very reverse of self-assertiveness which springs from egoity and makes for discord within man and within society. To wish to reduce oneself to zero reveals the utmost humility. The question was for Gandhi by no means a theoretical one. Constructive workers in the villages were advised to move among the villagers with humility. It could not be assumed that the townsman's ways were the best. 'A life of service must be one of humility.'[7] But this involves 'most strenuous and constant endeavour'. Humility is the condition of growth. 'When self-satisfaction creeps over a man, he has ceased to grow and therefore has become unfit for freedom.'[8] It was this impression of self-satisfaction that unfortunately struck him about all too many of the evangelical Christians he met and who boasted of being 'saved'. It was from the humility of the toiling millions of India's villages, deprived of the minimum necessities of life, the humility involved in the daily care of the mother for the child (for 'scavenging' is a natural part of this care), from the humble origins of India's mediaeval poet-saints, that Gandhi derived his paradigms of humility. When according to the law of stages in spiritual growth, the aspirant can only take one step at a time it follows that there can be no question of prescribing for others, of laying down the law. The supreme example of this is found in something for which Gandhi has been faulted by some, his deliberate abstention from prescribing what policy should be followed 'when freedom came'. It would have been against his life-long practice of careful study of current situations, of insisting that those actually involved should tackle the problems that faced them, to provide any kind of blueprint for independent India. There can be no magic formula for the future. Even one who knew his India as well as Gandhi did, was humble enough to avoid predictions and prescriptions. The only 'next step' that he regarded as essential was that the Congress Party be disbanded and that its erstwhile members should go back to the villages for constructive work. This fits in with what Mahadev Desai calls Gandhi's 'ideal of political sannyas'.[9] The *sannyāsi* has always been exempt from caste rules. Similarly, Gandhi is exempt from the usual obligation of political leadership, the obligation to prescribe a directive therapy, to switch to clinical language. The training in democracy which he gave his associates over a life-time of campaigns was a training in decision-making guided by truth and ahimsa. Even when the decision went against his whole life's work which had been directed to the creation of a free and united India, that is when Partition came, Gandhi was humble enough to accept the decision, and the non-violent social revolution, which was to have come, never took place.

We turn next to the theme of love. Gandhi says of satyagraha that:[10] 'Its root meaning is holding on to truth, hence truth-force. I have also called it love-force or soul-force.' The *bhakti* (devotion) tradition, as distinct from the *dhyāna* (meditation) tradition in India, speaks of love between man and God. The Vaishnava hymns Gandhi was fond of, celebrate this relationship. But Gandhi's language and idiom are peculiarly his own when he comes to elucidating what he means by love. The Radha/Krishna symbolism appeals to him far less than does the analogy of Rama and Sita, the idea of faithful consortship. But all mythologies are left behind when he identifies truth-force with love-force which are both to be understood as totally different from brute force. In 1925 he once addressed an audience in Cutch as follows:[11]

> What is worth learning from me is my love and not my strength to give a fight. My fighting strength is only a small fraction of my real life. And even that strength is the outcome of my truth, my sympathy, my love. All my fights, and fighting spirit are worth nothing without that love.

C. F. Andrews spoke with deep understanding of his friend Mohan when he wrote to Romain Rolland[12] that in his inner life 'it is the passion for others which is supreme'. Those close to him who saw how Gandhi allotted his time during the day have testified to the hours he devoted to listening to the woes of streams of visitors who consulted him on a vast range of personal problems, even medical ones. No letter was too insignificant to get a personal reply from Bapu, sometimes a brief message on a postcard. With the eye of love he was able instinctively to intuit the other's need. To women in East Bengal who had lost their husbands, sons and brothers he came with a message not of consolation, but of courage. In touring from village to village in East Bengal he went all the way back to give an ailing child the enema he needed. Such selfless giving attracted in full measure the rich friendship of men like Charlie Andrews, Rabindranath Tagore, Romain Rolland, Jawaharlal Nehru, Maulana Azad, and not only the giants of those days but the humble villagers with whom he identified himself in diet, dress, and style of life. So it came about that he drew so many to himself. Madeleine Slade (Mirabehn) was right when she wrote to Romain Rolland that:[13] 'with Bapu it is his life and acts (from the most important to the smallest) that speak more than words (that are more eloquent than words)'.

But it is part of our business to try and delineate the structure of his thought for the purposes of this study. We need to stress, I think, Gandhi's distinction between evil and the evil-doer, for the concept of 'moral evil' as we find it in philosophical literature is associated with the person, the doer. Gandhi's distinction comes out of the nature of his campaigns, his life-work, where he learnt to distinguish between a system and the people that operated it. The harshness which appears in *Hind Swaraj*, a very basic document for the study of Gandhi's thought, is directed against a certain kind of civilisation, a network of systems and institutions which, in his view, dehumanise man. But a system or an institution cannot be tackled head on. Principalities and powers have a human face. Whereas hatred engenders further hatred love has the special quality of eliciting love in return. Gandhi sees the modern malady as a malady of distances, the distance between government and governed, rich and poor, city and village, hills and plains, high castes and low. The distances between nations are but an extrapolation, what is writ large, of what we see before us wherever we may live. Love is the power which draws people closer together.

What he is talking about is far more like *agape* than it is like *eros* or *philia* or even *caritas*. Ahimsa is 'the largest love' because it is self-sacrificial love. We can compare it, then, both with *yagña*, ritualistic sacrifice which involves the taking of life, and the Vaishnava's close relationship between man and God celebrated so appealingly in India's devotional music. Ahimsa casts out cowardice; perfect love casts out fear. Gandhi never lost his faith in human nature in spite of having experienced man's inhumanity to man firsthand, both in South Africa and in India. The Hindu tradition spoke of the divine spark in man, the *Gītā* of the Lord as friend, and, as Gandhi put it, 'Buddha taught us to defy appearances and trust in the final triumph of Truth and Love.'[14] The Sermon on The Mount had also made an deep impact on young Gandhi, an impression fortified by Tolstoy's message of 'inward perfection, truth and love'. What Gandhi was looking for was a *manly* conception of love which he did not always find in the literature of his own Gujarat, much as he was devoted to it, or so it seems to me. He once wrote to Maganlal Gandhi, his nephew and close associate, that the love taught by Swaminarayan (towards the end of the nineteenth century in Gujarat) and

Vallabhacharya was 'effeminate sentimentality', and that there was more of *puruṣartha* (manly endeavour) in the couplets of Ramdas. As for the *gṛhasta* ties with their inevitable tinge of possessiveness, they appeared in the garb of bondage to one who had donned the mantle of a national mission or perhaps had it thrust on him by the course of events. Human love as seen in the ties of comradeship which bind workers in a common cause was perhaps the form of love most intelligible to Gandhi, a self-sacrificial love which was seen in a specially intense form in ashram life. But it was an out-going love which reached the village child, the riot-ridden citizen, the British constable, not excluding the 'tallest in the land'.

The Sanskrit words beginning with the prefix 'a' conceal a positive meaning behind their apparently negative grammatical form. Gandhi thought it was necessary to bring this positive meaning out, and this is why he says:[15] 'In its *positive* form, *Ahimsa* means the largest love, the greatest charity. If I am a follower of *Ahimsa*, I must love my enemy or a stranger to me as I would my wrong-doing father and son.' He is humble enough to include at the end of this statement what he at the time was finding a source of stress, his relationship with one of his sons. Gandhi's frankness about his personal relationships has often puzzled others. But this was all part of the pursuit of truth, of authenticity in so far as one was capable of it. How is authenticity to *manifest* itself if not in love. Here Gandhi seems to find a way out of the divide between a *Gesinnungsethik* and an *Erfolgsethik*.

There is a further dimension to this. The crying need for *peace* was never very far from Gandhi's mind. How can one 'live at peace with both friend and foe'[16] if it not be through making a friend of the foe? The central anguish that contemporary man has to surmount is the anguish of war. Archbishop Cosmo Lang once spoke[17] of Gandhi in unsympathetic terms as a mystic, fanatic and anarchist. I do not believe the first two charges are just. But there *is* an element of anarchism in Gandhi, an enlightened anarchism in which he gloried. He really believed that the efforts of ordinary people to multiply the bonds of love and fellowship around them operated as peace-making forces in the world. No organisation or world authority could be as effective. Enlightened anarchists would function as leaven leavens the lump.

The concept of *dharma* involves a chain of duties rather than a chain of love. The Jain concept of the unity of all living things provides a sanction for non-injury to all beings, great and small. The

Mahayana Buddhist concept of compassion, of return to the world out of concern for those still in bondage, exemplified in the lives of bodhisattvas, brought more strongly into the tradition of India the sense of the positive transforming power of the gentler virtues. The purificatory role of both fire and water are familiar in the traditions of many peoples. Likewise also the purificatory role of austerities. At what point then does Gandhi bring in something new? It would be easy to say that Gandhi's encounter with Christian communities had introduced him to the idea of the power of love. The answer is unfortunately not so simple. In this history of the Crusades and in the rapacious economic structures he observed in South Africa the influence of the Sermon the Mount was conspicuous by its absence. For Gandhi it is not the Holy Family which provides the paradigm but a capacity for a long-suffering bearing with others which he found in the *human* family and perhaps even more in the village of his dreams. His first encounter with the New Testament and, in particular the Sermon on The Mount made him 'simply over-joyed',[18] for it chimed in with what he already believed to be true. The language of I Corinthians, Ch. 13 is strangely echoed in the following:[19] 'Satyagraha is gentle, it never wounds. It must not be the result of anger or malice. It is never fussy, never impatient, never vociferous. It is the direct opposite of compulsion.' Gandhi is full of surprises. He assimilates the idioms of others and they come out in his writing as if they were his own, even, for example, an echo of Spinoza when in speaking of 'this grand Law of Love' he asks wonderingly 'are not all good and great things difficult to do?'

Gandhi believed that the 'law of love', as he called it, was actually at work. That life goes on in spite of death and destruction, he took to be evidence of this. But, as in the case of *dharma*, we encounter here a principle which at once sustains all things and yet which requires man to guard and tend it. The cohesive force which already exists among men needs to be *utilised*. In other words Gandhi believes we have at our disposal a power whose full potential has yet to be drawn on. There is an interesting Jain echo of the notion of subtlety in his opinion that:[20] 'The more efficient a force is, the more silent and the more subtle it is. Love is the subtlest force in the world.' But although Gandhi so often spoke of soul-force on the analogy of other forces, his intention was really to point out how different it was from other forces. The ultimate test of the satyagrahi is his willingness to die, the *choice* of death, the adoption of self-suffering to the extremest limit. Can such a spirit of self-sacrifice be possible for one without faith in

God? Gandhi believed that non-violence in the positive sense, that is, love, can only 'permeate' the man who has 'a living faith in God'. It was for this reason that Romain Rolland had many misgivings about the prospects of non-violence as an active principle in a de-sacralised world. Was a belief in human solidarity a sufficient base from which to build a new order? In an age when the scientific intellect shows its polished surface for all to see what becomes of the heart whose powers are invisible and whose radiance penetrates in hidden ways?

So far I have tried, as far as possible, to avoid talking of God, for Gandhi was himself very aware what a stumbling block the concept can be especially if we _remain_ at the level of concepts. Wrestling and experimenting with Truth is put forward as something which those can understand who baulk at the very mention of God. The satyagrahi, who has been presented for the most part as a political activist of a particular kind, is actually, as we strove to see in this chapter, a religious type. Gandhi even speaks of Christ as the Prince of Satyagrahis. Devotion to truth and ahimsa is the _tapasya_ required of the satyagrahi. He has _faith_ in truth and ahimsa and he has faith in man. Qua religious type the satyagrahi is neither cast in the form of leader or led. In the non-violent army of satyagrahis a kind of collective leadership emerges which recalls the togetherness of the primitive church. Should we at all pose the question whether or not the phrase 'atheist satyagrahi' is self-contradictory? Here, in keeping with Gandhi's train of thought one might say that not all who cry 'Lord! Lord!' are prepared to feed His sheep or die for them. Devotion to truth and ahimsa is shown not with our lips but in our lives. The satyagrahi in fact appears as a humanist with a rich inner life to which his 'outer' life is witness. The satyagrahi is _dedicated_ rather than merely _committed_, to truth and ahimsa. Amidst the urgencies of twentieth century living Gandhi indicates a role for man alternative to that of victim or observer, a salvific role which even the weakest can take upon himself. Gandhi as a satyagrahi himself was no doubt one who 'relies upon God as his sole refuge'. His inner life was nourished by a very deep faith which was as idiosyncratic as we have found the facets of his religious thought already considered to be. God, he once said, can only appear to the poorest of the poor in the form of _work_. This is straight speaking for anyone who is looking for a sophisticated theology in Gandhi's thinking. He will not find it. If God appears in the form of work it means that _love_ appears in the form of work. Work had traditionally been regarded as a punishment or penance in many world systems of thought. But Gandhi finds work a privilege, because in his own country not every man *has* productive work to do. Gandhi's inner life, his relationship with God as he experienced Him, takes as unorthodox a form as we would by now expect. What was the inner life of this man for whom religion seems to be coterminous with service, with a public life utterly taken up with affairs of the world?

6 Waiting On God

There is a genuine sense in which Gandhi's life was an open book; another sense in which it is not at all easy to read the signs, to penetrate the mystery of this most complex personality. Let us go back a little. Although some have tried, to search for a characteristic mode of Hindu spirituality is, in my opinion, a major blunder. Even to speak of mainstream Hinduism is to speak of something problematic. It was for this reason that the second chapter of this study went in detailing some of the strands that are woven into the fabric of Hinduism and the movements, orthodox or otherwise, that form parts of its pattern. The very words 'religion' and 'spirituality' have no counterpart in Indian languages. The second hard saying is that if the central concern of Indian religion is *dharma*, as I believe it is, then the question of God's existence, his nature etc., becomes ancillary. For Gandhi, however, the question is *not* ancillary. But he attaches no great importance to which word we may care to use, God (whether personal or impersonal), Truth, Allah, Ram or whatever. If his Vaishnava affiliations make it natural for him to worship the divine as Bhagavan (he prefers the word Rāma, or when he is using English, the rather neutral word 'God') his Jain associations make it equally natural for him to regard the religious life from our end of it as it were, that is, as a process of self-purification. This is to say that Gandhi falls in a class apart in that if we make a distinction between those religions which aim at an enlightened consciousness and those which aim at a special relationship, that between man and God, Gandhi in a sense straddles the two. The religious life is a life of self-purification, but it is also a dedicated life, dedicated to God and man.

For Gandhi godliness (a word he uses and which strikes me as singularly appropriate) was a fragrance which expressed itself in humour, in kindly acts, in stubborn self-questioning, in courage, and in humility – a strange amalgam of elements. But in none of these was there a trace of humbug. Like St. Paul, he was no stranger to inner struggles and he believed these were part and parcel of the life of any man with a strong conscience. Gandhi did not hear voices, see visions, go in for meditative techniques, nor was he in any sense a mystic. Idolater and iconoclast (he idolises the common man in whose face he sees the face of God), it is almost with an innate sense of mischief, something which was never far from him, that he presents himself to us, challenging all categorisation, pooh-poohing the analysis of religious language, religious talk, chuckling at any attempt to put under the microscope his religious 'thought' because for him it was not a question of *thought* at all, but the very breath of life.

Traditionally, Hindu religious behaviour centred on *yagña* (sacrifice) and *pūjā* (worship). As I see it, Gandhi puts soul-force in the place of the former and prayer in the place of the latter. The link between the two is what he calls 'the inner voice'. The power which is released through self-sacrificing acts, specially when embarked on collectively (what he calls satyagraha), was examined in Chapter 5. We shall next need to explore his understanding of the inner voice and his experience of prayer.

Gandhi was not a temple-goer, nor as was mentioned before, does temple-going have quite the role it does for the Hindu that going to Church or to the mosque does for the Christian and Muslim respectively. On this matter he did not claim any special merit for himself. There was a strong element of rationalism in Gandhi which told him that bathing in holy rivers or visiting holy places were as futile as the bath of the elephant (a traditional metaphor which expresses futility, as so little water actually falls on the animal!) without right thought and right conduct. The very importance which Indian traditions give to ritual observances including ritual acts of charity, might have been in his mind when he said this:[1] 'Works without faith and prayer are like an artificial flower that has no fragrance. Plead not for the suppression of reason, but for a due recognition of that in us which sanctifies reason itself.' But he was very sensitive to the special need for symbolism in religious life in so far as man seeks to give embodiment to what is invisible to the naked eye but many-hued to the eye of imagination. Indian religious life is particularly rich in such symbolism, the symbolic objects and acts of *pūjā* (worship), the symbolism of food, of dress, the symbolism of the repetitive rounds of *kirtan* (singing), the natural symbols of fire and water which purify. Gandhi was so much a man of the people that he was always alive to the beauty of much of traditional worship. But when this was accompanied by unhygienic surroundings, cruel practices such as untouchability, or exploitation of the animal kingdom, his anger was no less than that of Christ when he saw the money-changers sitting in the temple. Gandhi himself introduced a great deal of new symbolism, instinctively sensing his people's need for it. The stress on sanitary arrangements in the ashram and at All India Congress sessions provided a counter-symbol to the traditionalist's obsession with pollution; the wearing of *khādi* (homespun cloth) is a symbol of self-sufficiency and of the value of doing things which one's hands – at one go a counter-symbol to helpless dependency and looking down on those who do manual jobs; the very ordering of time in a disciplined way throughout the day is a symbol which redeems the cyclical endlessness of the daily round and common task. None of these things, we must remind ourselves, fall outside what Gandhi understands the reach of religion to include.

But what did Gandhi mean by the 'inner voice'? It seems to have echoes far back in time, echoes which include Socrates' 'daimon', the candle of the Lord of the Cambridge Plationists, and Protestant 'conscience'. Gandhi had written a Gujarati version of the trial and death of Socrates, giving it the title *The Story of a Satyagrahi*. His own deposition in Champaran before Sir George Rainier strangely echoes the tone of Socrates' speech at his trial. There is a common nobility about them both. Each was an educator, a crusader whom history cast in the role of subverter. Each appealed to 'the Court of Conscience'. Each was profoundly misunderstood. Each suffered for his beliefs to the extreme limit of death.

I myself believe that Gandhi had been imperceptibly influenced by the evangelical concept of 'guidance' during his long years of association with men and women in non-conformist circles in South Africa, and that this eventually emerged, characteristically, in something peculiarly his own, what he called his 'inner voice'. He absorbed a good deal of their vocabulary and constantly drew out oddly appropriate lines from hymnals of the vintage of Sankey's and Moody's, unconscious that he was doing so. Even today, those unfamiliar with non-conformist collections of sacred songs will be unable to recognise the origin of some of the things Gandhi says. I suggested earlier that Gandhi felt himself to be *addressed* by events. Sometimes he was taken unawares by a sense that a particular course of action was imperative in a certain situation. At other times it was more like the slow growth of conviction. But in any case the inner voice was the way in which *dharma* appeared to him. If we say 'it struck him that . . . ', something of the force with which Gandhi's experience of the inner voice occurred is conveyed in this familiar phrase. A man can only be addressed by events and situations if he knows a lot about them, cares deeply what happens and is prepared to plunge into them through action aimed at making things better than they are. There is a strong trace in Gandhi's form of activism of what Simone Weil has discussed in contexts many of which were very similar to those that concerned Gandhi. There is no guarantee that our intervention will be the best possible, but we should seek to *improve* a situation, to make things better than they are, rather than worse. The uninformed inner voice, or the inner voice of the undisciplined man, would lead to disaster, as all moralists who have cast a critical eye on the fallibility of conscience have been always ready to remind us. Gandhi's position on all this does not fall neatly into either the *Gesinnungsethik* or the *Erfolgsethik* basket. The subjective or attitudinal pole is provided by his commitment to non-violence in thought, word and deed. The feasible, the possible and probable results of alternative course of action, are carefully estimated with special attention focussed on the human imponderables. The rest depends on fellow-workers, the way they are able to enlist the dormant powers of others involved, for example, the villagers along the route of the Dandhi march, and, without using this mode of speech in any light-hearted way, all are committed to the hands of God.

The inner voice for Gandhi was a vehicle of insight, a call to action, and a source of strength. The last of these marks off his position from that of the pure *Gesinnungsethiker*. He is nonetheless different from the *Erfolgsethiker* in his assimilation of the *Gītā*'s teaching of non-attachment to the fruits of action. Gandhi has left on record mention of when the inner voice began to play a key role in his life:[2] 'The time when I learnt to recognise this voice was I may say, the time when I started praying regularly. That is, it was about 1906.' The days spent in jail in the Transvaal in 1908 allowed him long hours of reflection. Moreover, this was a period in his life when the various influences which had been at work in his inner experience resulted in a distinctive shape, a synthesis peculiarly his own. He had already come to have a kaleidescopic vision of a world which only he could see. On at least two occasions in later life he speaks of his embarking on a fast in response to the inner voice. The 'call' (again a term familiar in non-conformist circles) to undertake the fast of 6 April 1919 came to him in a dream. As for his twenty one day fast in Yeravda jail in 1933 for the removal of untouchability, he told Dr Mott, founder of the YMCA movement, that this was embarked on in response to his inner voice.[3] But he was very conscious of the dangers involved. He writes: 'The "Inner Voice" may mean a message from God or the Devil, for both are wrestling in the human breast. Acts determine the nature of the voice.' It is an illuminating passage. The first part reflects the God/Satan dichotomy familiar in the hell-fire style of preaching. The last sentence indicates that what we have already done determines what we are and hence the direction in which the voice tells us to go. The voyage within may reveal monsters and demons. Gandhi's own consciousness of warring forces within him made him value that silence without which the still small voice could not be heard. It also strengthened his determination to follow 'the proper training' (the vows) without which 'God's will' could not be known. In 1933 he described in some detail how the voice of God, of conscience, of truth, appeared to him. It was:[4]

> like a Voice from afar and yet quite near. It was as unmistakable as some human voice definitely speaking to me, and irresistible. I was not dreaming at the time I heard the Voice. The hearing of the Voice was preceded by a terrific struggle within me. Suddenly the Voice came upon me. I listened, made certain it was the Voice, and the struggle ceased. I was calm . . . not the unanimous verdict of the whole world against me could shake me from the belief that what I heard was the true Voice of God.

To those who had reservations about the phrase 'inner voice' he suggested[5] they could use the expression 'dictates of reason' which should be obeyed. Gandhi was well aware that each man had his own stumbling blocks and that there was no harm in each choosing whichever expression seemed to him appropriate. The combination of expressions only seems puzzling if we associate reason with *argument*. Gandhi believed that the inner voice possessed both authority and power, but only to a man who had undergone the purificatory discipline of the satyagrahi and had faith in God. To such a man God gives His divine grace. The inner voice, moreover, spoke with accents of sympathy, enabling a man to put himself in the other's place, inducing in the listener an outreach towards the other. It is also interesting to note that in an essay written in 1906 entitled 'The Bond of Sympathy' Gandhi associated lack of imagination with the various weaknesses that human beings have. In the context of the Indian classical analysis of human finitude in terms of various *passions* Gandhi's mention of weakness of imagination as a fault is innovative. The outreach was at one and the same time an outreach towards God. It is not of the Mimamsaka 'witness' that he is speaking when he says the following:[6]

> There is not a moment when I do not feel the presence of a witness whose eye misses nothing and with whom I strive to keep in tune. . . . I have found Him nearest at hand when the horizon seemed darkest – in my ordeals in jails when it was not all smooth sailing for me.

The mixture of images illustrates very well his whole story of inner quest. He must have seen many a time in non-conformist homes the text 'Thou God seest me'. The sense of being in tune or out of tune was for him a very familiar metaphor, likewise the image of nearness, the overcoming of distance, and yet (this is important) which ipso facto excludes identity.

Gandhi derived the power to stand alone from a sense of being in tune at the deepest level of his being with the universe. This sounds a little odd to one not familiar with the concept of *dharma*. *Dharma* is above all what sustains. But it is man who is called upon to uphold *dharma*. Here is the paradox. That which sustains man itself requires man to sustain it. This being in tune (Gandhi seems to have read Trine) brings about an influx of strength. So the solitary man who takes a stand against injustice is not in fact alone. He has all the positive powers that work together for good on his side. He draws on their strength. It is no wonder, then, that Gandhi was so fond of a song of Tagore's which was very popular during the independence movement, a song which encourages the lone worker who struggles for freedom even though no one else responds to his call. Both Gandhi and Tagore had faith in a sustaining power at work in the universe and for this reason, in the words of one of Tagore's most memorable poems, man must keep his wings unfurled. The inner voice enabled a man to tell whether he were in the right direction or not. I quote now from a letter Gandhi wrote about a year before his death. The voice says: 'You are on the right track, move neither to your left, nor right, but keep to the strait and narrow way.'[7]

The various senses provide revealing metaphors which open up a little for us the nature of Gandhi's inner quest. One must be prepared to listen. Hence, the importance of silence. He writes in 1938:[8]

> Silence is a great help to a seeker after Truth like myself. In the attitude of silence, the soul finds the path in a clearer light, and what is elusive and deceptive resolves itself into crystal clearness. Our life is a long and arduous quest after Truth, and the soul requires inward restfulness to attain its full height.

Silence enables us not only to listen but to *see* the path. It provides kindly light, odd though this may sound. The outcome is something dynamic, an indication of the direction in which to *move*. He speaks of 'the communion of silence' and this communion was for Gandhi both with God and with the other members of the 'congregation' at his prayer-meetings, a congregation which included people of many faiths. What 'communion' could there be if any were excluded, be they Muslims, untouchables, or members of this sect or that? We are *drawn* to a centre through temporary *with*-drawal from the pressing cares of life. Indeed we are drawn *with*-in. This requires a withdrawal from speech. Gandhi, we must remember, had many Quaker friends. He always insisted on pindrop silence before the congregational prayers began, and his own presence invariably brought it about whether the group were a small one or a gathering of thousands. The practice of the Jain munis (monks) and the Trappists had become second nature with him. The image of the three monkeys, who speak no evil, hear no evil, and see no evil was much beloved by Gandhi but of course provides a far more negative model than actually fitted Gandhi's own practice. Without seeing evil there can be no chance of tackling it.

There still remains the sense of touch, which for Gandhi, in a long life of service, was a matter of great complexity, ranging from touch as the gate of temptation, to the cause closest to his heart as a Hindu, the removal of untouchability. The inner voice calls upon him to exercise a healing touch, whether it be in economic relations (the fast undergone in Ahmedabad), the withdrawal of the non-cooperation movement, or the strenuous endeavour to bring about communal harmony. Touch was a crucially important factor in Gandhi's personal life, canalised in a life-long interest in the nursing of others, expressed very explicitly in his valuing of manual work, and reflected in his personal need of contact, his habit of walking in later life supported by two younger volunteers, one on either side.

Underneath were the everlasting arms, his own consciousness of the supportive power which no human power could rival. Gandhi, it strikes me, was wise enough to see that reason is wrongly conceived as a human endowment working against the other God-given powers which we have. There is a sense in which the various powers become internalised for him. Seeing becomes inner vision, hearing means listening to the inner voice, touching means being touched by divine grace. But Gandhi does not stop there. If he had, he would have been a mystic in the contemplative tradition, and that, I have already tried to stress, he was not. He thought poorly of those who turned their backs on the world from no matter how worthy a motive, because, as he saw it, it meant they were shirking *work*. The life of service needs the enlisting of all our powers. Indian philosophical thought had been no less hag-ridden by seeing man's faculties in a compartmentalised manner than had the western.[9] Gandhi, it seems to me, out of his very homespun commonsense rather than for any philosophical reason, sees man's life as all of a piece. If there is a tendency to dichotomy in his thought it is that between soul and body (rather than mind and body), a view he inherits from Jainism. But this is tempered by the need to keep the body in good working order if one is to be a fit instrument for service. The seeing of man's life as a totality (for which sanction can be found in the *Gītā*'s stress on the possibility of combining the various *mārgas*) does not exclude recognition of the extent to which man, because he is a thinking and above all *feeling* human being, experiences inner struggle. The old Adam is represented in Indian thought in terms of egoity, self-centredness. Hackneyed though it may sound, and Gandhi's speeches were always full of proverbial wisdom some of which is of late Victorian vintage, God helps those who help themselves.

Have we moved too far away from the inner voice? Does he manage to avoid the old chestnut of the fallibility of conscience? There is a semantic way out. The inner voice of a Genghis Khan or an Al Capone is no inner voice at all, but a travesty of it. In a way the problem is the same as the one the existentialist faces when he insists on authenticity. But the semantic answer will not do, and Gandhi has more to offer than just that. In a prayer speech in 1944 he said:[10] 'The struggle between the forces of good and evil is ceaseless and eternal. The former have Truth and *Ahimsa* as weapons against the latter's falsehood, violence and brute force.' What Gandhi is suggesting is not a set of *criteria* but a weaponry of safeguards, *satya*, ahimsa, faith, reason (the classical *buddhi* re-thought as a power which enables us to see what *needs to be done*), and the imaginative sympathy which enables us to put ourselves in another's place. This is to say that the inner voice is not to be heard without necessary preparation. The delicate tuning[11] that is required is the outcome both of personal endeavour and divine aid. What did Gandhi mean by practising the presence of God, a phrase he himself uses, and which gives the title to a selection of Brother Lawrence's prayers and letters the English translation of which appeared in 1926. Employed as a cook in a Carmelite monastery Brother Lawrence believed that it was possible for a soul to live constantly in the divine presence and that formal prayer was but an extension of this. Gandhi and the seventeenth century lay brother seem to be of one mind here.

Anyone who studies Gandhi's life and thought cannot but be struck by the terms of familiarity and yet humility with which Gandhi speaks of God. If we are to derive a philosophy of religion out of all this it will be something intimately confessional, not a thought-out structure which can be presented in a tidy framework. He was extraordinarily *rooted* (I use the word in the sense in which both Simone Weil and Gustave Thibon use it) and extraordinarily *open*. This is a rare combination, for the rooted man usually speaks of commitment, a factor which keeps him on a single track, and the open attitude often sends a man awash, 'floating' in a Jasperian sense. Gandhi's childhood background and training was such as to foster both rootedness and openness. His conception of God was shaped by Vaishnava influences, but he had witnessed the spirit of devotion in people of other religious traditions as well and it was something to which he was immediately responsive. Devotion, however, for Gandhi, was intimately related to quest and it was this which drew to him two other giants of those days, Rabindranath Tagore and C. F. Andrews. Gandhi never liked the titles with which those who revered him, endowed him – *karmavīr* (a hero of action, the word here being one characteristically used in Jain ethico-religious thought) and Mahatma (great soul). He saw himself as a humble seeker after truth, a devotee of God.

In 1934 a famous controversy took place between the two friends who admired each other so much, Gandhi and Tagore. Truth called them differently, and Tagore was distressed at Gandhi's interpretation of the Bihar earthquake, linking, so it seemed to Rabindranath, what was purely a cosmic phenomenon, with the practice of untouchability, and seeing the disaster as a punishment for human iniquity. Gandhi's famous reply included an interesting statement about his religious beliefs, only part of which I shall quote here:[12]

> If God is not a personal being for me like my earthly father He is infinitely more. He rules me in the tiniest detail of my life. I believe literally that not a leaf moves but by His will. Every breath I take depends upon His sufferance.
>
> He and His Law are one. The Law is God. Anything attributed to Him is not a mere attribute. He is the Attribute. He is Truth, Love, Law and a million things that human ingenuity can name.

It contains one of the fullest theological statements that Gandhi ever made on any occasion. The context needs to be borne in mind. It was common practice for the Brahmos to refer to God as Father in their prayers, and many of the most striking hymns in the Brahmo 'hymn book' had been composed by Tagore's father, Devendranath Tagore. The father analogy, as I mentioned before, is not one which is common in Hindu thought. Gandhi's first comment then, sets him apart from the Brahmos whose role as reformers of the Hindu community, including their protest against animal sacrifice, however, no doubt earned his respect. But it was a respect which made room for disagreement, for, among other things, he did not share their fondness for western education. The immediate controversy concerned the relation between the moral law and the physical world, in which, whatever we may think of Gandhi's idiosyncratic line on the earthquake, roots him in the tradition which sees *dharma* as a principle operative at both the cosmic and human levels. Gandhi is here extending the personal experience of the *bhakta*, the experience of complete surrender, so as to see the entire cosmos, all that is, as *dependent* on God. The idea that not a sparrow falls to the ground without His knowledge is translated by Gandhi into the language of the people of Aryavarta, those for whom the forests are a blessing, for whom the offering of leaves is part of the ceremony of worship. Not a leaf moves but by His will. The use of upper case 'H' becomes necessary as Gandhi's article was published in English. Indian languages do not have upper and lower case letters, a point that enables us not to make too much of the distinction between truth and Truth, god and God and so forth.

Gandhi next comes out with an interesting comment on the language of attribute. We may take it (I hazard this opinion, I may be wrong) that Gandhi was quite innocent of any knowledge of the ontological argument. Yet here he is surely saying something which has complex theological overtones. God is not the *source* of Law (cf. Kant's discussion of the moral law and the Divine Legislator) but He *is* the Law. Whatever we attribute to God we do so out of 'human ingenuity'. The background of this, I venture to suggest, is not a Spinozistic insight into the limitlessness of the Divine attributes, but a sense of the *inadequacy* of all attribute language in speaking of Divine Being. That Being is Divine is taken for granted by Gandhi. Hindu philosophical thought distinguishes between *nirguna* Brahman (Being as quality-less) and *saguna* Brahman (Being as the devotee sees Him, that is, with qualities). Gandhi does not get involved in philosophical discussion about the nature of the Absolute. He often uses the image of being wide-awake, a term which has philosophical resonances if we think of the classical distinction between the various modes of consciousness, including dreamless sleep. But the philosophical overtones prove to be a red herring, for Gandhi speaks of being wide-awake in talking about *conscience*. We are not called to a higher state of consciousness where the mesh of *māyā* will disappear. We are on the other hand very much in-the-world and need all our wits, our conscience, and the total resources of being human, to enable us to play our part in it.

Gandhi's references to Advaita are illuminating in this regard. His language is strongly reminiscent of that of Swami Vivekananda who has been described as a neo-Vedantin and who spoke of Daridranārāyan, or 'God the poor'. In 1924, Gandhi wrote:[13] 'I believe in absolute oneness of God and therefore also of humanity. What though we have many bodies? We have but one soul. The rays of the sun are many, through refraction. But they have the same source.' In the same year he uses the word *advaita* explicitly:[14]

> I do not believe that an individual may gain spiritually and those around him suffer. I believe in *advaita*. I believe in the essential unity of man and for that matter of all that lives. Therefore I believe that if one man gains spiritually, the whole world gains with him and, if one man falls, the whole world falls to that extent.

The two uses of 'therefore' in each quotation invite attention. In the first, since God is one, so also is humanity one. The argument is not mediated through the posit of the fatherhood of God. Indeed it is not certain that for Gandhi it is an argument at all. The 'therefore' is more like the Cartesian 'ergo', drawing attention to what is taken to be a self-evident truth. The idea of one soul is advaitic no doubt. But the image of the rays of the sun is pluralistic. To speak of a common source is not to speak of identity. In this statement, Jain and Advaitic themes seem to strive for predominance in Gandhi's mind. The second quotation finds Gandhi on surer ground. He is speaking on the matter closest to his heart, and incidentally, in an idiom which is in tune with the central message of Mahayana Buddhism. The point he is making, moreover, does not tie in with the Jain belief that an individual *can* gain spiritually on his own. Gandhi is advaitic only to the extent that he believes in the oneness of all that lives, and that this oneness has to be realised by man in the sense that he has to become *aware of* it. But at this point the enlightenment motif comes to an end. Unity for Gandhi, strictly speaking, is *shown* in the way we live rather than merely *known*.

Let us note the stress of the second 'therefore' before we go further. Since there is an essential unity in the living world (the Bihar earthquake discussion, we saw, extends this to the non-living world too) this becomes the ground of the belief that the spiritual gain of one man will lift up the rest. The matter is tied up neatly, for the spiritual gain of the individual has already been defined as that which alleviates the suffering of those that surround him. The tradition once more needs to be borne in mind. For centuries the common people of India had revered holy men. The man who opted out of society and took to what C. D. Broad once described (if my memory does not fail me) as the life of spiritual specialisation, was not regarded as a parasite. As a mendicant he was supported by society, and he in turn bestowed blessings on those who filled his bowl with rice. But there were holy men and holy men. Indian religious consciousness and behaviour is curious in its tendency to classify in a graded way those who pursue the road of self-realisation, and deem 'great souls' those who succeed in their quest. The title of Mahatma had been thrust on Gandhi and he was never very happy about it. 'Bapu' (Father) was a name which suited him better and it was reserved for those with whom he was intimate. He did not in any way see himself as coming in the line of holy men who claimed to have achieved self-perfection and whose blessings were invoked by those whose miseries they had done nothing to alleviate. Almost each day his correspondence included requests from those

who, in the Indian manner, sought his blessings for this or that.
Again the cultural context must be remembered. In India not only
a holy man, but any senior person whether teacher, guru, or elderly
relation, can be called upon to bestow blessings on those who are
junior. On one occasion when his rather hard-pressed secretary was
inundated by the volume of written requests for blessings and was
inclined to consign some of them to the waste-paper basket,
Gandhi's sharp eye noticed what was in his mind and stopped him.
A number of postcards were to be bought and each correspondent
was to be told that if the project for which blessings were requested
was a worthy one then Gandhi's blessings could be taken as
bestowed on him. It was a clever move. The onus of consulting
conscience was laid fairly and squarely on the shoulders of the
inquirer!

In what sense is identification with all that lives *shown* rather than
known? Gandhi writes:[15]

> Man's ultimate aim is the realization of God, and all his activities,
> social, political, religious, have to be guided by the ultimate aim
> of the vision of God. The immediate service of all human beings
> becomes a necessary part of the endeavour, simply because the
> only way to find God is to see Him in His creation and be one with
> it. This can only be done by service of all. I am a part and parcel
> of the whole, and I cannot find Him apart from the rest of
> humanity.

In short we can only find God by serving humanity. That the
identity towards which human effort is directed is not conceived by
Gandhi in Śaṃkara's terms is clear from this quotation:[16]

> I subscribe to the belief or the philosophy that all life in its essence
> is one, and that the humans are working consciously or
> unconsciously towards the realization of that identity. This belief
> requires a living faith in a living God who is the ultimate arbiter
> of our fate.

I have chosen the last two quotations, *inter alia*, for their inclusion of
the word 'realization' which always occasions some difficulty in
analysis when used in the context of any Indian system of thought.
Those who teach philosophy in Indian universities are often
embarrassed by earnest seekers from overseas who are anxious to

meet some 'God-realised' men. The present writer was even requested (the request was, needless to say, not complied with!) to furnish some statistics of the percentage of people in ashrams who could be said to be God-realised and the numbers of those who were still trying. It is not surprising that the overseas visitor should be tantalised by the prospect of meeting such curiosities.

As we have noticed by now, there is an apparent simplicity about Gandhi's statements. But on analysis they bristle with possible meanings and one has to see *through* the language, used almost invariably in off the cuff responses to concrete situations or in question and answer sessions with serious inquirers. Gandhi does use the word 'realisation' quite often. In this respect he is not unlike other Indian writers on religion. But we have already seen that, as a karmayogin, he does not belong to the tradition of those who see liberation in terms of the attaining of a superior state of consciousness beyond good and evil and which may or may not (depending on the particular school of thought) be accompanied by a condition of bliss. The vision of God, and listening to God, presuppose a discreteness, a distance which is to be bridged both by devotion and grace, but which does not terminate in a state of identity. Gandhi is not a mystic, nor is he a philosophical monist. He speaks so often of his longing to see God face to face.

What does he mean by saying that human beings are working consciously or unconsciously towards the realisation of the identity, the oneness of all life? One interpretation is that the identity is already there and that, as in the classical story of the prince brought up in a lowly environment who discovers who he 'really' is, we have to 'wake up', as it were, to this identity. The other interpretation is that the identity has to be brought about by our efforts. There is, in the second quotation, an implied contrast with the non-human world. The environment, of which ecologists these days speak is, in its natural state, a world which possesses a unity, a system of interconnected parts into which only *human* activity has brought a discordant note, an imbalance. Gandhi often uses the idea of evolution, of progress. There is a genuine sense in which we are called upon to *become* something for which we have the potentiality but which still struggles against much in us which pulls in an opposite direction. 'Becoming' language, it must be remembered, is not compatible with the Advaita Vedanta understanding of oneness. Gandhi's stress on service as worship, service as the way of identification with others, his conviction that it involves a self-sacrificing dedication to *work*, provides, I believe, a good antidote (perhaps this is too strong a word) to the language of self-realisation and God-realisation which indeed even he himself on occasion uses, but which calls up an ātman/Brahman identity which I do not believe actually enters into his religious thought. The entire evidence of his favourite hymns, whether Vaishnavite or Christian, witnesses to his relation to a Being who is supremely Other, and yet nonetheless dwells in the human heart, and whose face is seen in the faces of the poor. Man *finds* himself by losing himself in the service of others and this service is none other than the service of God. The image of he who serves is a familiar one in Vaishnava devotional literature. It is also no less familiar in the Old and New Testaments.

Romain Rolland and Rabindranath Tagore both had the impression (at times, not always) that Gandhi, with all his rigorous self-discipline and continuous self-giving, missed an element in the life of worship that had usually been stressed in the Hindu tradition, the element of bliss. The distinction between happiness and bliss in the context of Indian religions is something like the distinction between happiness and beatitude in the west, in the sense that the latter of the two terms is of a different *order*, a state not possible without much prayer and seeking, accessible to all but attained by a few. All who were close to Gandhi have testified to his irresistible sense of fun, his bubbling spirits which seemed to well up from an inner spring in the face of all adversity. No man with the gift of laughter is devoid of joy and it is a joy of a specially mutual kind, for a man does not laugh by himself. There is also, paradoxically, the joy that Gandhi experienced in jail, again brought about through a sense of closeness to his band of fellow-workers, sharing experiences together. Gandhi's joys were always very human joys. Where the Advaitins in particular had held out the possibility of an *ānanda* which would be literally out of this world, Gandhi experienced the exhileration of non-violent combat, the joy of winning over an erstwhile opponent, the moment of mutual understanding in discussion with a sincere inquirer, the feeling that the people were *with* him. There is a saying in Sanskrit which says that without suffering there can be no joy. Gandhi most surely experienced both. Perhaps at the heart of his experience was something like this – the sense that when the vast mass of people are living in misery, when they are not even as well provided with food as the birds who greet the dawn with song, *enjoyment* as such, is a luxury. This is a recurring theme in his exchanges with Tagore which were always at a profound level, that is, not at the level of mere exchange of opinion. Tagore once said of Gandhi:[17] 'An ascetic himself, he does not frown on the joys of others, but works for the enlivening of their existence day and night'. Gandhi remarked, in a book written on the subject of health that 'without salvation there can be no true happiness.'[18] Of his 'most exacting Master' he wrote that 'The greater the surrender to Him, the greater has been my joy.'[19] But it was a happiness which was 'not dependent on external circumstances'.[20] He uses the word delight in a revealing passage about the man who gives himself up to God in complete self-surrender:[21] ' . . . he immediately finds himself in the service of all that lives. It becomes his delight and his recreation. He is a new man, never weary of spending himself in the service of God's creation'. Tagore once commented that:[22] 'The secret of Gandhi's success lies in his dynamic spiritual strength and incessant self-sacrifice.' This dynamic spiritual strength was fed by Gandhi's experience of prayer. Gandhi has himself testified that the factor that enabled him to recover from despair, for he had his share of bitter experiences both public and private, was invariably his practice of prayer.

Prayer for Gandhi was a major means of self-purification. In a characteristic metaphor he likened the role of prayer in the purification of the mind to that of the bucket and the broom[23] in the cleaning up of our physical surroundings. Prayer arises from the hunger of the soul, he said. Gandhi seems to have experienced this hunger very forcibly during his South African period, especially during the time spent in jail. He had attended many Christian prayer-meetings, and recognised the earnestness of those who besieged the mercy seat, especially those who made earnest supplication for the saving of the soul of their erring brother. But on the whole he was put off by their almost total stress on petitionary prayer. His own life of prayer witnesses to an unfolding in which the prayer of supplication, like the cry of David out of the depths of his distress, was certainly present, but which did not provide the dominant note. Gandhi, early in life, had already adopted a mantric prayer, Rāmnām, as part of his devotional practices. The vow also can be regarded as prayerful dedication to a way of life which indicates both repentance and a casting of oneself on God who alone can give the strength needed to keep a vow. Gandhi knew that there can be prayers of thanksgiving and prayerful acts of propitiation. Propitiation and supplication are characteristic forms of prayer in the various Indian traditions. As far as petition was concerned, the proper petition, as Gandhi saw it, was for the purification of the soul. 'The real meaning of prayer', he said, 'is devoted worship'.[24] Gandhi's conception of worship must be seen against the backdrop of the traditional notion of *pūjā* which involves invoking the presence of the deity, followed by the making of offerings (including the offerings of right feelings and good actions). For Gandhi, worship is both internalised, communing with God as the Indweller, and externalised in the sense that work is worship, the service of others is worship.

One further reason why Gandhi found petitionary prayer inadequate was the personal difficulty he felt in putting thoughts into words. In one of his prayer speeches he said:[25] 'The very attempt to clothe thought in word or action limits it. No man in this world can express a thought in word or action fully'. He confessed that 'words won't come to me'. For this reason, Gandhi found silent prayer an invaluable aid to that 'inward restfulness' which prepared the devotee for the still small voice. As Romain Rolland with all his sensitive understanding of his friend realised, Gandhi was a stranger to the passionate ecstasies of the inner life. But the words Gandhi uses to describe his own experience of prayer echo the experience of men of many faiths – being filled with the presence of God, a yearning of the heart to be one with the Maker, turning towards God, a conscious realisation of His presence within us. Man is:[26] ' . . . a creature of God striving to realize his divinity. Repentance and self-purification are the means. . . . True repentance is an essential pre-requisite of prayer'. Gandhi does not distinguish between meditation and prayer. He speaks of meditation, prayer and worship interchangeably, but he insists:[27] ' . . . They must be seen in every act of ours.' He does not set out a sequence for prayer as in a liturgy, but we find the elements are all there, praise and thankfulness, confession, repentance and intercession.

Gandhi has also reflected on associated problems raised by philosophers of religion. Prayer is not a *substitute* for effort, even though it is a natural human phenomenon for a man to pray to God to lift him up when he is in distress. Does prayer make a difference? Can prayer move God? Does not God know best? He wrote to Madeleine Slade about her prayers for Romain Rolland's health:[28]

I do not know that those prayers add a single second to the life prayed for. But they elevate those who pray and comfort those for whom the prayers are offered. The comfort has the appearance of prolongation of life.

Prayer is 'a daily admission of one's weakness'.[29] But this does not mean that the strong man does not need to pray. Prayer is both an expression of trust and a source of strength. It is an appeal for God's blessing on human endeavour. By implication Gandhi has a word of counsel for those who find it hard to pray, or who exclaim that they are not men of prayer. For one thing, prayer does not have to be in the form of words. Furthermore, the man who finds it hard to pray is often seeking for a dimension set apart from mundane activities, social, political and economic. This is a mistake. Writing to ashramites and those involved in active campaigns, where there was no time for prayers at the regular intervals, he reassured them that their labour was equivalent to prayer. If human life is an undivided whole, no line can be drawn between praying and other daily activities. As for the problem of praying to what or to whom, Gandhi understood the need that most people felt for symbolism. But for his own part this was the position:[30] 'I do not forbid the use of images in prayer. I only prefer the worship of the Formless.' If this sounds like meditation of a rarefied type, Gandhi sets us right by putting this alongside 'spinning and other daily duties' all of which can be reckoned as a 'spiritual lighthouse', that is, an agency which sheds light in darkness. Through every activity of life man can become aware of that 'indefinable, mysterious power' that pervades everything.

What is of special interest in the context of Indian religions is the role that Gandhi gives to congregational prayer. The Brahmo Samaj apart, the Hindu tradition does not accommodate congregational prayer in quite the way in which Gandhi made it a special feature of his daily routine. A private matter became part of public practice. Furthermore, instead of a homily or sermon, Gandhi would give a 'prayer address' which dealt with a very practical matter which had arisen in the day to day running of the ashram, the political events of the day, or the social challenges that needed to be met. If the congregational prayer situated worship firmly in the context of the everyday it no less situated the everyday in what others have described as 'le milieu divin'.

Some of the stages on Gandhi's life's way throw a little light on how he came to feel the need for congregational prayer. In 1896 the Gandhi family sailed from Calcutta to Durban, and as the ship neared the coast of Madagascar it ran into heavy seas. On all sides rose the sound of the prayers of men of different faiths. At a time of need sectarian differences melted away and all cried aloud the name of God, each in his own tongue. This was undoubtedly one of the formative experiences of Gandhi's religious life. Congregational prayer was introduced by Gandhi in his South African ashrams, the Phoenix Settlement and Tolstoy Farm, 'as a means for training in the use of the weapon of Satyagraha or soul force' before the beginning of the South Africa Satyagraha struggle. The custom was kept up in the ashrams he founded in India and indeed wherever Gandhi and his volunteers happened to be staying. It was, in fact, a natural outgrowth of Gandhi's pedagogy of sharing, of nurturing the fellow-feeling which would make men feel other's sufferings as their own, a further exercise in that releasing of powers which came about when men acted in unison. Late in life Gandhi puts it this way:[31] 'The secret of collective prayer is that the emanation of silent influence from one another helps in the realization of one's goal.' Prayer was the greatest binding force, he said on another occasion. To be in tune with God is to be in tune with one another. This point becomes specially significant, as we shall see in Chapter 7, in understanding Gandhi's attitude to religious diversity, for his prayer-meetings were very often inter-faith gatherings. Apart from the ashram prayer-meetings, especially towards the end of his life, Gandhi had *mass* prayer gatherings which, from all accounts, were as complete a contrast to the Billy Graham revivalist meeting as they were different from the Papal auidence.

Before the prayer gathering Gandhi suggested all shut their eyes in order 'to turn the gaze inward'.[32] In a letter to Sardar Patel he wrote:[33]

> The congregational prayer is having a magical effect. I am witnessing it every day. The crowds run into thousands – sometimes hundreds upon thousands. Yet there is perfect order and pindrop silence during the prayer – no jostling, no noise. It is a revelation.

The mass gatherings were certainly an object lesson in self-discipline. Gandhi, the educator, knew what he was about. In days when violence was very near the surface 'even the weakest would enjoy perfect protection'. The entire gathering would acquire a God-given freedom from fear, and those whose faith was weak would be strengthened. Why did the crowds come? Was it just to have *darshan* (literally 'sight of', but implying a blessing) of the Mahatma? Gandhi was humble enough to say that, even if this was so, the crowds came because they wanted to join a man of prayer.

The congregational prayers at the ashrams (first in Sabarmati and then in Wardha) took place at 4 a.m. and 7.30 p.m. The morning prayer began with recitation of *shlokas* (verses) printed in the Ashram *Bhajanāvalī* (hymnal). This was followed by one *bhajan* (hymn); *Ramadhun* (a hymn consisting of repetition of Rāmanāma) and a recitation from the *Gītā*. In the evening there was recitation of the last nineteen verses of the second chapter of the *Gītā* (Sthitaprajñasya kā bhāṣā), one bhajan, Ramadhun, and a reading from a sacred book. The evening prayers on the day before his 1924 fast was broken included a passage from the *Gīta* recited in unison, a hymn by Kabir sung by one of the company and an exposition of the Kaṭha Upanishad by Vinoba Bhave.

C. F. Andrews noted that while no images were used in Gandhi's religious observances and they were not held in a temple or special place, in fact more often than not under the open sky, everyone present took great joy in devotional music. The repertoire included Gandhi's favourite Christian hymns, 'Rock of Ages', 'When I survey the wondrous Cross', 'Abide with me', 'He who would true valour see', 'Lead Kindly Light' and hymns from Gujarati and Maharathi sources. Ramadhun was invariably part of the 'order of service'. Gandhi regarded it as prayer reduced to its simplest terms. Incidentally, there are two interesting variations on the trinitarian theme in Gandhi's religious thought. One is the trinity of evil thought, words and acts against which prayer is a shield. The other is what Gandhi calls 'the triple accord of the voice, the accompaniment and thought' which is found in the singing of Ramadhun. In keeping with the nature of Indian music, which does not accommodate harmony, Gandhi uses the image of music sung in unison as a symbol of human unity, something which echoes inner unison, and this in turn is both a unison of powers *within* the soul (absence of conflict) and a unison *between* men, a oneness of heart. He believed, there is no doubt, that congregational prayer generated power, since all waited on God together, and the atmosphere which resulted he characterised as possessed of sweetness, fragrance and strength. The link between prayer, power and peace was a very real one for Gandhi. So also was the link between individual and congregational prayer. Each fed the other. We find herein clues to two further important dimensions of Gandhi's religious thought, his understanding of religious diversity and his practical experience of it, and his vision of a transformed community.

7 Diversities of Gifts

It is necessary to say straightaway that Gandhi was not concerned with 'the problem of religious pluralism' in the sense that Christian theologians wrestle with it today. His was not the task of assessing rival truth claims, of reconciling apparently disparate visions, of formulating an intellectual model wherein theology can somehow or other be conceived in a global form. Pluralism never presents itself as an intellectual problem for Gandhi. Anyone with a Jain background takes it for granted. It always puzzled him that those who professed to follow the man for whom all alike were the children of God should set up barriers of allegiance between man and man, between saved and unsaved, between one sect and another, between the Christian *vis-à-vis* men of 'other faiths'. The Hindu takes it for granted that there are diversities of gifts but the same spirit, that the tree of mankind has many branches and each branch a myriad leaves. There has never been, throughout the long history of the Indian peoples, anything like (to borrow a phrase) a Ptolemaic standpoint. The danger, if at all, has been of the opposite kind, a tendency to find a sameness which can underplay the genuine differences which have been shaped by history, to proclaim an essence which does not sufficiently recognise the quiddity of traditions, all those elements that are not to be classified as accidental.

Gandhi was never very happy about St Paul's extrapolation of Christ's gospel. It was the *Ur*-message that appealed to him – love of God and one's neighbour. Without quite realising it, as a result of his contact with evangelical Christianity in South Africa, it was often the very Jewishness of the New Testament message that he responded to, the central teaching which was already there in the Old Testament. He speaks quite naturally of 'the Pillar of Fire in front of us',[1] and avows of God that 'He is a jealous Lord'.[2] Indian as he was, he was too aware of the fact of religious pluralism for any thought of a possible Omega point to appear as either feasible or desirable. Doke's assessment,[3] that of a friend and one who had observed him at close quarters during his South African period, is as valid of the young Gandhi as it was of the Mahatma of later years: Gandhi's sympathies were so wide and catholic that he seemed to have reached a point where the formulae of sects had no meaning for him. In a sense no greater tribute to Gandhi than this has ever been made. But Gandhi did not reach this point, which Doke has identified with such unfailing insight, through any kind of secularist temper, nor from a humanist outlook which was grounded in naturalism or which relegated the life of the spirit to superstructure or to irrelevance. Gandhi's relations with men of different religious persuasions must be seen in the light of his experiments with truth. We should not look upon him as a pioneer labouring on theological frontiers, for the frontier mentality, whether in relation to geography or anything else, was quite foreign to his way of thinking. God never made frontiers, he once put it. Also to be borne in mind is the practical context of the situations he faced from day to day where it was absolutely vital, both in South Africa and later in India, that all conditions of men, regardless of differences of caste or creed, should be able to work together for the great causes that engaged them, where indeed these very differences could become sources of strength, a pool of talents on which all could draw. There is a confessional quality in Gandhi's sayings about his inter-faith experiences which should not be forced into the straightjacket of theorising. We need also to bear in mind Gandhi's own knack of often finding his own deepest convictions reflected in what he read. When this happened, as most notably when he first came across H. D. Thoreau's essay on civil disobedience, he greeted with joy this further testimony to what he already believed to be true, and spoke of his convictions being thereby deepened and confirmed. I mention this, lest we think of Gandhi as a man who was unduly open to *influences*. When he comes across something which strikes him as new (as in Ruskin's teaching that the life of labour is the life most worth living) he acknowledges it as such. In religious matters his own special gift was the ability to see a common human striving, a common human response to a power beyond all understanding, in people bearing diverse religious labels. In refusing to be intimidated by the latter, he was all the more ready to recognise and, even more, to welcome the different ways in which the spirit becomes articulate in men and moves them. Commitment to common ethical values was, he found, in no way incompatible with diversity of religious belief.

It may seem strange that a national leader, one indeed in whom nationalist aspirations found their most eloquent voice, should have believed so deeply in the unity of mankind. The oceanic circle metaphor referred to earlier lends itself to an expansion of wider and wider circumferences, without limit, so as eventually to embrace the whole world. The unity of mankind, Gandhi thought, was based first of all on the common imperfections which all men have. To realise that others can be jealous, acquisitive, selfish and so on, and that we have these same weaknesses in ourselves, is a step along the path of understanding. Next, Gandhi believed that all men have within them certain positive powers for good, a heritage of non-violent strength, fearlessness and nobility, which needs activating through a discipline of self-purification and practical training in constructive work. This introduces the element of hope within the human condition. Thirdly, all are subject to the same laws of growth, a sense of expansion which informs us when we are on the right track, a capacity (almost in the Aristotelian manner) for habits of virtue to become second nature, confirming good resolution and enabling man to progress. The laws of growth involve both a deepening of faith, a rooting in the tradition to which we belong, and a broadening of sympathies which sets no limit to man's reaching out to his fellows and which for Gandhi was founded on the ability to put oneself in the other man's place.

Gandhi's faith in the unity of mankind was linked, moreover, to his belief that the nations complemented one another. This was an insight born out of his imaginative and generous recognition of the good qualities of others. A microcosmic form of this was often mentioned by him in his speeches up and down the country, that people should acquire the wisdom of the *brāhmin*, the fighting spirit of the *kshatriya*, the business acumen of the *bania* and the spirit of service of the *śūdra*. A natural corollary of this would be the idea that the different religions in some sense are complementary to each other. After all an important implicate of the trusteeship idea is that of the pooling of talent and this can surely include the pooling of religious insights. If we take the speeches he made to different communities as evidence, some such idea seems to have been in the background of his thought. The ground motif, however, would always remain the tradition into which we were born. If God had wished us to be other than we were surely He would have created us accordingly. Where some may see a factor of geographical for-tuitousness about the faith a man happens to have, Gandhi sees no such thing. The concept of *swadharma* provides a rationale for working out one's salvation in the community into which one is born.

But how far can the vision of a common humanity take us? Gandhi's own experience told him that within one and the same community there can be great inhumanity to man. The leading example for him was the situation of the untouchables, who were, after all, members of the Hindu community. An example of a rather different kind but still an example of discord between members of one and the same community, would be the relations between Catholics and Protestants today in Ulster. But as far as the encounter of *separate* religious communities was concerned it was the relation between Hindus and Muslims that concerned him most, a situation which was eventually to lead to the partition of the country. In both cases, that is, discord within a community and discord between communities, Gandhi's initial reaction was invariably to detect the economic and social basis of the discord. Matters which, on the surface, were matters concerning belief, were often found to have an unmistakably economic content. It was the economic grievance (or the social or the political) which cried out for redress. When this was satisfactorily tackled Gandhi was perhaps optimistic enough to believe that other matters would fall into place. But the grievances of centuries could not be settled overnight, nor could fear, prejudice and habits of over reacting to provocation be tackled through exhortation, and without the patient example of constructive workers whose example the masses would gradually learn to follow. Gandhi's untiring efforts in the cause of Hindu–Muslim unity have now become part of the history of a sub-continent, and historians deem him to have failed. Even so, Gandhi's relations with Muslims are from the point of view of this study very crucial evidence of that outreach of the spirit that I have been trying to point up.

Before we come to this, however, we need to look again at Gandhi's stand *vis-à-vis* secularism and secularisation. For good or ill, these terms have become closely associated with a number of other concepts such as modernisation, westernisation, the scientific outlook, materialism, this-worldliness, a desacralised view of the universe and so on. That whether in western countries or in India it is not found easy to plot the relation of all these to each other is perhaps witness not only to the semantic confusion of our times but, even more, to the social pressures and changes that are operative in the twentieth century. We need to go back a bit in order to understand Gandhi. The sequence of historical events was such that his ability to discriminate between western culture and imperialism came slowly. *Hind Swaraj* finds him identifying the two. But his own adoption in practice of two typically western culture-components, a work ethos and care for punctuality, showed he was willing to make his own whatever was, first of all, worth emulating, and next, capable of being adopted by the poorest of the poor. His attitude to materialism can by no means be identified with the blanket disapproval sometimes mistakenly attributed by scholars to Hindus. He was against the rapacious acquisitiveness which he had seen writ large in the faces of those who had come to South Africa to make their fortunes. But no modern Indian leader has laid such stress on *artha* (wealth) as a value as Gandhi did, and, with the possible exception of Swami Vivekananda, no one else has seen through the clap-trap of high thinking in the context of human destitution better than Gandhi. He by no means turned his back on modern science, but he wanted it to be used for the service of man, and above all for it not to lead to a displacement of labour, a vital point in a country where, as he put it, the only form in which God dare appear to the poor was the form of work.

We have to tread warily if we are to see in Gandhi's religious thought any attempt to come to terms with the process of secularisation, for such coming to terms is no doubt a notable feature of much of contemporary theologising in the twentieth century. The secular powers with which Gandhi was engaged in non-violent combat all his life were forms of exploitation such as racialism and imperialism. These powers he saw as forces which could be more than matched by other forces which lay within man himself, although for the most part the latter lay dormant. His adding of new symbols to India's cultural life, symbols such as the spinning wheel, shows, if anything, a reverse process to that of secularisation. Economic life is seen by Gandhi to fall within a religious framework. This is not by any means a new grafting as far as Indian thought is concerned. Cow protection is the classic case of economic common sense being endowed with a religious halo. But the realities of life, poverty, deprivation and exploitation, could easily drive out the aura of religiosity with which the Renaissance thinkers of India, in whose train Gandhi comes, invested the day to day task of nation-building. It was not secularisation that was to prove to be the dominant tendency in India but politicalisation. But this happened after Gandhi's time and we must not anticipate.

It was to Gandhi's everlasting credit that the realities of life, those which affected the teeming millions, were not swept by him under the convenient carpet of *māyā*, or made in any way subordinate to that darling of traditional philosophers, ultimate reality. Gandhi provided no re-thinking of *sanātana dharma* in the light of *science*, something which would have been a sort of parallel exercise to what some Christian theologians engage in in response to 'the challenge of secularisation'. As it happens, Gandhi made an interesting comment about new interpretations of scripture in 1927 when he wrote that many things in the Bible needed to be interpreted 'in the light of discoveries – not of modern science – but in the spiritual world in the shape of direct experiences common to all faiths.'[4] This is in keeping with the Hindu stress on the authority of *anubhūti* (inner experience), the inner light which lightens one's path. He did not differentiate between religion and politics, again something which a good secularist does. He drew freely on the matrix of religious ideas of everyman in India, just as Bankim Chandra Chatterjee and Sri Aurobindo had done. There was nothing in India parallel to the proletarian pop culture that has accompanied, tandem fashion, the secularisation of life in the west. There was a continuity between beliefs and practices in India's villages in Gandhi's lifetime and what they were hundreds of years ago, and this is so even today. Gandhi's religious thought, then, is firmly rooted in his own environment. Unlike some of his 'universalist' contemporaries, and certainty unlike Swami Vivekananda, he had no ambition to export his own way of thinking elsewhere. His healthy Jain pluralist philosophy ruled that out. The thing which he hoped India could show the world was not a new-look form of Hinduism, not, as some contemporary enthusiasts, mostly outside India, would have it, a new sort of 'spirituality', but a non-violent way of life, old as the hills, which would be able to neutralise what he saw to be the bane of our times, aggressive nationalism and its inevitable concomitant, war. If there is any paradox in Gandhi's life and personality it is not that of the saint and the canny politician but that of the nationalist leader and the confirmed internationalist for whom frontiers were utterly contingent and man-made. His natural confrères were not 'holy men' but all who believed in the fellowship of reconciliation whatever their professed religious affiliation and whatever their nationality might be. Putting it another way, one can say that Gandhi was deeply committed to the redemption of quantitative democracy. Politics to him was neither an art nor a business, still less a game (a word once used by Tilak). It was a mission.

Secularism and secularisation in the Indian context have certain features which need to be borne in mind. It was not in the context of demarcating the range of state versus clerical power that India's constitution-makers opted for a secular state. The question was a very different one, that of keeping the peace between various communities, given that India did not subscribe to the two nation theory. A demarcation of a different kind, that between sacred and profane is as foreign to the Hindu way of thinking as it is to the Muslim. Gandhi knew his India. Indian *society* is not, and never was, secular in outlook if by secular we mean keeping religion in a compartment of its own. In contemporary India the state spends considerable sums on the provision of various amenities on occasions like the Kumbha Mela when the majority community is involved in large numbers. If the Hindu and Jain ideas of purification are given full play, beyond the ideal of individual *ascesis*, if the idea of the interdependence of the economic, social, political and religious factors in society is thought through, we begin to see that Gandhi's approach was on a very different wavelength from that of those who see the main *religious* problem of the twentieth century as that of coming to terms with secularism. There is, moreover, a further warrant for Gandhi's refusal to separate religion from politics. The *Gītā* shows the validity of various paths to the attainment of the highest. This suggests that politics too, a human activity which is built into man's living in community, is a valid path. Gandhi's own *ascesis*, there can be no doubt, was not worked out through a life of meditation but through thorough involvement in the rough and tumble of political life. The purification of politics was to be brought about through an infusion of the non-violent spirit into it. There was no frontier between the things that were Caesar's and the things that were God's.

Secular man, in a western context, has tried to extract a moral core from religious tradition and reject the rest. Such a move overestimates men's rationality and underplays the role of selfishness and violence in human life. Gandhi does not make this mistake. In his own society he found that ethical principles, whether Jain or Hindu, were inextricably clothed in a religious garb. The very ambiguity of the word *dharma* (as both an ethical and a religious concept) brings this out. Secularism for him, therefore, does not mean an aseptic allegiance to the rational and the scientific, a careful avoidance of the sacred, but respect for all men and all faiths. Just as capitalism and socialism could be transcended, so Gandhi thought, similarly religious difference could be transcended. The

secularist function of religion was none other than the activism of
religion when it had been purged of obscurantism, superstition, and
doctrinal barriers. The religious instinct could be harnessed to bring
about conflict resolution, for this instinct bore within itself the seed of
sensitivity to social injustice.

What worried him in his later years was not materialism (for
nothing less like an affluent society could be found in India) but the
violence that was inherent in societies where there was social and
economic injustice. Paradoxically, secularism as he understands it,
that is, respect for men of all faiths, *depends* on men who care first and
foremost, about their own faith. There is a link, I suggest, between
Gandhi's dislike of all forms of compartmentalisation, whether it be
among the gifts and powers which men possess in their inner being,
among the social, economic political and religious dimensions of life,
or as indicated by any of the labels which mark off one man from
another. Wisdom lay in an interpenetration, a mutual fertilisation, a
give and take, and this alone can make for a healthy society.
Religion, Gandhi sees as a saving power in so far as it is through our
fragmentary visions of something higher that we aspire to change
ourselves, to change our environment. This insight of Gandhi's
provides the basis for his view of democracy, a redeemed democracy
in which each man grants to those whose vision is other than his own
a validity no less than what he attributes to his own.

Gandhi's own experience seems to have gone even further than
this. Like Swami Abhishiktananda some years later, he was able to
enrich his own experience through contact with those who had
different visions. He was able, as I see it, to go beyond both
encounter and dialogue to something which is hinted at in the
Upanishadic poetic utterance that all is food. He was able to feed on
diverse traditions and nourish himself thereby. Such a capacity
differs as much from belief in convergence towards an Omega point
as it does from theoretical allegiance to 'the universal in religion', the
essentialism of a Bhagwan Das. It indicates at once recognition of
diversities of gifts and a capacity for growth that accommodates both
the assimililation of new idioms and what, in a deeply suggestive
phrase, Gabriel Marcel has called inner accretion. I shall not try to
illustrate this in a case where it could be done without any great
difficulty, Gandhi's response to Christ and his teaching, but what
was for Gandhi, Hindu as he was, an even bolder 'experiment', his
response to Islam, his attempts to bring about reconciliation
between Hindus and Muslims. It was in the context of rejection of

the view that the two were separate nations that the modern Indian conception of secularism was worked out. Gandhi's own personal ventures in communication, however, went deeper than this, and it is with these that I shall be concerned, however inadequately, next, and not with the failure of his political mission as seen in the partition of the country.

Gandhi's contact with Muslims first began in his childhood where men of all communities were made welcome in his father's house. It may seem a small matter, but the same could not be said of all Hindu households in the last quarter of the last century. When Gandhi arrived in Durban in 1893, he was met by Abdullah Sheth who had engaged his services as a young lawyer. Gandhi recorded that contact with the Sheth gave him 'a fair amount of practical knowledge of Islam' and that they often discussed religious topics. The vocal element in the Natal Indian community was mostly Muslim. He could find in the hard working Muslim merchants from Gujarat, as he went about his campaign, the same 'bania' virtues that he often referred to later in life, and these included honesty and the careful keeping of accounts. Incidently he was very aware that banias were traditionally known for other qualities as well. Perhaps he also saw a resemblance between Muslim ardour, the Jain notion of heroism and the kshatriya sense of honour. Experience on a sea voyage had shown him that in distress all men cry out to God, calling Him by different names. Reading the Koran and Carlyle on the Prophet he again found confirmation of what he already believed. Years later he wrote:[5] 'I learnt from him (Mohammed) that only he can fast who has inexhaustible faith in God.' His experiences in the so-called Zulu Rebellion, when he nursed the sick and wounded, also left their mark. Those who attended the Cawnpore session of the Indian National Congress in December, 1925 were told:[6] 'I have seen that any Zulu embracing Christianity does not *ipso facto* come on level with all Christians; whilst immediately he embraces Islam, he drinks from the same cup and eats from the same dish as a Mussalman.' From time to time he gave an indication of what he admired about the Muslims – the fervour of the first followers, their Puritanism, the Prophet's practical reformism, 'unadulterated belief in the oneness of God', practical application of the truth of the brotherhood of man (no doubt for those who are nominally within its fold). He was open-minded enough to start using Islamic language, sometimes in rather surprising contexts. The battery of criticisms of western civilisation in *Hind Swaraj* (1909) was boosted by the comment: 'Accordingly to the teaching of Mahomed, this would be considered a Satanic civilisation.'

Back in India he was constantly aware that without Hindu-Muslim unity there could be no freedom for India. This was made very clear in a letter he wrote from hospital to Mahomed Ali, the Congress President:[7] 'An indissoluble bond between the various communities must be established if we are to win freedom'. But how was this bond to be brought about and what kind of bond was it? Gandhi felt his way over this, and each step was a different kind of experiment. 1918 was an interesting year in this respect. Here are some of the landmarks. He wrote from Sabarmati to Pandit Hridaynath Kunzru at the time of Kumbha Mela, which he was not able to attend;[8] 'I was looking forward to having an opportunity of seeing Hinduism at work, both in its devilish and divine character.' A month later, Mahadev Desai records this:[9] 'Hinduism will captivate Muslims by the power of its compassion, which is its very essence. This red-letter day of heart-unity, however, will come only when Hindus regain their spiritual heritage.' Both these statements are in keeping with Gandhi's frequent injunction that the search-light of self-criticism must be turned inwards by each community; that each must put its own house in order. 1918 is also the year in which, involved with the Ahmedabad millhands' campaign for the redress of their grievances, Gandhi advised them to take a solemn pledge to keep up the strike until a just settlement was reached. The oath was taken 'with Ishwara or Khuda (Hindu and Muslim words for God) as their witness'.[10] A simple pledge was not enough. It must tap the reservoir of power inherent in each man's religious faith. Gandhi, like Tilak, had not been invited to the conference of national leaders called by the Viceroy, Chelmsford. The Ali brothers were still interned. He wrote to the Viceroy on his own initiative, pleaded on behalf of the Ali brothers, and also for a settlement of the Khilafat question, and eventually attended the conference convened about recruitment for the war effort. It was a year when Gandhi addressed many Muslim gatherings and identified himself with Muslim political causes – all in the hope of bringing the Muslims into the mainstream of the national movement. Whether pan-Islamism could ever be compatible with nationalism, still less with the internationalism which Gandhi so passionately believed in, are quite different questions which cannot be entered into here.

The fast undertaken in September 1924 to bring about Hindu-

Muslim unity was regarded by Gandhi himself as an act of penance. How can a fast help to bring about peace and goodwill? Through the persuasive power of showing one's willingness to die for what is believed to be right. The detailed story of the twenty one day ordeal certainly shows how people of different faiths flocked to Gandhi, all equally anxious for this painful act of self-punishment to come to an end.

Sources of friction continued, cow-slaughter, conversions, the issue of separate or joint electorates, music played before mosques, and Gandhi continued his on-all-fronts attempt to create a peaceful climate where all communities could sink their differences in the national cause. The language he used in his public discourses over the decades reveals his desire both to put himself in the other man's shoes and even to see with his eyes. In Jallianwala Bagh, addressing the crowds in December 1924, he goes so far as to say that if he is not to disrespect Quran-e-Shareef he must 'look up to it with the eye of a Muslim, must do what they do when I am in their midst. . .'. This really goes further than recognising that God has many names, stressing our common humanity etc. and raises the whole question of the extent to which a person belonging to one faith can share the experience of another who belongs to a different tradition. It would seem as if much of Gandhi's life and teaching was imbued with the pedagogic intent of enabling men of diverse persuasions to *understand* each other. This came out of his own lifelong willingness to learn from others – Briton, Boer, all conditions of men, including the poorest villager whose endless patience mirrored the patience of God. This ran parallel with another motive to which it was by no means subordinate, the showing up of the economic base behind differences and the attempt to find a practical way of dealing with the exploitation/injustice involved. It is not that ideational, even ideological, differences were relegated to superstructure, but that the contestants were persuaded to look again, and this time, at the total matrix of discontent, rather than to allow apparently 'religious' aspects to obtrude as sources of friction.

The way in which Gandhi conducted his prayer-meetings provides a valuable source for any student of his religious thought. His occasional inclusion of readings from the Koran in 1947 brought down a shower of criticism on his head. He was taken to task by Hindus for being 'a slave of Jinnah-Saheb and a fifth columnist.' Some Muslim friends also objected, feeling he had no right, as a non-Muslim, to read verses from the Koran. Gandhi had written in

Harijan that when Vinoba and Pyarelal had studied the Koran in jail their Hinduism had been enriched thereby. Here again, a different claim is being made, that study of another's faith can enrich one's own. Gandhi's own criterion had been mentioned clearly to a Muslim scholar, that one should 'remain absolutely faithful to the text' and approach it 'with a prayerful and open mind'. He went on to say that no one had a monopoly of truth and that Biblical texts 'are still being corrected'.[11] Gandhi had been taken to task much earlier in his career by *Hindus*. One such occasion was when he read the New Testament to the students of the Gujarat National College.[12]

Switching back to the South Africa days, a Christian priest, an Imam and a Jew once accompanied Gandhi to visit the wife of the Tamil leader Thambi Naidoo who was in prison, and Doke records they all 'bent together in prayer'. What was possible in South Africa was impossible in the deteriorating communal situation of 1946 and 1947. Gandhi's heroic campaign in Noakhali from November 1946 onwards to bring about peace in East Bengal is now part of history. It shows him appealing to those who had been wronged to show courage and not run away, encouraging them to build a new life after they had lost all that they had at the hands of the other community. It found him urging people to realise their common concerns as weavers, fishermen and farmers rather than to think of religious labels. It was a time to forget 'religious affiliations'. This is the language he used in September, 1947.[13] The country had become free from British rule. The country had also been vivisected (in Gandhi's own words). What did Gandhi mean by forgetting religious affiliations? How could he advise this, a man for whom every act of life was a matter of *dharma*? The time had come to see that there could be no conflict of interest between Hindus and Muslims in the context of revenue, sanitation, justice – in fact in the vast task of satisfying the minimum needs of the toiling millions.

Gandhi's healing touch was not to remain for long. One of the most illuminating incidents from the last phase of his life tells of his attempt to console a poor Muslim woman whose son had perished before her eyes in the Calcutta riots. He spoke in the idiom that she would immediately understand. Allah had given her the son. Allah had taken him away. A hard saying. Perhaps no other saying could have reached her in the depth of her grief. It was not for nothing that Gandhi had tried to look up to the Koran, as he said in Jallianwala Bagh in 1924, 'with the eye of a Muslim'. It was a Hindu fanatic who assassinated him, someone who represented a group that thought Gandhi was too fond of the Muslims. He had in the last days taken the Hindus to task for their retaliation against what was happening to Hindus in what had become Pakistan. He had urged the Cabinet to transfer to Pakistan 55 crore rupees as her share of the Indian assets which had been promised. These were the last acts of a Hindu who was faithful unto death in the cause of Hindu–Muslim unity, a man who did not possess the scholarship of a Raja Ram Mohun Roy or a Maulana Azad and could not have held his own in any debate with a Muslim theologian, but who saw in the Islamic idea of brotherhood a principle capable of infinite expansion, beyond the confines of immediate affiliation and community. It was a heart-breaking experience for Gandhi to find in the twilight hour of his life that so far from India being a beacon light in this respect the forces of hatred had prevailed. He lived long enough to indicate the lines on which rebuilding must start – patient reconstruction of humane living at the village level, the righting of wrongs, the rediscovery of the dignity of neighbours and the enriching possibilities of fellowship with them.

In what remains in this chapter Doke's insightful remark about the catholic character of Gandhi's sympathies will provide something of a guiding thread. If Gandhi's South African experiences provided him with ample examples of the range of human conflicts (between indentured labourer and the authorities, between Briton and Boer, between Zulu and white) they also provided him with a training that gives us an important clue to the catholicity of which Doke wrote. I refer to his legal experience. The young Indian lawyer made a name for himself, other things apart, as a man who could settle matters out of court, who could unearth common ground where it had been thought that none existed. Peace-making, even in his legal practice, I am suggesting, went beyond conflict-resolution, to a setting up of human relations on a new footing. Such an approach requires a frank recognition of difference and a willingness to go on from there. This, I believe, enabled him to see in the meeting of people of different faiths not scope for litigation between rival systems of belief but the opportunity for mutual enrichment. We need to close in now on some of the issues involved.

Gandhi believed firmly that '. . . No one has a monopoly of truth.'[14] Since this was so, it was possible for us to learn from each other. This learning can come about in several ways. One is the study of different scriptures in a prayerful spirit. Gandhi shows a certain shift in emphasis over the years with respect to the attitude to be taken to scriptures of 'other traditions'. Addressing missionaries in Calcutta in 1925 and referring obviously to an earlier stage in his life he said:[15] '. . . I said to myself that if I was to find my satisfaction through reasoning, I must study the scriptures of other religions also and make my choice.' An example of what, in Gandhi's view, does not satisfy reason is the Christian belief that Jesus was the 'only begotten Son' of God. The importance of the appeal to reason was always stressed by Gandhi. In 1946, for example, we find the same theme again:[16] 'Religion never suffers by reason of the criticism fair or foul of critics; it always suffers from the laxity or indifference of its followers.' The context of this remark is worth mentioning in the light of our previous discussion of Gandhi and the Muslims. The Government of Sind had banned the Sindhi translation of Swami Dayananda Saraswati's *Satyārtha Prakāsh* on the ground that the fourteenth chapter was offensive to Muslims. As a veteran journalist, writer and believer in freedom of speech and of the press, Gandhi's reaction was both bold and fair.

But appeal to reason was not the only criterion given by him. Let us return to the Muslim scholar's objection to 'a non-Muslim citing the scripture for his own purpose' (the Koran) and Gandhi's reply: 'Surely there is no harm in it so long as I remain absolutely faithful to the text and approach my task with a prayerful and open mind.'[17] Here, no doubt, some difficulties raise their heads. The whole idea of being faithful to the text is question-begging, some may say, in the context of post-Schleiermacherian hermeneutics. But do we not have the key in the quotation itself? To be prayerful and to have an open mind is precisely what being 'absolutely faithful to the text' involves. But is a Muslim in a better position to do this (for the Koran) than a Christian or a Hindu? The indications given are various. Prayer and indeed the non-violent action of the satyagrahi, could be both an individual experience and a collective one. Apart from his own personal readings and studies, Gandhi, especially towards the end of his life, tried to introduce readings from the Koran into his prayer-meetings. What kind of effect would this have? He said in an after-prayer discourse[18] in New Delhi in 1946 that the secret of collective prayer was the emanation of silent influence from one another and that this would help them in the realisation of their goal. If we try to spell out what this might mean, bearing in mind the year in which it was said, it seems to me we find Gandhi drawing on the Quaker idea of the sense of a meeting, the belief that being together in a prayerful context releases power, and that there would be practical results brought about thereby. It is common knowledge that not many Muslims attended Gandhi's prayer-meetings. When those who came raised objections it was sometimes Gandhi's practice to pass on to the post-prayer speech which centred on events of the day. What was in the way was not a challenge to reason but a matter concerning the heart, a failure of heart-unity in Gandhi's own terminology, brought about through a variety of causes including economic disparities, sufferings undergone directly at the hands of others, fear etc.

An indication of a different kind can be located in the following. Gandhi translated the hymnal used in his ashram, the *Ashram Bhajanāvalī* into English for his friend and close associate Mirabehn. One verse runs 'Jaya jaya karunānidhi,' O Shri Mahadeva Shambho (Victory to Thee, O Shri Mahadeva Shambho, Ocean of Mercy). Gandhi translated 'Jaya, jaya' as 'Thy will be done', explaining to Kakasaheb Kalelkar[19] that 'For a Christian, the best rendering of this can only be "Thy Kingdom come" or "Thy will be done".' He went on to say that the central intent of prayer is that 'God should be ever victorious in our own hearts'. The method of 'translating' the vocabulary of one religion into that of another seems to have had largely a pedagogic purpose and, effective teacher as he was, the 'translation' was specially geared to the needs of the pupil. A much earlier interpretation of a cognate term runs like this. In Amritsar in December 1924 when the crowds were repeating 'Hindu-Muslim-ki jai' this is what Gandhi said:[20] 'This "jai" means that wrangling is *haram* (an anathema) to us. In Hinduism, in Islam, in any religion for that matter, a quarrel with another religion is *haram*.' In this example, the meaning of a popular slogan (whose content, subsequent years were to show, could be all too shallow) becomes almost a candidate for inclusion in 'religious language' and the meaning of 'jai' is pointed up by using strong language intelligible to both communities in order to drive home the message that certain sorts of action are at all costs to be avoided. We may not touch theological profundities in mentioning such sayings of Gandhi's, but to leave them out would be, I believe, to miss a lot that was part and parcel of Gandhi's religious thought.

So far it is clear that Gandhi not only stressed the vital importance of harmony between different religious *groups* in the interest of national unity but believed it was possible for men of different faiths to come close together. This is to say that he did not confine himself to seeing communal relationships (I use the word 'communal' here in the way it is used in the Indian context) in terms of the avoidance of conflict but in a very positive fashion. The metaphysical presuppositions are the common humanity which all men share and the common accessibility of Truth to all, each of course according to his own light, that light in turn being illuminated by particular traditions. This is the source of Gandhi's saying:[21] 'Our prayers for others ought never to be: "God give them the light Thou hast given to me." But "Give them all the light and truth they need for their higher development".' The kinds of indication given by Gandhi do not point to theological reconstruction but to things that any man of good will can do. Here perhaps we have a very characteristic feature of Gandhi's thought, whether religious or otherwise. Let us look at some of the various ways in which diversities of gifts can be fully drawn on, seeing this as closely related to the whole idea of pooling of talents which Gandhi constantly reiterated both in the economic context of trusteeship and elsewhere.

Excrescences are to be eliminated from one's own tradition. For the Hindu the leading excrescence or *upādhi* was 'the sin of untouchability'. It was no part of anyone's business, however, to remove the mote from another's eye. We should rather try to 'practise the truths' to be found in other faiths. For example, instead of pointing out that the Islamic idea of brotherhood appears to be confined to those within the fold, we can try to apply the principle of brotherhood in our own lives, treating no man as an outsider. The pursuit of such an ideal, if we are Hindu, can be further inspired by the loyalty of Rāma and Lakshman, and will enable us to turn the searchlight inwards (a favourite phrase of Gandhi's) and realise that untouchability is incompatible with brotherhood. The assimilative capacities of Hinduism as a cultural complex have been noted by almost all researchers into this intricate phenomenon. Gandhi is really at this point advocating the cultivation of this assimilative process more consciously and beyond the confines of the Hindu community. It is unfortunate that the word 'tolerance' has been so frequently invoked both by Hindus and their critics. What Gandhi is getting at, it seems to me, is much more dynamic and far-reaching than mere tolerance.

In this out-reach Gandhi finds reason and science staunch allies of religion. This in itself is a mark of Gandhi's originality. It is usually taken for granted that the scientific outlook encourages scepticism, one-level explanations, and fosters impatience with mysteries. But if we recall the discussion on Gandhi's experiments with truth it will be noted that Gandhi used the word 'experiment' advisedly. He believed it to be possible to advance in knowledge of the truth progressively on the lines on which a scientist controls his laboratory conditions in order to verify or falsify a particular hypothesis. This 'empirical' approach has always been part of the Indian tradition. The story of Gandhi's experiments is his story of self-purification. Even his fads and fancies, as they may strike some observers, were part of his *ascesis*. The scientific outlook fertilises the religious impulse, that is the self-purificatory impulse, the desire to follow *dharma*, when we verify for ourselves (here are two examples) that control of the palate is closely associated with other kinds of self-control, or when we find that there is no factual basis for racial discrimination. Reason enables us to see that the sacrifice of an innocent creature, a goat, can in no way be regarded as a means of acquiring merit, nor can it be compatible with our most sensitive intimations of what would be pleasing to the deity. Gandhi used this example (after experiencing a feeling of revulsion when he visited Kali Mandir in Calcutta) to identify 'positive irreligion'. But it was no less positively irreligious to treat a whole section of people in an unjust way, whether they be women or untouchables or any other underprivileged group in society. Reason, however, has its limits. These are not the Kantian limits of a mind deprived of an intellectual intuition, but a limit of a different kind, the fact that reason is unable to *move* us. One of the Gandhi's most illuminating sayings brings out this point.[22]

> I have come to this fundamental conclusion that if you want something really important to be done, you must not merely satisfy reason, you must move the heart also. The appeal of reason is more to the head but the penetration of the heart comes from suffering. It opens up the inner understanding in man.

Two contemporary examples of how reason fails to move us may be mentioned here. It is irrational to destroy food while there are people who do not have enough to eat. Again, it shows inconsistency if the economic prosperity of a country rests on its armaments industry while its citizens pay lipservice to the value of life. Gandhi was, fortunately, not a professional philosopher. The vocabulary he inherits is the unsophisticated everyday language of reason, understanding, the heart. If there are defects of understanding, there are also limitations of the heart too.

Bearing these points in mind the following quotation can be turned to next. It was after the study of different religions, he said,[23] and this included both the study of scriptures and the lives of prophets and other religious leaders, that he: ' . . . came to the conclusion that all religions were right, and every one of them imperfect, because they were interpreted with our poor intellects, sometimes with our poor hearts, and more often misinterpreted'. This was what he said to missionaries in Calcutta in 1925. In Colombo he suggested that one remedy for 'broadening' the heart was the study of the teaching of other faiths. There are signs in all this of Gandhi's rejection of the compartmentalisation of human faculties, grounding them all in a human nature which decades of philosophers and psychologists had tried to dissect into separate functions. There is a link, I believe, between his refusal to compartmentalise religion, economics and politics and his insight into the interlinking of human powers. From this follows the need to purify and strengthen *all* these powers. This process could be furthered if each in humility were willing to learn[24] from the other, both consciously and through the unconscious influence which he believed to be at work through collective prayer. Such an enriching of our life (I deliberately do not say religious life, because for Gandhi this was in no way isolated from the myriad aspects of every dimension of life) would greatly increase fearlessness, a virtue on which Gandhi laid great stress and which he diligently sought to cultivate in the course of his own *ascesis*. To know and love the other is no longer to fear him. What would result is not unlike what in ecumenical circles these days is spoken of as renewal where this includes both a rooting and an outreach. It is perhaps significant that Gandhi made very frequent use of the tree metaphor for the tree is perhaps the most powerful natural symbol of grounding and outreach, a symbol too of the connection between outreach and blossoming. He wrote:[25] 'I regard the great faiths of the world as so many branches of a tree, each distinct from the other though having the same source.' It was his belief that all the branches were growing and that each leaf, (as we are told from the standpoint of science also) is different. The ideas to examine here are those of sameness of source and the resonances of development. The source for Gandhi is not the Fatherhood of God – although this metaphor is not absent from Hindu devotional literature or even from his own usage – so much as the common aspiration of men, this being in turn a response to the divine reality manifested in diverse forms. Gandhi also did say on many an occasion that 'we have but one soul'. The context, however, was not a Advaitin one but Gandhi's sense that he must not, as he once put it, detach himself from 'the wickedest soul',[26] but involve in his satyagraha experiment 'the whole of my kind'. This 'gathering in' (borrowing the language of George Matheson's wellknown hymn which was a favourite of Gandhi's) anticipated in microcosmic form that wider community which could be looked forward to as an outcome of both human effort and Divine grace, or more strictly, Divine grace at work in us. Depending on his audience, Gandhi sometimes used language of a different kind, speaking of God as 'the sum-total' of all souls. In any case the message was the same, the need for service of others, the identity between service of others and service of God.

To develop is to move in a certain direction, to grow. One of the things that Gandhi found uncongenial about Christianity, perhaps based on a misconception about what it involved, was the notion of a once-for-all salvation dating from a conversion experience and manifested in various forms such as 'confessing Christ as one's Saviour', expression of credal belief and the like. It was probably not until he met C. F. Andrews that he came close to a Christian fellow-seeker for whom religious aspiration was an endless *striving*, an endless quest, as agonising as Gandhi himself had found it to be. The concept of *swadharma* gives metaphysical and ethical ballast to the idea of *individual* quest, a path unique to oneself. In this way, there was built into Indian tradition a respect for human individuality it is not always given credit for. Salvation does not come about through the acts of a Saviour but through the salvific faith and works of the aspirant, assisted by Divine grace. Development for Gandhi is gauged by an increasing conquest of egoity, progress in the attempt to reduce oneself to zero, and the sense of expansion which Gandhi experienced both through personal *ascesis* and through what, in the language of another tradition, is described as the bonds of fellowship. The infinity which beckoned, and which for his brother in the spirit, Rabindranath Tagore, was ever the leading source of inspiration, was mirrored for Gandhi in the infinite powers of the human being. To develop, therefore, was both to reach out towards that ocean of being which had through the ages inspired the deepest nostalgia in India's venturing souls and to join hands with *all* one's fellow human beings, no matter at what stage of development they might be. Like Swami Vivekananda, Gandhi found in the poorest of the poor the greatest exemplars of that patience and humility which he was always seeking to acquire. For Gandhi, if there is equality in imperfection, since all products of human culture reflect our finitude, there is also the equality to be seen in all human efforts to develop. The *Gītā* had taught him that the *yogī*, *jñānī* and *guṇātīta* look with an equal eye on all, especially including in this both friend and foe. There is also another very significant context in which Gandhi referred to equality. In his Belgaum Congress Presidential address he said:[27] 'God's grace and revelation are the monopoly of no race or nation. They descend equally upon all who wait upon God.' Today this may appear as an extraordinary remark to make in a political gathering. But it was perhaps one of Gandhi's own special gifts that he could see no limits to the possibility of human growth. No doubt what was of immediate relevance for him was always the next step to be taken. The developmental idea is not accompanied by the idea of an eschatology worked out in any detail. But it was closely tied up with how he envisaged the ideal human community, as we shall see in the next chapter, something which would in the very nature of things accommodate great diversity.

Looking with an equal eye on all, however, was for Gandhi perfectly compatible with the recognition of and respect for diversities of gifts. The particular experiments with truth which Gandhi carried out were not in way seen by him as models for others to follow. For example right at the end of his life his *brahmacharya* experiments were seen by him as a last-ditch weapon against Jinnah's attempt to bring about the 'vivisection' of India. The point, however, that each man's experiments will be peculiarly his own and in accordance with his own light, and that the experience of generations had shown that disciplines such as that of fasting resulted in inner strength, were matters which were generally valid. His extensive correspondence shows him sharing his own ex-periences, but urging the inquirer to discover what suits him best, whether it be on questions of diet, the spending of time or the practices of private devotion. His concerns with bodily conditions were in no way peripheral to the other issues raised by his correspondents and one gets the impression above all of a man who is anxious to advise in order to bring about efficient functioning of the psycho-physical organism. This was the basis of the coming into effective operation of whatever personal gifts we may have. The Christian will at this point recall Christ's practical concern with the feeding of the five thousand.

Mahadev Desai, Gandhi's secretary, once wrote[28] of Gandhi's role in 'toning down differences by creating a climate of understanding between men of varying views and thus increasing amity all around'. This could most of all come about through the undertaking of common tasks, for then differences of caste and creed would fall into proper perspective. In these common tasks each man would find an opportunity of putting into practice what he professed. Gandhi himself spoke of his task in his last phase as that of:[29] 'bridging social distance consistently with religious belief . . . by going out of my way to seek common ground on political fields'. The common-or-garden phrase 'sinking of differences' is not inappropriate in this context. One does not sweep differences under the carpet by engaging in common tasks, but one prevents them from serving as obstacles to nearness, to that community of spirit which Gandhi himself experienced in his friendships with so many different kinds of people and which foreshadowed what a transformed society would be like. Translated in terms of the ecumenical language of today, Gandhi was talking about combined witness, except that he saw this not as confined to the rapproachments between denominations which belonged to a single tradition (falling under the Christian rubric) but cutting across all barriers, all labels. It is for this reason that Gandhi seems to me to go beyond both encounter and dialogue, envisaging a sharing which is but natural since God dwells in every man.

Gandhi had no truck with the *māyā* doctrine of Advaita Vedanta. He does, however, regard as a veil of illusion the ignorance and prejudice which divide man from man and to which our separate religious allegiances unfortunately often make their various contributions. Significantly, he was fond of an old hymn sung by an earlier generation and which contains the line: 'We shall know each other better when the mists have rolled away'. In Gandhi's own mind many mists had rolled away. The outcome was evident in a mingling of religious language drawn from various traditions and which found expression in his day to day sayings. So it was that he could speak of a true votary of the *Gītā* as one who ' . . . ever dwells in perennial joy and peace that passeth understanding'.[30] Rather puckishly he asked a Catholic Father:[31] ' . . . is not the whole universe a mosque? And what about the magnificent canopy of

heaven that spreads over you? Is it any less than a mosque?' And
here is an even more mischievous one. He said to an American
opponent of organised religion that man's body ' . . . has been
rightly called the temple of the Holy Ghost . . .'.[32] Brother
Lawrence's phrase, being 'filled with the presence of God' and
Trine's being 'in tune with the Infinite' were constantly on his lips. It
was, in fact, no wonder that he quoted Rabindranath Tagore's
speech at the Parliament of Religions in Calcutta approvingly.[33]
Tagore had said:

> God is generous in His distribution of love, and His means of
> communication with men have not been restricted to a blind lane
> abruptly stopping at one narrow point of history. If humanity
> ever happens to be overwhelmed with the universal flood of a
> bigoted exclusiveness, then God will have to make provision for
> another Noah's ark to save His creatures from the catastrophe of
> spiritual desolation.

The eschaton Gandhi had in mind was a community on earth of a
rather special kind. It is to this vision that the diversities of gifts
which have the same spirit, the combined energies of men of
goodwill, must be devoted. We shall next try to see what the main
contours of this vision were like.

8 The Vision Splendid

Gandhi often had occasion to pinpoint the fact that, only too often, living and speaking, practice and profession of faith, went out of step with each other. The conscious pursuit of spiritual experiences, whether mystic or otherwise, where this is seen as divorced from the activities of everyday life, was quite foreign to Gandhi's way of thinking. In this respect he departs radically from the pattern set by many Indian 'holy men' and those from other cultures who seek to copy them. He once said:[1]

> Spiritual experiences are shared by us whether we wish it or not – by our lives, not by our speech which is a most imperfect vehicle of experience. Spiritual experiences are deeper even than thought.

Although Gandhi brought speaking and singing into collective worship, including in the *Ashram Bhajanāvalī* bhajans of Muslim Sufis and fakirs, Guru Nanak's poems and Christian hymns, it was for him *living* that brought people closest together. As for spirituality, if one must use the word, Gandhi likened it to the fragrance of a flower, not something of which the flower is itself aware, but of which *others* are aware. Gandhi, then, is an implicit critic of styles of religious life which see this as something distinct from ordinary life, and this in spite of his keen sensitivity to the difference between lower and higher, the natural and that which strives to go beyond it. The spiritual experiences which for Gandhi are deeper than thought are not the rarefied kinds of things one might suppose. They include tending the sick, the giving of hope to those bereft of it, the experience of realising the nobility of the dispossessed, the silent comradeship of those who watched with him not one hour but many hours and days in jail and during his fasts. Gandhi did not start life as someone who found it easy to make friends. Yet there is, one feels, a golden thread of endeavour that runs through his lifework – the quest of a new art of living, a togetherness, which the humblest could share. It forms, I believe, a leading characteristic of his 'religious thought', something in fact deeper than thought. The pursuit of it made him look on familial ties and some of the human and very natural bonds of intimate relationship (here he resembles St. Paul) as forms of human association which have to be transcended if community in the ideal sense is to be brought about. Many have seen in his successive experiments with ashram life and, outside these, in his own great variety of human relationships, surrogates for family life. His acceptance of the title 'Bapu' lends some credence to this. Such matters cannot occupy us here. We shall rather be on the track of what he envisaged the ideal community to be like and to support the hypothesis that such a community was the vision splendid which he profoundly believed could shape human living in a new way, a way as old as the hills but which had not as yet had a fair trial. The vision did not come, in Pauline fashion, as a conversion experience. It came slowly, the steps of the pilgrimage that were left behind leaving their mark. There was however, much more to it that what may seem to some as a madcap scheme of founding celestial villages on earth. Nor was the situation simplified by demarcating what was Caesar's and what was not, for Gandhi admitted no such demarcation. Gandhi's vision enjoins praxis to such an extent that at times he seems to be joining hands with the Marxists. But it is not a praxis determined by 'naturalistic misconceptions' nor uninformed by intimations of goods, 'immaterial things' in Ruskin's phrase, exceeding those of material plenty. All this makes Gandhi's religious thought not more easy to grasp, but less so, and therefore all the more challenging.

The vision is grounded, I believe, in a metaphysic of existence which embraces the inorganic, the organic, the individual and society – all environed in the divine dimension in which they have their being. That the inorganic and the organic have claim on man had been pointed out by Ruskin in his *Fors Clavigera*:[2]

> *Modern Painters* taught the claim of all lower nature on the hearts of men; of the rock and wave, and herb, as a part of their necessary spirit life; in all that I now bid you to do, to dress the earth and keep it, I am fulfilling what I then began.

Mr Henry Polak had given Gandhi a copy of Ruskin's *Unto this last* to read on his journey from Johannesburg to Durban in 1904. Gandhi records in his *Autobiography* that this was the first book by

Ruskin that he had ever read and that Polak was well-versed in Ruskin's thought. Whether or not Gandhi ever read Ruskin's other works he does say that he found some of his 'deepest convictions' reflected in *Unto this last* and it is evident that he had discussed Ruskin's work pretty thoroughly with Polak. In any case the tiller of the soil and the craftsman are involved in a commerce with the organic and the inorganic which the 'brain-worker' does not share.

Gandhi had already reflected on the distinction between the inorganic and organic in the context of the Jain tradition. His dietetic experiments and his interest in compost are but two instances which illustrate his awareness of the interplay of the two. That Gandhi also personally found a therapeutic value in manual work (in his own case it was spinning), is also quite clear. Man is peculiarly *dependent* on inorganic and organic nature. For Gandhi, as for Gustave Thibon, the soil provides man's deepest rooting in the inorganic. It is the soil with which the agriculturist contends and which he tends, and it is the soil which also provides the primeval symbol for nationality. The mountains symbolise aspiration, and the sea and sky infinity, and these are key symbols not only for Tagore the poet but for Gandhi the man who collects dust on his feet. The organic is the concern of the farmer who tends living things, the vegetarian whose special concern is with the vegetable kingdom as a source of food, the Indian villager who endows certain trees with special virtues. The animal kingdom is dependent on man, directly in the case of cattle and indirectly in the case of the wild life who rely on a habitat unspoilt by human agency. Here it must be admitted that Gandhi speaks in different tones of voice about the animal kingdom, sometimes reverting to an ancient but outworn idiom when he refers to 'the beast' in man and yet finding in the cow a 'poem of pity', a mother symbol signifying bounty and humility. But there is no mistaking the fact that he thought of man as a being whose role it was to *tend* the powers that are in inorganic and organic nature, and whose own noblest powers were released above all when he was in association with his fellows.

Gandhi's interest in the idea of *forces* has surfaced from time to time in preceding chapters. His thinking on this theme has a sophistication it is not always given credit for. Traditional Hindu thought, especially at the more popular level, attached importance to *alaukik* or supernatural powers. To exhibit control whether over nature or over one's own personal functions has, in the popular mind, and especially in the Tantric tradition, excited admiration.

The miracle which Gandhi believed in was of a very different kind; the capacity of ordinary people to discover and use their non-violent strength in the cause of transforming human society. Indeed to him it was no miracle in the sense of a rupture of nature's laws. It was rather an evidence of natural law in its highest manifestation. The powers of inorganic nature are released to their maximum extent through fission of the atom. This is what we have learnt since Hiroshima and Nagasaki. The powers in man, however, are released through the very opposite process, the process of combining, of living in harmony. In both cases force is seen as something which brings about change, which achieves a new equilibrium. It was precisely because conflict released forces of disharmony that a new *tapasya* was called for; not a *tapasya* which only aimed at individual perfection but one which had within it resources sufficient to transform society.

Gandhi's experiments with the new *tapasya* of community living involved him in founding a series of settlements both in South Africa and later in India whose importance as keys to Gandhi's religious thought cannot be exaggerated. For it is these communities that in one way or other served as *exemplars*; it was here that the necessary elements in the training of the satyagrahi were worked out; here also that in the choice of members of different races and of those who professed different creeds Gandhi sought to vindicate his belief in the possibility of a unity of design which lay in the diversity of colours (to paraphrase language he used in 1947). Traditionally the ashram was a forest retreat, cut off from the world, the flesh and the devil. The idea was transformed in modern times by several of India's key figures. Gokhale's Servants of India Society, Tagore's Santiniketan and Swami Shraddananda's Gurukula at Kangri, Hardwar, each owed something to it. C. F. Andrews once threw out the suggestion that the core personalities involved found an extension in other lives. This is as may be. But it is important to note that Gandhi's own position in each of the settlements and ashrams he founded was not that of a 'guru' figure. This has been stressed especially by Mirabehn. It is in the settlements he founded in South Africa that he was first called 'Bapu' (Father) and it was there that his *motherly* qualities were first manifested most fully. The Gandhian ashram, moreover, was not a retreat from the world but very much in it.

The ashram, it may be worth pointing out, is distinct in concept from the *ecclesia*. It does not constitute a mystical body from which those outside the fold are excluded. It is a kind of extended family embracing people of different faiths and diverse gifts. Qua institution it is both peculiarly elastic in respect of those who can join it, and peculiarly stringent in terms of the style of life enjoined on those who do. The Gandhian ashram was intended above all to be a storehouse of energy, of soul-force, a place where batteries were recharged. But this is to anticipate the full-fledged ashram concept of Gandhi's Indian experience. The pioneering task began in the Phoenix Settlement and in Tolstoy Farm in South Africa, the concretisation of Gandhi's response to Ruskin and Tolstoy respectively. The story of these experiments gives us the first stages of Gandhi's quest of *true community life*, a simple phrase perhaps but one which combines key elements of Gandhi's religious thought.

It is recorded in Gandhi's *Autobiography* that his immediate reaction to reading Ruskin's *Unto this last* was to shift the press of *Indian Opinion* to a farm 'on which everyone should labour, drawing the same living wage, and attending to the press work in spare time'.[3] Gandhi is sometimes referred to as an anti-intellectual by his critics, but the account of how the paper was actually brought out on this isolated farm in a jungly and snake-infested stretch of land fourteen miles from Durban is moving evidence of how manual work could be combined with a typical intellectual task, the labour of educating the public. True, Phoenix was a settlement rather than an ashram. Gandhi could not remain in Phoenix continuously himself. During this period of his life his experiments and changes in ideas came in quick succession. The desire for a simple life which was exemplified in the Phoenix settlement was also expressed in the way the Johannesburg household was run. Not very long after he had encouraged members of his 'heterogeneous family' to marry, Gandhi was to undergo a turning point experience in his life, his service with the Indian ambulance corps attached to the Natal forces during the Zulu rebellion in 1906. Gandhi had already served in an ambulance corps before, during the Boer war, in a six week stint after the action at Spion Kop, and the entire corps earned high praise both from General Olpherts and General Buller for their fearlessness. Gandhi, who always had a flair for nursing throughout his life, saw the occasion as a further opportunity for service, and his experiences of the miseries of those he nursed gave him an insight into the destiny which awaited him in the future. One who aspired 'to serve humanity with his whole soul' would have to impose a strict discipline on himself. He writes in his *Autobiography*:[4] 'In a word, I could not live both after the flesh and the spirit.' Gandhi's 'conversion' experiences so often took the form of a fresh personal *ascesis*, an *ascesis* occasioned by the demand of events as he saw them and his own particular role in relation to them. If the first ambulance corps service developed a quality he much desired to acquire, fearlessness, the second period of service led him to the view that the pleasures of the *grhasta* stage were incompatible with the life style of a man who was devoted to humanity. It is also noteworthy that he himself valued both periods of ambulance work for the way they brought about a close relation in the first case, with the indentured Indians, and in the second case with those whom he described as 'Zulu friendlies' i.e. those who had been flogged as suspects but not wounded in battle, and also with the white soldiers whose job it was to quell the rebellion. The Phoenix Settlement carried on while Gandhi was busy in all these other ways, increasing his self-imposed discipline through the vow of *brahmacharya* and seeking closeness in the new encounters which his day to day experience brought him. Hindu traditional lore shows the extent to which Hindus admire continence, associating this with the conservation of power and the ability to do *alaukik* acts. There is of course a great deal in Hindu culture which pulls in the opposite direction. But it is important to remember that, for Gandhi, *bramacharya* is not an end in itself, although he is traditional enough to speak of it as 'full of wonderful potency'. Gandhi sees it as a necessary part of the self-purification required of a servant of society, a renunciation which was the prerequisite for the total involvement in the affairs of men which was to be his destiny. The Phoenix Settlement example already tells us quite a lot about Gandhi's early glimpse of his vision. It takes the following form: firstly, founding of a pioneering community of which he remains the leader (but not a guru figure) although he is not always able to be physically present; secondly, widening engagement in affairs outside this community; thirdly, personal *ascesis* in the interest of full utilisation of energies for practical tasks which appear to him as God-given work. It must be noted that there is a constant interplay between all three factors.

The transcendent dimension which environed his vision is perhaps more explicit in the founding of Tolstoy Farm, his second experiment in community living, embarked on in 1910. *Hind Swaraj* had already been written two years earlier, and Gandhi's mind, ever positive in orientation, turned to what kind of society could be nurtured as an alternative to the acquisitive society which, in his view, went along with modern civilisation. Gandhi and Tolstoy were already in touch through correspondence and felt themselves to be co-workers in propagating the gospel of non-violence. Each was drawn to the pilgrim spirit of the other; each believed that the human characteristics of envy and hatred could be neutralised by other powers that dwell within the human individual. Like Tolstoy, Gandhi believed that the kingdom of God is within. Both men believed in the law of love. The immediate occasion which led to the founding of the new experiment was the need to maintain the families of the satyagrahis who had gone to jail as a result of their campaign against the Immigrant Act. The Phoenix Settlement was too far away from Johannesburg and could not satisfy this need. At this critical stage, Gandhi's friend Hermann Kallenbach came to the rescue and bought a farm some miles outside Johannesburg and several families moved in. A number of interesting problems arose which may seem strange to anyone unfamiliar with Indian life. But the ways in which Gandhi dealt with them provide significant evidence of how he thought everyday life could be simplified and a spirit of equality brought about among members of a community. We find him tackling questions such as that of different diets, disposal of waste, what language was to be spoken and what kind of education the children should be given. It was, moreover, at Tolstoy Farm that Gandhi decided that women too could court arrest. Here mention will only be made of Gandhi's experiments in religious education.

The children belonging to Hindu, Muslim, Parsi and Christian families, Gandhi thought, should be instructed both about their own tradition and about those of the others. But this was on the intellectual level. Gandhi looked upon what he called 'training of the spirit' as essentially character building rather than just involving scripture lessons or the singing of hymns (both of which were part of his school routine). The training, then, centred on 'the exercise of the spirit'[5] and Gandhi likened it to physical exercise. As it happens some have discerned an element of athleticism about Gandhi's religious life style. But the flexing of muscles was not an end in itself. The satyagrahi had practical tasks ahead of him. Notably it was out of his South African experience that Gandhi made one of his most outspoken pronouncements about the role of religion in life:[6] 'Religion must either occupy the highways as well as the by-ways, the whole of life or abdicate.' Shuttling between Phoenix Settlement, Tolstoy Farm and Johannesburg, Gandhi was fully engaged as teacher, guardian and leader. He was also at this time directing the publication of *Indian Opinion* which shifted to Tolstoy Farm and, in addition, both for his own education and in order to teach the children in his care, studying the major religious traditions of the world. A few years earlier, in 1906, he had written his essay on 'The Bond of Sympathy' which in a very perceptive way links up the consolidating bond of sympathy with the cultivation of imagination. In Tolstoy Farm he was specially situated in respect of becoming aware of the sentiments of others. The idea of participating in the observances of others took a concrete rather than a ritualistic form, since Gandhi was always impatient of rituals, especially when they served no practical purpose. Non-Muslims agreed to have one meal a day in order to keep the Muslims company during Ramzan. Incidentally it was ironical that Gandhi, even in this early stage in his career should have come in for criticism by a Muslim friend. His copy of the Koran lay on the table along with the other books he was studying. When it was pointed out that this showed disrespect Gandhi hung it up on a bag on the wall in deference to Muslim sentiment.

Each settlement founded by Gandhi came about in response to a particular practical situation. The Satyagraha Ashram was founded in May 1915 in Kochrab village near Ahmedabad. Gandhi's work in South Africa was over and he was eager to try out in India the methods he had experimented with outside India. In keeping with his sensitivity to locality and tradition Gandhi henceforth now used the word 'ashram' rather than settlement or farm. A code of rules and observances were drawn up. Ahmedabad was a centre of the mechanised textile industry. Gandhi scenting challenges in the air, non-violent war horse that he was, immediately found it proper to make hand-spinning a major activity in the ashram. This seemed good sense economically. But it was not long before there was a flutter in the dovecotes. An untouchable family joined the ashram. Again this is a matter which to a non-Hindu may seem of small account. But Gandhi's non-violent war against untouchability was to be, throughout his life, his major way of purifying the Hindu community. In the first of his ashrams in India the inmates were to learn the major lessons of self-help and self-purification. The latter involved yet another irony. The orthodox Hindus whose minds were obsessed by fear of pollution were to learn that for them self-purification would involve going 'the length of dining with the untouchables.' Herein lies another important strand in Gandhi's religious thought. There can be no rapprochement between men and women of different persuasions, let alone a genuine *sharing* of the life of each, until each has put his or her own house in order. The ashram was a testing ground for those who claimed to be seekers of truth, a home or base from which trained people went out as satyagrahis and constructive workers, and particularly in the case of untouchability, it was to be an examplar for the rest of the community.

When plague broke out in the village the ashram was shifted to a site near Sabarmati Central Jail where it remained until 1933. Gandhi liked the idea of moving near the jail, not only because the location was clean but because 'jail going was understood to be the normal lot of satyagrahis'.[7] No less than the early Christians under the Romans, the satyagrahis of India were constantly in and out of jail for their convictions. The symbolism of bondage has many overtones. In Hindu philosophical thought life in the everyday world is, ipso facto, a life of bondage. Gandhi's personal *ascesis* was a quest of liberation from the bondage of egoity. There was, in addition, the bondage of subjection to an imperial power. In contrast to all these there is the voluntary bondage undergone by those who court arrest in the course of non-violent resistance to various injustices, the voluntary bondage of those who take upon themselves the disciplined life which membership of the ashram entails. In subsequent years Gandhi was to refer to Yeravda Jail as Yeravda Mandir ('mandir' means temple) and it was from this jail that he conducted the independence movement at a critical period of history and from where the weekly *Harijan* was launched. For Gandhi a place of service was a place of worship. As for the early Christians, the place of physical bondage was the place where those concerned (and this includes the jailers) were in closest fellowship with each other and with God; it was the place where loving bonds were strengthened. The new society could not be born without suffering. But, as was seen earlier, there was a big difference between suffering imposed externally, and suffering voluntarily undergone in the interest of a selfless cause, and undergone moreover not in the arrogant pursuit of individual perfection, but in a spirit of humility and for the good of all.

Gandhi's ashrams need to be seen in the context of his own particular diagnosis of the tragedy of twentieth century religious life. For Gandhi the tragedy consists not in the inadequacy of concepts but in the existence of belief systems which have little or no impact on actual life. He sees this, not unnaturally, from the perspective of his own age and situation. Imperialist policies were practised by countries which professed to be Christian. The Hindu community which paid lip service to the unity of all life treated a large section of its members as untouchable. Those traditions which make a big thing of brotherhood are careful to exclude from their fold those who do not subscribe to certain doctrinal tenets. Not only is man in chains primaevally but man forges new chains for himself in the shape of unjust economic systems and credal packages which defy reason. The Gandhian ashram was a pioneering community rather than a Utopian one. Gandhi's work took him all over India. But it was to the ashrams that he returned, and his direction of them was maintained, in periods when he was not in residence, through a voluminous correspondence. We need to look a little closer now at the kind of collective *tapasya* that ashram life involved and see in what sense the ashrams could be regarded as the spearhead of the new society.

It is often said of Hinduism, and correctly, that it is not an institutionalised religion. Gandhi, however, was a great believer in the institutional nurturing of constructive attitudes and this fitted in with his pursuit of truth both as inward realisation and outward transformation. Of existing institutions his view was that they should be as open as possible. As a symbol of this may be mentioned the fact that the prayer-meetings and the discourses which followed them were open to the public. Whatever took place in the ashrams was a matter of common knowledge and the ashrams were often the venue of important meetings during the national movement when decisions of moment were taken. Over a period of decades he founded a number of institutions for particular purposes (especially in the context of rural reconstruction) and we can gather from the history of these just what Gandhi envisaged their role to be in the following way. An institution should make an impact on those outside it; it should be as innovative as possible; it should evolve projects which will bring people of different communities together; and, significantly, it should be wound up when its purpose had been served. Gandhi had learnt that vested interests tend to dominate institutions and this was why he laid such stress on openness. The ashrams can be seen in the light of these overall perspectives, and also in the context of his conviction that the pursuit of perfection, that is, reducing the self to zero, and the building up of a good society are not alternative strategies but can be carried on pari passu. Addressing the ashramites in 1925[8] Gandhi said that ashrams like theirs were founded with a view to propagating conduct that is in conformity with *dharma*. They must have in them the spirit of the brahmin, meaning truth and faith, as well as that of the kshatriya, that is, strength and non-violence. Mahadev Desai, who of all his secretaries was probably closest to Gandhi, and was in the best position to understand the style of life at Sabarmati Ashram, noted that each member had his own work and common principles, but that it was common *activities* that brought them together most of all, and these were spinning and prayer.

Between 1926 and 1929 Gandhi wrote a series of letters to the ashram sisters, the keynotes of which were the importance of community life, that education was essentially a matter of character-building and development of skills for everyday living, that one should not be a burden on society, and that no evil should enter in. The methods to be followed were physical labour, industriousness, simple living and self-control. Other things stressed by Gandhi were punctuality, concentration, the memorisation of verses, and correct pronunciation. The ashram vows sent to members of the Sabarmati ashram while Gandhi was in jail included allegiance to truth, non-violence, continence, non-possession and non-stealing, and Gandhi regularly made these the subject of his discourses. The remaining vows enjoined control of the palate, fearlessness, removal of untouchability, bread labour, equality of religions, and swadeshi. All this was intended to nurture an outlook which went beyond family attachments. From his letters the reader gets the impression of a man who knew very well how many frictions arise when people live in a community. For example he advised:[9] 'The first step in purifying oneself is the admission and eradication of whatever bad feelings one might have about others.' This is the first step in what Gandhi called the education of the heart, something, incidentally, which he thought intellectuals were particularly in need of. There is a New Testament ring to the following:[10] 'Speak with one who does not speak with you; visit those who do not come to you; make up with someone who is angry with you.'

There was no temple in any of the ashrams founded by Gandhi. How could there be, when people of different faiths were its members? There could be no image-worship, for the same reason. Since peasants and labourers have to rise early so should 'a worshipper of Truth or servant of the people'. The ashram prayers at 4.20 a.m. and 7 p.m. provided a framework for the day's activities.

The morning prayer consisted of a recitation of shlokas from the *Ashram Bhajanāvalī,* one bhajan, Ramadhun (Gandhi's favourite hymn, which speaks of the many names of God) and a recitation from the *Gītā.* In the evening prayer there would be first of all the last nineteen verses of the second chapter of the *Gītā* (which deal with the qualities of a *stithaprajña* and which a satyagrahi must become), one bhajan, Ramadhun, and a reading from a sacred book. After the evening prayer there would be a roll call of the daily *yagña* (sacrifice), that is a tally of how much each had spun. The coordination of work and worship, seeing *dharma* as service, Gandhi's own after-prayer discourses on both the day's affairs in the ashram and the political situation of the moment – all point up the ways in which the ashram was intended to be a power-station for the rest of the community.

Throughout history societies have made provision for the training of leaders who stood apart from the rest of society. The types of cadres range from those trained in military affairs, scholars, and priestly initiates to bureaucrats, technocrats and ideologues. To classify the worldly and non-worldly elites that mankind has fostered would take us too far afield. India's hierarchically ordered society has not accommodated the idea of a community within a community whose task it should be to leaven the lump. Nor, for that matter, have competitive societies been conspicuously hospitable to the idea. Yet history shows evidence of the impact of the pioneering efforts of monastic communities on the world outside, whether it be in agriculture, chemistry, wine-making or education through the written word. Gandhi's ashrams, for all the rigour of their discipline, were not monastic communities in the sense in which this is usually understood. A look at some of the activities of the satyagrahis may clarify this point.

Soon after Gandhi's brush with the orthodox sensibility of some of the ashram inmates over the induction of untouchables into the little community, and a no less vigorous brush with potentates attending the inaugural ceremony of Benaras Hindu University, Gandhi was called to Champaran in Bihar for a campaign of a very different kind, the battle of the peasants who worked on the indigo plantations. It was a cardinal principle with Gandhi that those who suffered the brunt of a particular injustice should themselves offer non-violent resistance to it. In Champaran he was at the beginning of his career as a pioneer of a new method of righting wrongs. Local volunteers were slow in coming forward and there was a great deal to be done. Along with collecting evidence for the inquiry, constructive work must be carried on, for example, instructing the villagers in elementary hygiene, running kitchens and opening schools for the children. Not only were Kasturba and Mahadev drafted from Gujarat to come and help out but, as one of the volunteers, Acharya Kripalani has described it, all taking part 'started living an ashram life'.[11] This is to say no servants were employed, food was of the simplest and the routine of the day was organised so that each had the opportunity to perform the maximum of service. The point is that the quality of life of the satyagrahi is seen not only in the ashram but in society at large. Situations call for a response from those that have ears to hear. Or, to modify language used by George Eliot, human activity is a response both to the solicitations of circumstance *and* the density of circumstance.

I have mentioned Champaran not only because it shows Gandhi in action for the first time on a major scale after his fact-finding study of the Indian scene embarked on at Gokhale's advice when he arrived in India, but for two other reasons. It is sometimes said (and I am not entering into the merits of this assessment) that Hindu thought stresses duties rather than rights. This may appear in various lights according to how one views it. A standpoint which prescribes a whole network of duties, including duties to the gods, and to all living creatures, may at first sight indicate a world-view where egoity is kept successfully under control. On the other hand the liberal may well regard with dismay an outlook which seems to leave little room for protest or for protection of the individual *vis-à-vis* loci of authority. Champaran finds Gandhi encouraging the dispossessed to speak up for their rights as well as enjoining them to put their own house in order. A great deal of Gandhi's life work can be seen in terms of a campaigning for rights, social political and economic, with the proviso that this should always be matched by what he called constructive work, that is the painstaking labour of doing what one can to remedy one's situation, of building up what should replace the old structures of society. How else would people have an idea of what they were fighting *for*? The other thing is that in his *Autobiography* Gandhi sums up his Champaran experience in the following remarkable lines:[12] 'It is no exaggeration, but the literal truth, to say that in this meeting with the peasants I was face to face with God, Ahimsa, and Truth'. To expand the space of the heart is to see all creatures as links in the chain of being. In Gandhi's own words:[13] 'All creatures are interlinked. And if one link of the chain is weak, the whole chain is weak.' If all men's activities constitute an indivisible whole and if all created things are so interconnected that when one member suffers all suffer, activisim will not be regarded as a religious policy to be opted or not opted for; rather it will follow as a natural flowering in one whose heart is not a cave of retreat but who finds in the 'with' the deepest confirmation of the 'within'. It was from Motihari, district headquarters of Champaran, that Gandhi wrote[14] in reflective, almost poetic, vein to his old friend Hermann Kallenbach with whom he had shared his early experiments in community living. He wrote of the leaves of the tree each of which have their own life, which depend on the tree and yet which drop and wither. The tree is a part of the forest. In spite of the change and decay noted in one of Gandhi's favourite hymns what abides is 'the eternal in us'. Gandhi writes that he 'derived much comfort' from this thought. Before leaving Bihar Gandhi was anxious to put the constructive programme on a firm footing. How far the work would prosper once he had gone back to Gujarat was anyone's guess. But the spirit of man, in the long run, would always triumph. It is this that Gandhi found comforting.

I have discussed Gandhi's ashrams in some detail because the role of communes, churches and other communities within communities occupies many thinking people in this last quarter of the twentieth century. There is a sense in which institutions of such kinds – and there are, of course, great differences between them – are symptoms of a withdrawal from a state of affairs believed to be unjust. Gandhi, no doubt, in his experience of evangelical congregations in South Africa was familiar with a concept of 'the world' where the latter is looked on as something to be eschewed by the faithful. No doubt such a view, in so far as it surfaced from time to time in western societies, did not prevent the go ahead from accumulating capital any more than the philosophical doctrine of *māyā* prevented Hindus from being concerned with *abhudaya* or prosperity. The point is that Gandhi's whole vision of a new society went against any kind of Noah's ark view. His conception of the small non-violent and largely self-sufficient rural community can further be contrasted with the militant trade union with its concentration on bargaining for *rights*, and also with the romantic small group as conceived by Rousseau and de Toqueville. Gandhi made no distinction between the sacred and the profane. He speaks of the message he carried on his Harijan tour in 1933 and 1934 when he urged the caste Hindus the length and breadth of India to expiate for centuries of exploitation of the untouchables, as a 'spiritual message'. Although he was no temple-goer himself he campaigned for the right of the Harijans to enter them for without this how would they feel they had any stake in the free India of tomorrow? All profession of egalitarianism would indeed be a mockery. This is all of a piece with his conviction that each man must have his rightful place in his own community, before there could be any question of reaching out towards those of other faiths. His differences with Ambedkar on this question are now part of history.

The ashrams, moreover, point up Gandhi's views about the sanctity of work. Gandhi's insistence on the dignity of work, especially of manual work, must be seen in the context of his own situation, in surroundings where those who did unclean tasks were looked down on, and manual work in general was rated lower than the intellectual pursuits of the lawyer and the teacher. Gandhi did not come from farming stock, but he kept the condition of the vast majority of his countrymen, who were villagers, always in the forefront of his mind. His analysis of the nature of modern industrial civilisation and the facts of the agrarian scene in India led him to believe that India, and indeed we could extrapolate this to take in what is now described as the Third World, could so organise its economy as to avoid the dilemma facing western economies. The dilemma can be put quite frankly in contemporary terms, decades after Gandhi's death – that of a political economy which has to date only flourished through the boost given it by the machinery of war, something which goes against the deepest insights of all religious traditions and nullifies man's highest aspirations and creativity. The logic of Gandhi's thinking is relentless at this point. If intensive industrialisation goes along with the centralisation of power, imperialist trade policies and political conflict, the remedy must lie in precisely the opposite direction. Gandhi was well aware that it was not possible to put the clock back in economies which were already on the industrial escalator. It was not for him to prescribe if or how they could cry a halt to the consumerism inbuilt in such societies. It was of India that he was thinking when he said:[15] 'To a people famishing and idle, the only acceptable form in which God can dare appear is work and promise of food as wages.' The teaching of Ruskin and Tolstoy about manual work found a ready response in one familiar with the *Gītā*'s stress on selfless labour. Gandhi goes as far as to think of bread labour (that a man must earn his bread by labouring with his own hands) as a divine law, again evidence of how the religious, for him, is interwoven with the warp and woof of everyday life. Those who in many countries today make their own bread, spin wool, and find a great release of creative energy in crafts which have been neglected for generations, are on the same wavelength as Gandhi. For him, such activities moreover had a further dimension as an expression of solidarity with the mass of mankind who labour with their hands and on whose efforts the further strivings of other men must always depend. There is more in all this, again, than yet another plea by disillusioned twentieth century man for a return to nature. The alternative is what we already have before us, a world carved up by national boundaries and where human greed is writ large, taking a visible form in overt conflict.

Gandhi's mature reflection on the concept of work brings out how differently he regarded religious life from the way of mysticism.[16] It also has much to do with how he saw the role of women in society, a topic which currently exercises certain circles of clerical and lay opinion. It would not be an exaggeration to say that Gandhi's vision of the future was strongly influenced by his hope of the part women would play in it. If his thinking includes certain stereotypes, for example, that women embody the affective side of life more than men, and if he shares with St. Paul a tendency to self-flagellation in the interest of 'higher things' there is much else as well. He thinks of woman as the 'incarnation of "ahimsa"' in that ahimsa stands for infinite love and this in turn means capacity for suffering. It is not just the fact that women's role is traditionally, as Simone de Beauvoir has put it, to make an environment for living. Gandhi was the person who more than any other Indian national leader encouraged women to come out of their homes, and take an active part in politics. When on his tour of East Bengal, he was asked to console a group of women in Noakhali, whose menfold had all be slaughtered in communal conflict, his face hardened as he replied that he had not come to bring a message of consolation but of courage. Courage was a quality which was essential for the satyagrahi, a quality which Gandhi himself constantly sought to foster in himself. In spite of the customary association of courage with militancy Gandhi associated it with qualities of a very different kind, not with what some have dismissed as 'monkish virtues' but with patience and steadfastness. The society of tomorrow would need to draw on the total resources of the human family and Gandhi himself had great confidence in the capacities particularly

associated with the keeping of a house (housekeeping has unfortunately a narrower connotation) and the rearing of a family –
competence, firmness and a forgiving spirit. In holding such a view
Gandhi drew on his own childhood experience of a saintly mother,
the long-suffering character of his own wife and a heritage which
often pictures the divine in the Mother form, help of the helpless, a
source both of love and strength.

Gandhi's conception of the total man grew over the years. But he
was strikingly contemporary in crossing the boundaries which most
societies have in the past drawn between the roles of men and
women, and a consistent and constant feature of his thinking is his
belief that the whole man is one who embodies many of the qualities
traditionally associated with women. Common activities such as
scavenging, spinning and other forms of bread labour were
incumbent on all alike. He was equally convinced that large
anonymous structures could not bring about the releasing of the
constructive forces within man. All these ideas receive their most
definitive statement in an article entitled 'Content of
Independence' which appeared on 22 July 1946 in *Harijan*, written
at a critical time in the history of India. The Viceroy's efforts
towards forming a coalition Interim Government at the centre were
going on and there was just one week to go before the Muslim
League decided to initiate 'direct action' to achieve the creation of
the new state of Pakistan. Gandhi had hitherto laid stress on the
methods to be followed in building up a new social order, with the
focus on satyagraha, a non-violent method of redressing grievances
which even the poorest could adopt, and the constructive programme which would provide training in setting up new institutions
which were to take the place of the old. He now spelt out the content
of the new order and the values it would embody. In the
decentralised economy of his dreams 'ultimately it is the individual
who is the unit'. For all its hierarchical structure, caste system and
the rest, Hindu thought has always been individualistic in so far as
the destiny of man was conceived in individual terms as liberation
from a particular cycle of births and deaths. But Gandhi's
individual was far from being a self-regarding creature. He should
know what he wants (a moment's reflection shows that this is not
always an easy thing) and 'no one should want anything that the
others cannot have with equal labour'. The following passage puts
in seminal fashion Gandhi's vision of the future:

Life will not be a pyramid with the apex sustained by the bottom. But it will be an oceanic circle whose centre will be the individual always ready to perish for the village, the latter ready to perish for the circle of villages till at last the whole becomes one life composed of individuals, never aggressive in their arrogance, but ever humble, sharing the majesty of the oceanic circle of which they are integral units. Therefore, the outermost circumference will not wield power to crush the inner circle, but will give strength to all within and will derive its own strength from it.

Gandhi here invokes many ideas and symbols from the Hindu tradition, putting them all in the context of a new vision. At the centre is the *stithaprajña*, but a *stithaprajña* who is very aware of his fellows' needs, ready to die for his friends and ready to win over his enemies through love. The model is neither linear nor hierarchical. Although the circle is a closed figure there is no limit to the proliferation of concentric circles. Horizons move as one moves. The destiny of the individual is a world of expanding horizons, a visual metaphor. Setting his sights on wider and wider scenes of involvement, even beyond national boundaries, he is yet par excellence the pedestrian, that is, literally, a man with his feet on the ground. His hands are engaged in practical tasks. His ears are alive to the calls of the needy.

No model could be further from what, to all intents and purposes, is operating in most countries today, where in fact the focus of power is as distant from the individual as bureaucracies and juntas can make it, and where the role of the individual is at most focussed on the ritual of the ballot box. Gandhi's conception is founded on his faith in the moral autonomy of the individual and his capacity for influencing others, that is, his role as a locus of power which operates in a way very different from material forces. Non-violence had been presented by Gandhi as a power which could successfully pit itself against authority when authority misused its power. Could it show no less efficiency in the promotion of mutual aid? Gandhi did not have before him the evidence we now have of certain unanticipated features of the welfare state; where goods and services pour *downwards* so to say from the coffers at the centre and there is little or no movement in the reverse direction (other than taxation plus the vote); where democratic communities find themselves unable to control violence (whether it be urban guerila warfare, the mindless mugging which threatens city life, or the revolt of deprived sections of the population), or to curb corruption. He saw clearly, however, that a one-way traffic between the state and the individual, whether in the interests of exploitation or the dispensing of benefits, was not a healthy state of affairs in that it would not ever make for the freedom of the individual.

In an even later document, his famous article entitled 'Congress Position' dated 27 January 1948, Gandhi made use of an interesting phrase, the 'difficult ascent to democracy', as if democracy were not a rock-bottom base from which to begin but the *goal* of all endeavour. There are two main keys to help us here. The first is that Gandhi's conception of democracy was based on his fragmentary view of truth which we discussed much earlier. It is *because* no man possesses the whole truth that we have no right to impose our views on others and the will of all must be consulted. The second is that the whole article, which takes up the burning question of the hour, the future of the Congress Party after the goal of national independence had been attained, centres round the link between democracy and service. A few hours before his death he was giving thought to the future of those he had trained in the nation's work. Economic, social and moral freedom were yet to be attained. The law of progress indicated that once a particular goal were attained further horizons beckoned.

We have not moved so far from Gandhi's religious thought as it may appear. It was Gandhi's belief that there was a mysterious connivance at work between the creative powers in man and the divine forces at work in the universe. To release, through cooperation and mutual aid, the positive forces in man was at once to tap the divine source of energy. There is an affinity between this way of expressing it and the language used by a twentieth century German scholar. How can twentieth century man 'become a vessel to receive the influx of transcendent forces'?[17] Gandhi's answer to this question will take us into the heart of the novel way (novel in the context of Indian traditions) he treated a central concept in the religious thinking of his own people, the concept of *moksa*.

9 Mokṣa Rethought

Some think that, for Gandhi, not *mokṣa* but *dharma* had the pivotal place.[1] We must see if this makes sense. In ancient Indian thought values are classified in a fourfold way, that is, into *artha, kama, dharma*, and *mokṣa*. No doubt, as far as orthodox Indian philosophers were concerned, *mokṣa* had as cardinal a place as justice did for Plato. Classically *artha* and *kama* are values as long as life at the everyday 'behavioural' level goes on. But without *dharma* even everyday life would be chaotic, for *dharma* is *samājik* (social), and without *dharma* there can be no possibility of *mokṣa*. The ideas of *dharma* and *mokṣa* have never been treated apart from each other nor are they such for Gandhi. But his treatment of *mokṣa*, associated as it is, for him, with *swaraj*, has many new features about it. Two major influences which shaped his thinking in this respect were his Jain mentor, Raychandbhai, and the songs of the poet-saints of India of whom he was so fond. One of the books sent by Raychandbhai to Gandhi during the seminal period of their correspondence from 1893 to 1894 was the *Mumukṣu prakaraṇa* of the *Yogavāsiṣtha* which enjoins *puruṣakāra* (human endeavour) in facing world problems. The Jains are believers in *videhamukti*, that is, liberation from the body, and this has a natural consequence, belief in the value of the ascetic life. The extreme form of this is fasting to the point of self-annihiliation. On such a view the body is not seen as the temple of the soul, but as its fetter. Gandhi had picked up sufficient Christian terminology for phrases like 'the temple of the Holy Ghost' to come naturally to him. It would clearly have been incompatible with a life of service to regard the body as something which is preferably to be shuffled off at the earliest opportunity. Gandhi's dietetic experiments are evidence not only of austerity, of a desire to minimise wants and share the deprivations of the poor, but also of a desire to find the most economical way of making the body function efficiently. The Jain influence persists, however, in Gandhi's emphasis on purification. For example, he wrote to his friend Sheth Jamnalal Bajaj from jail in 1942, saying:[2]

Moksha is liberation from impure thought. Complete extinction of impure thought is impossible without ceaseless penance. There is only one way to achieve this. The moment an impure thought arises, confront it with a pure one. This is possible only with God's grace, and God's grace comes throughout ceaseless communion with Him and complete self-surrender.

Interestingly enough he once told another friend that Bajaj was one of the few people he had known who closely approached being a *mukta*, or liberated soul. He said the same of Raychandbhai.

But Vaishnava sentiments are also at work in the complex structuring of Gandhi's religious thought. One of the Gujarati bhajans sung in the ashram runs:[3] 'But men of God ask not for salvation; they desire to be born again for everlasting service, praise and singing and to meet God face to face.' In contrast to this both the evangelical Christian's claim to once for all salvation and the traditional Hindu's desire to be liberated from the wheel of births and deaths have a self-regarding air, paradoxically, since in both cases the apparent basis of each is a striving for higher things. As for seeing God face to face, Gandhi, like Swami Vivekananda and Mother Teresa, sees the face of God in the poorest of the poor. Rabbinical wisdom and Hindu wisdom alike are replete with stories about the disguises of God. The devotee is always able to penetrate the disguise, to discern the identity of the unknown visitor, the beggar, the singing mendicant.

It is worth mentioning some other references which underline Gandhi's departure from the traditional Hindu abhorrence of rebirth and his seeing of rebirth as the way to extended spheres of service. The ashram hymn book also contains this:[4] 'Nishkulanand says: Blessed be he who gives up all desire for physical comforts and adopts sannyasa, he has left his family, it is true, but he has gained an imperishable family'. The *sannyāsa* of service, for which there is warrant in the *Gītā*, leads to wider and wider allegiances. For Gandhi, as for Swami Vivekananda, this meant the family of mankind. Narsinh Mehta the poet-saint of Gujarat sang:[5]

He is the Godly man who wants,
Not 'mukti' but repeated births.
That lustily, O God, he may
Sing thy glory and always pray.

Of all the arts Gandhi was fondest of music, and this, it might be mentioned, was one of the strong filaments in his bond of friendship with Romain Rolland and Mirabehn. It was a musical analogy he chose when speaking of the 'sadhana' of the spinning wheel. He said that just as countless devotees may get in tune with the Infinite with the help of their '*tanpoora*' (a stringed musical instrument) and '*manjira*' (a pair of cymbals), so he cherished the idea of becoming one with God in the continued strain of the music of the spinning wheel.[6] To any who may feel out of tune with this particular music it may be said that Gandhi saw the spinning wheel not as a sort of prayer wheel but as a means whereby the poorest of the poor could earn. The message is for captives of poverty, a message of self-help.

Another extract from the *Ashram Bhajanāvalī* cites Tukaram and runs:[7] 'I desire neither salvation nor riches nor prosperity; give me always company of the good. Tuka says: 'On that condition Thou mayest send me to the earth again and again.'

Surdas' bhajan 'Take Thou a lesson from the tree' utilises a symbol used very often by Gandhi. In a series of thoughts for the day written at his friend Anand T. Hingorani's request we find the following: 'The bhajan "Take Thou a lesson from the Tree" is worth laying to one's heart. The tree bears the heat of the sun, yet provides cool shade to us. What do we do?' The tree symbolism of Indian folk and classical traditions is very rich. That certain trees are especially holy, beloved of a particular god or goddess, or have life-preserving powers, are beliefs that come naturally to a people whose climate, like that of the people of the Old Testament, makes shade one of the chief goods. We shall return to the idea of rootedness and growth later. Here Surdas recalls the infinite long suffering nature of the tree which in spite of standing in the heat of the day yet provides cool shade to the tired villager. The Christian will find additional overtones in this. The Hindu associations, however, reach out to the heat of *tapasya*, of sacrificial suffering, the one-legged stance of the yogi (an image invoked by a famous poem written by Tagore referring to the *tāl* tree), the coolness of the *stithaprajña*, the brave and tranquil one who endureth all things. This suggests neither the *mokṣa* of escape from bondage, nor the idea of a destiny which involves going away from where one is (say, on pilgrimage) nor the reward of bliss for sufferings undergone, but the fulfilment of the performance of *swadharma*, something which a living tree epitomises.

The resonances of Gandhi's thinking, as we have already found, lead in many directions. They also stem from many cultures. The chords, however, are peculiarly his own. They strike as new and fresh upon the ear as the work of a path-breaking composer. Nothing illustrates this better than the working into *mokṣa* of his conception of *swaraj* or self-rule. Nothing, moreover, better illustrates the impossibility of prising away his religious thought from the main corpus of his personality, life and thought. As early as 1920 he declared:[8] 'Government over self is the truest Swaraj, it is synonymous with *mokṣa* or salvation'. He also maintained the following:[9] 'Swaraj of a people means the sum total of the Swaraj (self-rule) of individuals'. To proceed in the usual logical fashion, maintaining, say, that he is committing the fallacy of composition, will take us on a wrong track. We need rather, first, to get inside the skin of his way of thinking.

We have already seen something of the discipline required of the satyagrahi. He must be fearless, humble, self-restrained, know his own limitations, be unattached, selfless and compassionate. All these qualities require an endless process of cultivation. It was not for nothing that Gandhi distinguished 'spiritual knowledge' from 'spiritual attainment'.[10] Spirituality was 'a matter of heart culture' and the content of this is clear from his many references to the Gujarati Vaishnava poet's celebration of the man whose heart melts at another's woe. If this might seem rather joyless in contrast, say, to the Advaitin's prospect of *ānanda*, one has only to remember Gandhi's delight in the company of children, the way he refreshed his spirit in the company of the villagers, the intensity of his friendships, to be convinced that he was not someone to whom joy was a stranger. But the very examples are significant. Joy for Gandhi was not something rarefied. It was, I would hazard, neither *ānanda* nor *sukha*, neither bliss nor happiness. It was the warmth felt in the company of friends, the quiet jubilation experienced in everyday victories, the fulfilment felt in sacrifices cheerfully undergone. But victory could be achieved at too great a cost. When it was accompanied by violence it was in a fact defeat rather than success. Most notably Gandhi felt no jubilation when Independence came. The country had been bifurcated, thousands had been killed or lost their homes. Political independence had come about, but not *swaraj*.

What then was *swaraj*? Gandhi explains:[11] 'It seems that the attempt made to win *swaraj* is *swaraj* itself. The faster we run towards it, the longer seems to be the distance to be traversed. The same is the case with all ideals'. Two things will help us here. One is

Gandhi's belief in the continuity of means and ends and the other is the idea of horizon. Gandhi's view was that while man had control over means he had little or none over the end. He falls back once more on the organic analogy of the seed and the tree and likens the relation between them to that between means and end. There is an inviolable connection at work. One should know what one's goal is, and Gandhi himself had a clear idea of what this was both in his campaign in South Africa and in his long leadership of the Indian independence movement. But he attached supreme importance to the intermediate steps, believing that progressive use of good means (he usually spoke of purity of means) would eventually result in attainment of the objective. Although this is not mentioned in so many words the two factors which threaten the continuity of means and ends are firstly the time factor – the future is not in our control – and secondly, the actions of other men. After Jallianwalabagh no one could foresee the events at Chauri Chaura three years later. There was a setback and Gandhi devoted himself all the more assiduously to the work of preparation, of constructive work, that is, to means. It was easier to spell out the nature of Swaraj for the individual than it was to spell it out for groups in that in the latter case a progression of policies was involved. Gandhi, reflecting on his own spelling out of the content of Swaraj for the nation, recalled his successive stress on the spinning wheel, on prohibition, and on *swadeshi* (the use of home produced rather than foreign goods). But the qualities of fearlessness and the like that were needed were the same. The law of growth was the same for individuals and for nations. The freedom to err was the universal condition of all progress. It is remarkable that in a culture where the cyclical view of time scarcely accommodates a linear view of progress Gandhi should have had such faith in such an ongoing view of man and his destiny, such a sense of horizon. But Gandhi's understanding of the situation had no truck with the mechanistic conception associated with the nineteenth century idea of progress. We were not on a moving escalator which would inevitably take us to our goal. Herein lies the significance of Gandhi's frequent recourse to organic imagery. When something goes wrong in the individual or society it is likened to a disease of a living organism rather than to the malfunctioning of a machine or the arresting of a mechanical process. Man is not a robot. He has limitless possibilities for good. But these can only be fostered through forms of social organisation which thrive through a pooling of talents in small groups. Gandhi and Schumacher are one in their distrust of anonymous large-scale structures.

Gandhi saw the life of the free man in a multi-dimensional way, with his economic, social and political life ordered so as to eliminate exploitation and bring about the mutual welfare of all. It called for the translating of the ethico-religious values of fearlessness and so on into the fabric of everyday life, with all the structural innovativeness that this would involve. *Swaraj* would be 'the fruit of patience, perseverance, ceaseless toil, courage and intelligent appreciation of the environment.'[12] Once more we find Gandhi advocating a cultivation of the total man which goes beyond the advocacy of the rational outlook which we usually associate with modernism and a scientific world-view and this in spite of his insistence that the demands of reason must not be ignored. Each of the words used by Gandhi in the last quotation are significant, I think, in so far as they invoke the total resources of the human psyche instead of concentrating on man's capacity for thinking in a theoretical manner, still less on the circumstance that he is a talking animal. Life in the twentieth century is demanding in the sense that it needs man's total endowments in order to shape it according to the vision splendid. At the core of Gandhi's distrust of modern civilisation is his conviction that the impasse into which we have fallen (I reiterate his seeing of this impasse as that of a society which has knowledge in plenty, but which is yet unable to prevent war) is the result of the woeful neglect of those human gifts which foster creativity and release the potential for good within the toiling masses of every land.

The free man is the one who, progressively striving to attain self-conquest, is able to win over others through love. His reason and conscience are both alert. His prayerful mindfulness of all that is around him makes him a fit instrument of response to the appeal of events for human constructive intervention. Something in the manner of Simone Weil, Gandhi sees the capacities of the free individual tested most not in situations where there is a clear cut choice between good and bad but in the assessment of far more difficult circumstances where the choice is between goods or where we need to adjudicate between courses of action so that harm is minimised. Such occasions call for moral insight of the most informed and sensitive kind.

The utilitarian guideline could never appeal to a man who all his life cared passionately for the welfare of minorities. The criterion of non-violence, when employed in its most positive way, that is, in its connotation of the persuasive power of a love which is willing to suffer in order to heal the gulfs between man and man, is Gandhi's key to how the enlightened anarchist should proceed. The approach is meliorist if by this we mean a strategy aimed at bettering the prevailing state of affairs. But it is not meliorist if by this we mean a tinkering with existing structures in a remedial manner so as to soften the impact of inequalities, injustices, oppression and the like. What Gandhi's social philosophy indicates, and there is no doubt about this, is a radical reordering of society, a redistribution of wealth through the process of trusteeship, the bringing into being of a thoroughly decentralised socio-economic structure and a society whose health would be measured by the capacity of its humblest members to resist authority if it were abused. Gandhi was an anarchist in so far as he justified principled disobedience of the state and spoke of civil disobedience as 'the storehouse of power'. For all his own transcendental framework of thought, his belief that the law of love was actually at work in the universe, Gandhi by no means advocated theocracy. How could he, when he looked upon the free individual as the axis on which all hope of a new society turned?

Along with contemporary thinkers like Paolo Freire and Gustavo Gutierrez Gandhi regarded twentieth century man as dehumanised. What he has to offer as a remedy has much in common with Freire's idea of 'conscientization' and Gutierrez's theology of liberation. Dadabhai Naoroji and Bal Gangadhar Tilak had both used the word *swaraj* before Gandhi did. But Gandhi spelt out the inner resources of the free man in a way which went beyond freedom from political subjection and worked out in detail through the campaigns which he led on many fronts, social, economic and political, what self-rule amounted to in day to day living. *Artha* is not to be left behind in the pursuit of other-worldly values, but wealth is to be justly distributed and the poorest of the poor provided with work so that they can generate new foci of non-violent power. Political freedom would not stop at national frontiers for, as he pointed out, God had not made frontiers, but had as its natural extension an international polity where the oceanic circle had been expanded so as to include all men. This latter point distinguishes Gandhi's thinking from that of several thinkers of the Indian Renaissance, especially from that of Bankim Chandra Chatterjee who had invested patriotism with a religious aura. National leader as he was, Gandhi looked forward to the time when the idea of *swaraj* would inspire *all* men. The microcosm of the ashram, his own richness in friendships, his lifelong willingness to learn from Englishman as well as Boer, Jain as well as Muslim, made it possible for him to look upon the whole world as his home.

All this is sufficient to indicate that the context in which Gandhi thought of liberation was rather different from that, say, in which some twentieth century churchmen may see it. Hinduism is not an institutionalised religion. The decisions concerning involvement of a church with movements outside it stem from a distinction made between the things that are Caesar's and the things that are God's which is quite foreign to Gandhi's way of thinking and to the culture of which he was such an innovative exponent. Similarly strange to him would be problems concerning 'mixed' marriages, controversies over liturgy and whether the church should be 'involved' in X, Y, Z. His own prescription was clear. Each community should set its own house in order before attempting anything further. Secondly, he always advocated the message of simplication. The third clue is this. The satyagrahi is not enjoined to be apart and be separate. His call is to inspire others with courage to face the demands of their own situation, to join with them, but if none is prepared to listen, as in the words of Tagore's famous song, to tread his path alone.

As for the encounter with materialists, atheists and humanists, which has in recent times exercised churchmen, Gandhi had every sympathy with those who found doctrine a stumbling block. His famous conversion of 'God is Truth' into 'Truth is God' arose in the context of discussion with conscientious objectors in Lausanne who could not subscribe to orthodox belief but who were passionately devoted to peace. There were 'non-believers' in his prayer-meetings, present as a gesture expressing fellow-feeling with others involved in the common task of nation-building. To one who mentioned to Gandhi that he was not a man of prayer Gandhi replied that all that was needed was a readiness to die for the truth as one saw it. Through such would the kingdom of God be realised on earth. Gandhi was never alarmed by the corrosive intellect of the free-thinker (to use a rather old-fashioned word). What he was alarmed at was hardness of heart, lack of imagination and atrophy of sympathy. These were the really dehumanising factors in the twentieth century outlook of those who claimed to be modern. It was to a quickening of the atrophied powers within the human individual that Gandhi looked for the salvation of man, a salvation to be worked out in this world and none other.

The word *swaraj* no doubt has very definite political connotations. Gandhi certainly stood for the spiritualising of politics. Scores of speeches to Congress Party members and the public at large could be cited to support this. In his Foreword to a volume of Gokhale's speeches (and Gokhale was as near a political mentor for Gandhi as one could get) Gandhi wrote:[13] 'Everyone had realized that popular awakening could be brought about only through political activity. If such activity was spiritualized, it could show the path of *moksha*.' Right at the end of his life he clarified what spiritualised political activity and its converse were like:[14] 'Let the Congress proclaim to itself and the world that it is only God's servant. If it engages in the ungainly skirmish for power, it will find one morning that it is no more.' Similarly Gandhi spoke out against the *exploitation* of religion for political purposes in criticising Rashtriya Sevak Sangh (RSS) activities, saying:[15] 'Religion is a personal matter which should have no place in politics.' The context of Gandhi's saying must always be noted, for his remarks were invariably closely tailored to the audience and what needed to be said to it.

Gandhi's desire to spiritualise politics must also be seen in relation to his insight into the weaknesses of representative government, especially in a situation where hundreds of millions of voters were involved. This was why, in addition to the ritual of the five yearly ballot, he advocated bread labour for all, the practice of non-violence in resolving conflicts, the right of the weakest to resist authority when it has been abused, a work ethic which would give all a sense of having a stake in society, the exercise of the God-given powers of creativity which would give every man a sense of participating in God's work. The democratic spirit would grow, not under the protection of a bureaucratic umbrella but under two conditions, the generation of power from below, from street to street, village to village; and from within, by the cultivation of open and valiant hearts. *Swaraj*, for Gandhi, meant a continuous effort to be independent of government control, whether the government be foreign or national.

Gandhi did not survive to shape Indian political life after Independence. But there is sufficient evidence available in his long life of political leadership to show in what directions his thinking tended; for example, the setting up of peace committees in East Bengal at the time of communal riots, his belief that a party should be scrapped once its purpose has been fulfilled, his belief that the political educator should make people aware of their rights and duties, that the legal apparatus should be used to preserve constitutional rights, that methods of self-help are preferable to dependence on aid, that non-violent direct action should be a last resort when all other methods of persuasion have failed. The list could be extended, but these are some of the essential principles. Above all, and this gives a clearer picture of the presuppositions of his political thinking, he believed that man-made law could and should be overridden by the moral law which lies in the heart of man himself. Like many men in other traditions Gandhi identified the moral law with the voice of God. Such a framework of thought provides full sanction for the political activity of civil disobedience and no less for the constructive work that is needed if new structures are to be built up in place of the old. In neither case is there any room for niggardliness of spirit. Protest, penance and constructive work were for Gandhi inextricably bound together. They constituted the *tapasya* of the free man.

If life is seen as an indivisible whole no apology is needed for the entry of men of faith into the rough and tumble of politics. As Gandhi wrote in 1934:[16] 'My life is one indivisible whole, and all my activities run into one another, and they all have their rise in my insatiable love of mankind'. One can also see Gandhi's multiform involvement in every aspect of human life, ranging from diet and sanitation to efforts to unseat an imperial power, as an idiosyncratic way of tackling human imperfection. The flawed character of humankind is recognised by every religious tradition whether it be referred to as sin, weakness of will, or the bondage of ignorance. Man's flawed nature is writ large in all his activities, social, economic and political. What is special about Gandhi's response to man's perennial condition, we have seen so far, is his immense faith in the other side of the coin, in man's immense reservoir of positive powers which need quickening, in the hitherto unplayed chords which bear the promise of new music. This strong faith in the incipient greatness of man rings as new a note for cultures which dwell on the sinfulness of man, those which, more recently, take for granted the general decadence of the times, or, and here the reference is to India, see bondage as a cosmic net in which man is willy nilly caught up. The tendency had been to present the alternative as some form of other-worldliness or other. Built into Christian belief is the idea that man is a citizen of two kingdoms and that his ultimate destination is in the world to come. In a different idiom, the peoples of India too, traditionally looked forward to the cessation of births and deaths. Philosophers in India were quick to distinguish between the anthropomorphic popular conception of heaven and something higher, a state of consciousness rather than a 'place'. But Gandhi's reaction to imperfection is not to long for a putative state when all imperfections will have been overcome, but to set about the pursuit of perfection in what is nearest at hand, that is, himself and his immediate surroundings. Whereas this-worldliness had in India traditionally taken the form of pursuit of prosperity, of *abhudaya*, Gandhi's this-worldliness takes a very different form. The world is the place where I am, the opportunity for self-purification. The story of his self-purificatory acts reads like the story of the labours of Hercules, a long apprenticeship which for Gandhi was unceasing. How does this approximative view of *mokṣa* relate to his own tradition and what light does it throw on the life of faith as he saw it? We must now try to close in on these questions.

In 1929 Gandhi undertook a series of tours in various parts of India, addressing large gatherings wherever he went, urging people to use swadeshi articles, and impressing upon the Congress workers the need to improve its village-level organisation. The Meerut Conspiracy trial had started and plans for the Salt Satyagraha were yet to be formulated. It was a year of activity on many fronts for Gandhi, including the completing of his commentary on the *Gītā*. It was in July of this year[17] that Gandhi said that he considered it to be man's achievement to harmonise *dharma* and the ultimate aim of life, truth and *swaraj*; *swaraj* and government by all, the welfare of the country and the welfare of all; that this alone was the path which led to *mokṣa*, and this alone was what interested him. If we bear in mind that India's philosophical tradition, especially the Advaitic one, laid much stress on the *distinction* between the *vyavahārik* (mundane) and the *paramārthik* (absolute or transcendental) levels this statement of Gandhi's appears to have a special significance. I reiterate that he wrote it at a time when his involvement in the world of affairs could scarcely have been greater. There is a certain rhythm about his activities in this year. From Sind to Calcutta and Burma, from Andhra to Bombay, he is constantly on the move. He has periods of rest in Almora and Agra. The crowds are with him everywhere. Fund-collection goes on. The finishing touches to his *Gītā* commentary are given in the short respite of a week in the hills. The year would end with the famous 'Poorna Swaraj' (complete independence) Resolution in the Lahore session of the Congress. It is in such a year that Gandhi affirms that the greatness of man lies in his ability to harmonise what has to be done (*dharma*) with his quest of the ultimate. It is a sentiment which recalls Niebuhr's understanding of man as the being who stands at the junction of nature and spirit. Gandhi's eye is fixed on the path. It was a path which would lead to Dandi, to the Salt Satyagraha. The year was full of disquiet. Gandhi was not at all clear what should be the next step. Even in January 1930, when his friend Rabindranath Tagore visited him in Sabarmati, he told him[18] 'I am furiously thinking, I do not see any light coming out of the surrounding darkness.' It is not surprising that Gandhi found that Newman's well-known hymn echoed his own experience. How much of the path can in fact be seen? At most the next step presents itself in terms of what then we must do.

A man who thinks in such terms is not deliberately setting his sights on *mokṣa*. The *sannyāsa* of service necessarily dictates otherwise. Along the path as it unfolds, there are landmarks, but it is not given to man to see very far ahead. It comes naturally to Gandhi to use religious language in his recognition of the demands of the moment. The moment of truth lies in the dictates of *dharma* now. Divine grace comes to succour man when he feels most helpless and yet most ready to do His will. If this seems incongruous in the circumstances which I have intentionally given in some detail, we have only to remind ourselves again of how Gandhi sees the political quest of *swaraj* in the wider context of full liberation. Jain and Buddhist overtones are no doubt discernible. What is to be done is in accordance with our own light. The risk of error is always present. But he who grasps truth as he sees it and remains non-violent in thought, word and deed (a Gandhian reformulation of the teachings of the *Zend Avesta*) is on a valid path. The criterion thus amounts to far more than an existentialist appeal to authenticity. The ultimate destination is as hidden from us as the Himalayan peaks are hidden from the hardy mountaineer. To miss the next step is to risk a fall. The path allows at times only infinitesimal movements and often includes detours which seem to lead away from the goal. Such is the quest of *swaraj*. Such is the quest of *mokṣa*.

Gandhi's thinking here perhaps poses a challenge to those who polarise a *Gesinnungsethik* with an *Erfolgsethik*, and likewise to those who stress the autonomy of the ethical. The ethics of the *Gītā* rules out an *Erfolgsethik*, and Gandhi's own stress on truth seems to indicate an unalloyed *Gesinnungsethik*. But the Indian notion of path or *mārga* brings in a consideration of a different kind. The *mārga* idea straddles the deontologist's and the teleologist's position by positing neither prima facie duties nor a fully conceived telos of good or goods but indicates *principles* according to which one is to proceed. In the Jain and Buddhist traditions the principles are specified in detail. Gandhi uses the more general concept of *dharma* but gives content to it through his emphasis on non-violence. As for the autonomy of the ethical, Gandhi's own framework of thought is avowedly ethico-religious and the concept of *dharma* itself witnesses to the convergence of the ethical and the religious in Hindu thought. Like Kant he sees that the moral man is likely to be *led* to the thought of a *Divine* Being, not that this grounds doing good in fear of God; for both Kant and Gandhi this would nullify the good qualities our acts may seem to have. There is, of course, another sense of fear of the Lord, in the Old Testament and Kierkegaardian sense, where the doing of good is grounded in the knowledge that it is God's will, a sense which is often reflected in Gandhi's sayings. But Gandhi's accommodation of the ethical insights of the atheist and secular humanist within pursuit of Truth or living in the Truth may seem to tilt the scales more on the side of the ethical than the religious. If it does, there is a reason for it, or so it seems to me. In the context of his national work Gandhi enlisted the labours of all conditions of men. Not all could accept that God had many names, and there were those for whom the very concept of God was a stumbling block. The position is not all that different today. However that may be, the ideas of truth and non-violence seemed to him sufficient to inspire the allegiance of men of very different persuasions and without raising the kind of theological dust which obscures vision. Gandhi takes it for granted that we see in a glass darkly. But this is not to say we see nothing at all. He often spoke as if the sum of fragmentary visions would amount to a total vision. Although this summation idea may seem inadequate it is valuable for the way it recognises religious consciousness as a *human* phenomenon and suggests the need for a pooling of insights. The ultimate would not be for the Hindu conceived in terms of a vision *sub specie aeternitatis* in that, at that stage, the language of being rather than that of vision would be appropriate. Gandhi is humble enough to regard himself as one of the labourers in the cave. Here, though, reference to Plato can be misleading. The cave of the heart, in Hindu thought is the place of withdrawal, the domain of the within. How is one to interpret this statement made by Gandhi in *Young India* in April 1924:

I have no desire for the perishable kingdom of earth. I am striving for the Kingdom of Heaven which is *moksha*. To attain my end it is not necessary for me to seek the shelter of a cave. I carry one about me, if I would but know it.

Gandhi had been released from jail in February of that year. There were difficulties within the Congress party, with the so-called swarajist group under Chittaranjan Das and Motilal Nehru seeing no incompatibility between entry into the legislatures and non-cooperation. The world was much with him. Life in prison, in spite of illness, had been more peaceful. It was indeed necessary for Gandhi to carry his cave with him. The *ascesis* required, changed with the needs of the hour. A few months later, in September, he undertook a 21 day fast in Delhi as a penitential act for the communal violence that had broken out especially in the North West Frontier Province.

The rhythm of active involvement in satyagraha movements alternating with periods of constructive work (rural reconstruction) was matched by a rhythm of activity in Gandhi's life which extended to his daily routine. His prayers, periods of silence, his capacity for inner regeneration through many channels, especially those of personal contact and friendship, are witness to his ability to nourish himself in ways very unlike the 'life apart' of the traditional holy man or member of a religious order. The quotation cited is strangely revealing of Gandhi the person, his own personal aspiration for *mokṣa*, and yet his conviction about his own destiny as a man of complete involvement in human affairs. Although the world is too much with him it is in this world and none other that he must employ his powers. Both senses of the word 'cave' apply; the cave of the world, the place where he must be, and the inner cave, the cave of the heart[19] wherein he experiences both the welling up of energies and the influx of transcendental powers. One searches for language which will approximate most closely to the nerve of Gandhi's experience at this point. He seems to experience something very like what Gabriel Marcel describes as 'inner accretion' and, like Marcel too, he experiences it most in the bonds between man and man, the sustaining power discovered as a function of human relationship; he also experiences it in the bonds he has forged for himself, the vows, through which, like an athlete, he seeks to discipline himself. Soul-force, above all, is found in its most active form in common tasks undertaken jointly through the tapping of the non-violent powers of a group.

As far as the corpus of his writings is concerned it is mostly during the period from November 5 1926 to January 20 1927,[20] when Gandhi was having a sabbatical year in the ashram at Sabarmati, that he set on record most fully his understanding of *mokṣa*. The greater part of this comes in his *Discourses on the Gītā*. The idiosyncratic character of his interpretation of the *Gītā* has been remarked upon earlier in this study. The general trend of his comments concerns the *quest* of *mokṣa* rather than any speculation as to what the attainment of it would be like. The cultivation of *sattvik* qualities is stressed, and this is identified with serving others without feeling that one is doing so. The idea of fitness for *mokṣa* is introduced:[21]

> I have come to the conclusion that no one can be called a mukta while he is still alive; one may be said at the most to have become fit for moksha . . . the necessity for deliverance remains so long as connection with the body remains.

The image of fragrance is used, as it will be later in his writings:[22] 'Till the gate of the body prison has opened the fragrance of *moksha* is beyond our experience.'

That political acumen as well as moral insight is needed for the aspirant for *mokṣa* who sees the struggle for *swaraj* as part of his *dharma*, is clear from the following:[23] 'And when the interest of one's country is not in conflict with the interests of the world, service in the cause of one's country takes one towards *moksha*.' Gandhi believed that it was in the interests of the world that the people of each land should be free from exploitation. If this were so, the freedom struggle of a particular country could not be regarded as going against the interests of the people of another land. This did not exclude that it may go against the interests of another *state*. Gandhi noted that the textile industry hit not only the handloom weavers of India but that it had already dealt a death blow to the handloom weavers of the British Isles. Just as the whole world suffered (and this is true also at the level of economics) if there were suffering in any one area, likewise the spirit of non-violence and self-help shown by people in one country could not fail to benefit those elsewhere. Gandhi believed we were all members one of another. There is also a hint here of an ancient Indian assumption that the *tapasya* of a single man, or of a few, had repercussions on society which we were scarcely aware of. A well known Hindu scientist who was not religiously minded at all once told me that the prayers of all religious men, whether sadhus, saints, sannyasis or laymen could not fail to produce some result, according to the law of cause and effect, although we were not as yet in a position to say what this impact amounted to. Likewise the Sikhs believe that the sound of prayers being made benefit even non-participants who hear them (the microphone, a production of modern technology, thus acquires a religious halo!).

Gandhi's passion for Truth and non-violence, as we would expect, shows itself in his interpretation of *mokṣa*. Śaṁkara had spoken of the patience needed by one seeking *mokṣa*, and Gandhi of the patience needed by one seeking the ideal of perfect non-violence. In both cases genuine *vairāgya* (renunciation) would be required. The ideas of ahimsa, Truth and *mokṣa* are tied together thus:[24] '*ahimsa* means *moksha* and *moksha* is the realisation of Truth'. The idea of God also comes in, but in a way rather unfamiliar perhaps to the non-Hindu. He says elsewhere:[25] 'Non-violence means *moksha*, and *moksha* means realising Satyanarayana.' For Gandhi Truth and the Lord are one and the same. Non-violence is the way, the *mārga*, in that a man who has violence in his heart cannot claim to be goodly or godly. Just as the utilitarian concerns himself (especially in legislation) with obstacles to the general happiness, Gandhi concerns himself with obstacles to *mokṣa*. The philosophy of 'one step enough for me' necessarily involves this concentration on the task at hand. All symptoms of egoity, whether of self-indulgence, possession of property or the overt forms of exploitation, serve as obstacles to the pursuit of *mokṣa*. Gandhi is also sensitive to the inhumanity of letting die, the unspoken violence done to other men by deprivation, by the silence of indifference. Compassion is the essence of religion he says, quoting Tulsidas rather than the Buddha.

The pursuit of *mokṣa* involves a series of stages, or, more happily put, a life of endeavour. A helpful gloss on this is provided by Mahadev Desai, Gandhi's secretary, in an article written in 1926.[26] He writes that Gandhi speaks of gradations of spiritual freedom: the one who bows down before a temple deity and is 'lost in God', the one who exults in the sky without and needs no other symbol, and 'the man who can get all he needs from the sight of the sky within'. Desai suggests:

All these three states are in a gradation of greater and greater (spiritual) freedom. And all of them can and do exist in a man at one and the same time. The reason is that every individual is consciously or unconsciously going from the gross to the subtle.

If we examine Gandhi's own *ascesis* in the light of this we find, perhaps, something like the following. Gandhi had immense respect for the simple devotion of the villager, seeing through the symbolism of it and knowing very well that the simple folk of India do not 'worship stocks and stones'. The man who exults in the infinities of sky and sea is epitomised in his close friend Rabindranath Tagore. Gandhi himself is too much a man of the people to confine himself to the sky within. He is bound with the gossamer string of love (his own phrase, and which is perhaps a perceptive reformulation of the Hindu sacred thread idea) to the folk about whom he says that he feels he has become 'the vessel of their longings.' One of his letters takes us further in the same direction:[27] 'Life to me would lose all its interest if I felt I could not attain perfect love on earth. After all, what matters is that our capacity for loving ever expands.' We noticed earlier, in discussing Gandhi's oceanic circle metaphor, how he makes use of the idea of expansion in order to arrive at the idea of a just society which has no national boundaries. We must now see how in his thinking about *mokṣa* the language of expansion comes in once more, not counter to the idea of hierarchy this time, but virtually providing an alternative to the more familiar religious language of ascent.

We need to go back a bit. The extract from Mahadev Desai's article spoke of movement from the gross to the subtle. This language is particularly appropriate with reference to the Jain understanding of the gradual purification of the soul. One has only to think of the refiner's fire, and St. Augustine's analogy of the oil press to have the feel of how the Jains look at it. The language of ascent is more applicable to the Jain style of *ascesis* than it is to *ascesis* as conceived by any other branch of the family of Indian religions. While this could make for a breadth of perception which finds even in the seemingly inorganic the germs of life, the very pitching of the target, so to say, away from incarnatedness provides poor warrant for a compassionate life of human involvement. Furthermore, the very notion of the 'subtle' was conceived by the Jains in a rare manner (in every sense) as a kind of attenuation of the physical. Now although Gandhi speaks of his 'journey to the land of Eternal

Freedom and Peace'[28] he was no less convinced that 'we have to work within the limits of our strength with our feet on the hard earth.'[29] The Vaishnava poet-saints had left an indelible mark on Gandhi's consciousness, men of humble origin whose idea of the religious life centred on a horizontal expansion of fellow-feeling, and for whom God Himself was conceived as Friend. It is largely thanks to them that Gandhi is able to envisage man's destiny as that of becoming 'an ocean of friendliness'. This is not an ocean in which individual identity is swallowed up. Friendship presupposes discreteness. It also presupposes the possibility of reaching out, of forging the voluntary bonds of fellowship which, in their supreme form, are in India traditionally associated with sweetness.

Because the pursuit of perfection is an endless process, men find, in their pursuit of it, that the goal ever recedes. Gandhi's own experience was that when one was on the right track (that is to say when the criterion of non-violence was being applied in a particular set of circumstances) the aspirant would have a sense of expansion. The reference is here no doubt to the space of the heart, that growth of fellow-feeling in which he saw hope for the future of the human family. Gandhi was by no means a sentimentalist although he set great store by sentiment, especially in his stress on respect for the sentiments of others. Reasoned apprehension of the situation, sympathy with the sufferers, intervention such as will enable them to discover their own non-violent strength – such are the marks of the man who, helping others on the road to freedom (political, social and economic), finds therein a growth of his own consciousness, a milestone on his own progressive self-emancipation.

Almost at the end of his life and career Gandhi was asked by some friends to explain more fully what he understood by *mokṣa*. This is what he told the interviewer:[30]

> He said the desire for *moksha* was indeed there, but it was not meant for anyone other than the individual himself. The world was interested in the fruits, not the root. For the tree itself, however, the chief concern should be not the fruit, but the root. It was in the depth of one's own being that the individual had to concentrate. He had to nurse it with the water of his labour and suffering. The root was his chief concern.

We noticed Gandhi's fondness for the root/tree/flower metaphor earlier. The overtones, in the above passages are richly resonant.

There is, first of all, the *Gītā's* stress on non-attachment to the fruits of action. We need an inner acceptance of the fact that the results of our actions may often be other than we intended. Gandhi's own experience bore bitter testimony to this. Radical concern, which for Gandhi is the same as ultimate concern, is with one's own inner self-purification. The story of his own long pilgrimage, his experiments with truth, fills this out for us. But radical concern also involves being rooted in the community, in the land, in the work which we can do best. Here, it seems to me, he is a member of a brotherhood of thinkers that includes, among others, William Cobbett, Gustave Thibon and Simone Weil. The quest for *mokṣa* is not the *ascesis* of a solitary individual Jain fashion, in search of arhatship.[31] It is part and parcel of translating the vision splendid into actuality, a human community of free men, and it is the latter which would amount to *mokṣa* in a corporate sense. Gandhi believed that such a community could only be brought into existence by men imbued with a religious spirit, that is, by those who were inspired with a sense of devotion, and who believed that their efforts, at a level which cannot be captured in the net of conceptual thought, were matched by a transcendent power at work in the universe whose clearest evidence was found in the nobility inherent in the hearts of men.

10 Epilogue

In the foregoing chapters I have tried as far as possible to discuss Gandhi's religious thought in his own idiom so as to present him as a very exceptional personality whose thinking stretches back into the traditional religious life of India and reaches forward to times which are yet to come. Methodologically I have tried to eschew an analytic conceptual approach, believing this to be singularly inappropriate in considering a man such as Gandhi. I would like to think that, as a by-product, some sort of case has indirectly been made out for the feasibility of using a method aimed at identifying essential structures of thought, where this includes tracking the path of those structures on the move, so to say, and having a sense of context, a sense of history.

I do not believe it to be very necessary in a study of this kind that we should hunt in Gandhi's thought for standpoints which may seem to provide some kind of 'answer' to current philosophical and theological controversies. It is, moreover, a risky business to hazard hypothetical viewpoints which might have been elicited from a thinker had he been alive today. The matters we may consider important, from our own professional perspectives, may not at all have been those which were central to the thinker under consideration.

And yet it would limit us unduly if we were to put a frame round Gandhi, label him as a thinker in the Indian tradition and leave it at that. For even this will not do. Time and again we have found him contouring anew some of the pillars of the Hindu temple of religious thought in a striking way. Accepting *karma* and rebirth as a traditional Hindu would, he would *like to be reborn* as an untouchable in order to be of service to that downtrodden section of Hindu society – an extraordinary preference according to traditional lights. Furthermore, in spite of accepting the postulate of a round of births and deaths, his sights are set on what is to be done in this life, and not in the expectation of a good credit account in the life to come but because *dharma* requires it. Gandhi's religious thinking at this point has all the urgency associated with belief in a 'one life, one chance' framework. In spite of acceptance of the cyclical cosmology which Gandhi does not question, he has passionate faith in the possibility of a *new* life for man, a life governed by the law of love which itself is as 'old as the hills'.

He interprets the *Gītā* in an idiosyncratic fashion, seeing the message of non-violence in it, a message which belongs more properly to Buddhism and Jainism. While, like other Hindus, he draws no sharp distinction between sacred and profane, Gandhi sees man as the servant, not Lord, of the created order. Man is not in dominion over nature but called (a convocation of all men) to a caring involvement with it, a partnership which those who are close to the soil perhaps understand best. Such service is not submission to bondage, a willy nilly servitude to empirical reality, but the proper way for man to fulfil his destiny. This *mārga* can also be described in terms of therapy. Caring involves healing nature's wounds and also healing the wounds of humanity. Here Gandhi has much in common with Gutierriez. Where so many Indian philosophers had opted for an eschatology of transformed consciousness Gandhi opts for an eschatology of transformed relationships. To all who seek in Indian religion or, even more generally, in so-called 'eastern religions', paradigms of mysticism Gandhi's religious life provides salutary evidence to the contrary. Gandhi agreed with H. D. Thoreau's advocacy of the simple life but was not attracted to his nature mysticism. Gandhi's life was singularly free of ecstasies. There was no time for contemplation when there was so much work to be done. Just as there are material luxuries so also there can be luxuries of the spirit. Gandhi has no patience with either.

It may have been noticed that I have avoided using the word 'spirituality' as far as I could. The reason is that Gandhi drew no distinction between spirituality and social involvement and never thought of the religious life as a tricky tandem operation, a tightrope walk of life in the world under the wobbly umbrella of a private ascesis. He had an uncanny way of nosing out humbug, and many practices usually thought to have 'spiritual' value were for him as bootless as oblations on ash, to use an old Hindu analogy. He does talk of *mokṣa*, but what he has in mind is not freedom from the round of births and deaths but what seems to be a corporate *mokṣa* of a this-worldly kind, although unmistakably environed by a sense of transcendence. I use the idea of environing advisedly. It provides a 'grounding' image for the oceanic circle idea, an ontological base for something which is as distinct content-wise from the linear notion of secular progress as it is from the idea of secular history intersected by eternity in the form of a salvific incarnated Divine Being.

But let us now put Gandhi in a modern context and see how his thinking stands. One could say that Gandhi unwittingly constructed a modern Indian modification of what the three formative figures who shape twentieth century thought had preached – I speak of Freud, Darwin and Marx. Without being a Freudian Gandhi was acutely aware of the great variety of powers latent in ordinary human beings. His mission was to discover how these could be put at the service of humanity at large, thereby benefiting both the individual who discovered a channel for releasing his energies, and society which cried out for the development of new structures to meet contemporary challenges. In lieu of Freudian sublimation he advocated rigorous self-discipline, not for an ascetic purpose, but in view of the pressing tasks which called out for action. Responding to the needs of those around us, Gandhi believed, would canalise man's aggressiveness in constructive ways. It was not the Tagorean 'surplus' factor which would feed man's 'higher' activities but all man's endowments, his manual skill, his sense of personal and familial allegiances, his love of his own familiar territory, his natural desire to better his condition.

Unlike Darwin, he did not envisage development as an outcome of a competitive process. He was a passionate believer in the human capacity for growth. At a time when both in India and the west there were, and still are, many to bewail what seems to be man's entry into a dark age, Gandhi thought otherwise. He sees man as *navigator* in the high seas of historical process, man not as the plaything of circumstance, but gifted with the capacity to control his destiny.

Like Marx he looked forward to a time when the differences between man and man would no longer act as barriers to their communication, to the time when exploitation would end. But he believed that the vision of tomorrow could be, and must be, translated into concrete terms today, that it was possible to decide the next step keeping the overall vision in view. Unlike Marx he did not regard capture of the state machine as an essential step towards the classless society. Nor in spite of his insistence on the importance of an equitable sharing of *artha*, wealth, does he think of the desirable shape of things to come purely in economic terms. Most of all, and in a way which takes his thinking beyond that of the three seminal thinkers mentioned, what makes Gandhi's thinking unusual in a secular age was his conviction that man's efforts are matched by a connivance of powers in the universe, an influx which at the same time fructifies man's deepest aspirations.

He was bold enough to affirm that in today's pluralistic world it did not befit men of good will to confine what he once described as 'the sustaining energy of God'[1] by false limits of their own. He pleaded for a pooling of insights which would be yet another illustration of that pooling of talents so needed at a time of history where there was in every sense a crisis of resources. The resources were not as scarce as some imagined. What would result from such a pooling of insights would not result in a global theology, for Gandhi attached little importance to formulations and often took intellectuals to task for their 'analytic' outlook. Rather he had confidence that something more pertinent to man's present condition would emerge – a more humane society. In this respect Gandhi says something different from the pronouncements of those who see religious pluralism as a challenge for theologising, including in this those who speak in global terms, those who think in terms of a 'convergence' model which can be acceptable only to *some* Christians, and those who try to bypass the challenge of pluralism by encouraging a secular outlook. If all man's energies are to be enlisted it will follow that his religious instincts and sentiments are not to be relegated to the sphere of mere privacy, or alternatively, written off as of no consequence, still less seen as a curb on his efforts to improve his lot. Gandhi was in this respect one of the few men of his generation who was able to see all human strivings towards a better world as bearing the stamp of his reaching out to the transcendent. For example, whenever he commented on what was then known as Bolshevism he recognised in it a manifestation of that same aspiration which takes a more familiar garb in the religious quest.

Gandhi always had at the back of his mind the dreadful alternative which threatened twentieth century man – world conflict on a scale hitherto unimagined and in the maelstorm of which all would perish. For men of God to refuse to face the most pressing of all contemporary problems, our inability to prevent war, was in Gandhi's view for them to betray their calling. The unity of *bios* and *logos* which is found in the human being provides the ground for seeing man as a creature capable of being non-violent in the most

creative and constructive manner. Such a being has the power to see
the face behind the mask, the label, the stereotype. In the human
face, especially the face of the poor, Gandhi, like Swami
Vivekananda, sees the face of God. In moments when the world was
less with him he spoke of the stars and the sun as witness to his
thoughts, symbols of human aspiration. But it was for the most part
in saintly souls like Tulsidas, Surdas and Narsinh Mehta that he
found his beacon lights. Their words illuminated his way, the
encircling gloom is penetrated by their example, and the lamp
within is fuelled to burn bravely even in the windy spaces of the
twentieth century world.

Gandhi does not say it does not matter what you believe; rather it
does not matter what name you give to God. 'It does not matter' in
the sense that whatever you call Him you will never be able to
plumb the depths of His inexhaustibility. If the very concept of God
be a stumbling block, hold fast to what you are willing to stake your
life on, provided that you have the good of all in mind, have
undergone a discipline of self-purification and are as non-violent in
thought, word and deed as it is possible for a human being to be
while avoiding cowardice. These provisos take care of the single-
mindedness of a Genghis Khan or an Al Capone. Gandhi's
uniqueness here is his refusal to get bogged down in theological
debate, even in the more Indian form of it, that is in the discussion of
whether God is personal or impersonal. His life is his message, and
living is the test, not credal formulations. Human activities are girt
about with a nimbus which not only surrounds but sustains. It is not
Greek chaos, nor is it illusion. For Gandhi it was the love of God,
that is to say, the love of God towards man. Man is addressed by
events, and this includes also the very lacunae in the world of
circumstances (for example, that nothing is being done to combat
war, put an end to poverty and so on). In responding to the call for
human intervention man participates in God's work. He becomes a
co-worker with God.

For Gandhi what is wrong with us is not the inadequacy of our
concepts, although they are, heaven knows, inadequate enough,
but the weakness of our imagination, our inability to put ourselves
in others' shoes, the smallness of our hearts, and our unwillingness to
translate beliefs into practice. Breadth and depth, rather than
ascent, are the metaphors which suggest themselves as indicating
what Gandhi felt was the need of the hour. A reaching out,
combined with rootedness and inner discipline will all enable a man

to find a correspondence between whatever gifts he may have and what calls out to be done. The very cultivation of an inner life, what Gandhi calls self-purification, has its natural flowering in involvement with others. Any other kind of *ascesis* would be like a seed which starts germinating but never gets to the stage of showing a shoot above the ground.

The metaphors of breadth and depth need a little elucidation. They are metaphors of expansion for Gandhi. He is optimistic about the apparent *Grenzsteine* (I borrow a term from Frege, used in a very different context) between different religious traditions. We are after all speaking not of abstractions but of other men, that is to say, men with whom we share a common humanity. Even in the, at first sight, no-man's-land of unbelief he finds, as he did as Lausanne, a quest for truth, a healthy impatience with shibboleths. The formulation 'Truth is God' can be seen, if we wish, as a de-mythological innovation on the part of Gandhi. But demythologis-ation was not an issue for Gandhi personally. Indian culture presents the phenomenon of the coexistence of mythical thinking and 'high' philosophy. The ethical teaching of the *Gītā* is presented in a very mytho poeic form. Gandhi himself found neither error nor stumbling block in the simple rituals of his unlettered fellow countrymen. Myths in India are not pictures which are *used* but stories which are *lived*. Unlike those who in this century have occupied themselves with the so-called problem of inter-faith relations he used neither the method of encounter nor dialogue. The natural domain of the meeting of persons is not the noösphere but the tackling of common tasks. Mere dialogue cannot bring peace. What is needed is the labour of reconciliation. This is why he said:[2] 'Spiritual experiences are shared by us whether we wish it or not by our lives, not by our speech which is a most imperfect vehicle of experience. Spiritual experiences are deeper even than thought'.

There was no temple in the ashram either at Sabarmati or Wardha where he shifted in September 1933. This did not prevent men of various faiths from gathering together for prayer, reciting the scriptures and singing the hymns beloved of those present. What followed was not a homily but a discussion of what next needed to be done, whether the building of a road for the ashram inmates or the next move in the freedom struggle. Gandhi did not think of such matters as falling outside the domain of the spiritual for, as saw it, the spiritual was not a separate domain at all. The religious community is a caring, participating community. The breadth of experience which resulted from growth in such a community enabled Gandhi to pray that God should grant to the other the light that he needed on his path rather than the light that may be proper for himself. This frank recognition and welcoming of plurality comes in a refreshing way at a time when unity may seem to require singleness of belief or at least a common denominator of ethical principles. I have mentioned more than once Gandhi's preference for metaphors from the organic world. That world shows not convergence but further and further differentiation. India's ethnic and cultural diversity was never a bar to her assimilative powers or her sense of nationhood. National leader as he was, this awareness of India's great inner diversity was ever present in Gandhi's thinking at its deepest level. He was, at this point, in tune with another democrat, John Stuart Mill, who once said that the mark of the mature society was its welcoming containment of diversity.

But how could a man gain in depth of religious experience? Here again Gandhi has something new to say. It was natural that a man should be devoted to what he knew best, and nourish his spirit through those practices which belonged to his forefathers. Gandhi did not attach much importance to ritual observances himself. His tour in Noakhali could be seen as a pilgrimage of a very unorthodox kind. Decades earlier, in the Phoenix Settlement, he had tried to give the Hindu boys a sense of sharing in the life of the Muslim inmates by persuading them to restrict their own diet during Ramzan, the time of fasting for the Muslims. He found kindred spirits in Charlie Andrews and Rabindranath Tagore, although no three men could have been more different from each other. When enthusiastic fellow-workers from overseas wanted to become Hindus he dissuaded them, urging them to root themselves more firmly in their own faith. There is in fact evidence that Gandhi was able to nourish his inner life through his friendships with men of other faiths. It was this human contact with living faith, whether Hindu, Christian or Muslim, rather than his study of others' scriptures (which was very considerable) which sustained him and gave depth to his experience. Rooting itself again and again in the soil the great banyan tree reaches the living streams which feed other trees as well. The divine force[3] 'necessarily makes no distinction between kinsmen and strangers, young and old, man and woman, friend and foe'. Even after the clouds of communal conflict had already burst, Gandhi said in a post-prayer speech in November 1947 that there was 'so much in common between man and man that it was a marvel that there could be any quarrel on the ground of religion'.[4]

The fact was, however, that men belonging to different religious persuasions were, and still are, in other parts of the world in conflict with each other. One of the things that Gandhi did to diagnose this 'marvel', or rather tragedy, was to detect the economic disparities that lay behind communal conflicts. This is as true of India as it is of present-day Ulster or of racist clashes elsewhere. Gandhi's thinking involves both a method for de-fusing the causes of conflict, and beyond that, a vision of a society in which men of goodwill will nourish each other, each with his own insights. Such an approach seems to me to go both beyond encounter and dialogue and the stereotype of 'tolerance' with which Hindu culture is usually credited. Dialogue is supposed to be the next step after encounter. But it still falls short of combined witness, and tolerance can only too often connote indifference to situations which call out for protest.

There are signs (the experience of Swami Abhishiktananda is one example) that the ability which Gandhi possessed himself for seeing with others' eyes, the way he deepened his personal faith through drawing on the reservoir of experience of other branches of the human family, may well be characteristic of the religious consciousness of many men of faith in days to come. What Gandhi's religious thought offers is by no means an eclectic package, but a challenge to think through and live through the breadth and depth of opportunities for sharing, whether worldly goods or those deepest intimations which are the warp and woof of the inner life. So understood, religion can once more become a binding force (invoking one of the senses of its somewhat disputed etymology) which goes beyond national frontiers and which sees no barrier between one community and another. Religion envisaged as a way of life of the caring individual who participates in a multi-faith community, striving non-violently to establish a just society, would be close to the conception of the founder figures, saints and seers of the different traditions. We have clearly some way to go before our hearts are large enough to draw on the heritage of the entire human family and to live accordingly.

Notes

Gandhi did not use diacritical marks in his writings. He sometimes used capitals for the first letter of words like ahimsa and satyagraha, but not always. I have avoided diacritical marks for words in the standard English dictionaries, the two leading cases being ahimsa and satyagraha, and for common proper names. Elsewhere I have tried to use diacritical marks as uniformly as was possible in a book which includes technical discussion as well as passages which are rather less so. I was anxious to steer a course midway between pedantry and its opposite. This has resulted in what may strike the scholar as an unsatisfactory compromise, as in, say, *Ashram Bhajanāvalī*. I can only plead – *mea culpa*.

Preface

1. Anthropologist, and Gandhi's Private Secretary during his tour of Noakhali in 1946–7.

1 Introduction

1. See my Principal Miller Lectures, Madras University, 'The Meaning of History', Feb. 1976 (Published in *Journal of the University of Madras*, July 1976).
2. *Harijan*, 20 Apr. 1935, p. 74.
3. *Young India*, 8 Sept. 1927.

2 Gandhi's Religious Thought and Indian Traditions

1. See Mahadev Desai's *Day to Day with Gandhi*, vol. I, p. 132. The talk was given on 22 May 1918 (subsequent reference to these volumes will be made under Mahadev Desai's *Diary*).
2. 23 May 1925.
3. *The Collected Works of Mahatma Gandhi*, XLVIII, Publications Division, Government of India, Delhi, 30 May 1913. Hereafter referred to as *Collected Works*. p. 127.
4. *Collected Works*, L, p. 326.
5. *Harijan*, 24 Aug. 1934.
6. Quoted in *Prayer and Meditation*, F. C. Happold, Pelican, p. 126.
7. *Young India*, 24 Mar. 1927, p. 93.
8. Mahadev Desai's *Diary*, vol. III, p. 31.
9. *Harijan*, July 1940.

10. Mahadev Desai's *Diary*, vol. VIII, p. 275.
11. Ibid., vol. VI, p. 270.
12. Ibid., vol. V, p. 139.
13. Ibid., vol. V, p. 148.
14. *Autobiography* (1948 edn) pp. 47–51.
15. Mahadev Desai's *Diary*, vol. VI, p. 333.
16. *Harijan*, 29 Apr. 1933, p. 6.
17. *Delhi Diary*, Navajivan, 1948, p. 123.
18. Mahadev Desai's *Diary*, vol. VII, p. 307.
19. Ibid., vol. I, p. 139.
20. *Young India*, 21 Jan. 1926.
21. See Ashram Vows under 'The Vow of Celibacy'.
22. The references to Tolstoy are taken from Kalidas Nag's *Tolstoy and Gandhi*, Patna, 1950.
23. See Appendix I in *Prayer*, compiled and edited by Chandrakant Kaji, Navajivan, Apr. 1977. This includes some translations from *Ashram Bhajanāvali*, the prayers and hymns used in the ashram 'order of service'.
24. *Mahatma Gandhi at Work*, p. 251.
25. Quoted in Geoffrey Ashe's biography of Gandhi, p. 373.
26. Desai's *Diary*, vol. IV, p. 74.
27. Ibid., vol. VIII, pp. 149–50.
28. Ibid., pp. 149–50.
29. Ibid., vol. VI, p. 95.
30. Ibid., p. 332.
31. *Young India*, 13 Oct. 1921, pp. 324–6. The reference is to the classical parallel drawn between parts of the body and the four castes.
32. Desai's *Diary*, vol. VIII, pp. 155–6.
33. Ibid., vol. IV, p. 239.
34. Legend has it that the swans on Manasa Lake on Mount Kailas drink milk, leaving the water. The allegorical meaning is that a man should be able to distinguish between the good and bad elements in his mind (*manasa*) and so live on Mount Kailas, the abode of the gods. The contemporary Indian will of course note with wry pleasure that the practice of putting water in the milk seems to have a long lineage! The speech referred to was made in Vankaner on 20 February 1925 and is recorded in Desai's *Diary*, vol. VI, p. 18.
35. See my paper on 'The Concept of Seva' in *Approaches to Religion* published by the Guru Gobind Singh Department of Religious Studies, Punjabi University, Patiala, 1973.
36. See my book *The Language of Philosophy*, Allied Publishers (India) and Martinus Nijhoff, 1981, for more in this vein.
37. Desai's *Diary*, vol. VII, pp. 236 f.
38. Desai's *Diary*, vol. VIII, p. 48.
39. Quoted in *The Moral Challenge of Gandhi*, by Dorothy Hogg, Allahabad, 1946, p. 19.
40. *Young India*, 5 Apr. 1925.
41. *Young India*, 12 Nov. 1925.
42. *Young India*, 3 Nov. 1927.
43. *Young India*, 30 Apr. 1925.
44. Desai's *Diary*, III, p. 20.

45. *Young India*, 9 Apr. 1925.
46. Desai's *Diary*, vol. v, p. 204.

3 The Impact of Christianity on Gandhi

1. *Harijan*, 17 Apr. 1937.
2. Mahadev Desai's Weekly Letter, *Young India*, 12 Jan. 1928.
3. *Young India*, 6 Aug. 1931.
4. *Young India*, 11 Aug. 1927.
5. *Harijan*, 31 Dec. 1931.
6. Desai's *Diary*, vol. vii, p. 186.
7. *M. K. Gandhi – An Indian Patriot in South Africa*, Joseph J. Doke, reprinted by Publications Division, Government of India, Sept. 1967.
8. Ibid., p. 100.
9. Ibid., p. 106.
10. *Young India*, 19 Jan. 1928.
11. Desai's *Diary*, vol. viii, p. 289.
12. Ibid., p. 326.
13. *Harijan*, 26 Jan. 1947, p. 517.
14. *Romain Rolland and Gandhi Correspondence*, tr. of vol. 19 of *Cahiers Romain Rolland*, Publications Division, Government of India, ed. Sept. 1976, p. 255, entry dated 4 Feb. 1932.
15. *Harijan*, 30 Jan. 1937.
16. Desai's *Diary*, vol. vii, p. 135.
17. Ibid., vol. viii, p. 11.
18. Ibid., p. 235.
19. Ibid., p. 239.
20. Ibid., p. 242.
21. *The Modern Review*, Oct. 1941, p. 406.
22. *Harijan*, 11 May 1935.
23. *Harijan*, 18 Apr. 1936.
24. *Harijan*, 12 June 1937.
25. *Gandhi Marg*, Apr. 1959 (rpt).
26. The letter is dated 2 Aug. 1932. Quoted in Hugh Tinker's *The Ordeal of Love*, OUP, 1979, p. 257.
27. *Harijan*, 1 Sept. 1946, p. 286.

4 Experiments with Truth

1. Desai's *Diary*, vol. iv, p. 168.
2. *Harijan*, 23 Feb. 1947.
3. Desai's *Diary*, vol. i, p. 145.
4. Desai's *Diary*, vol. i, p. 229.
5. Desai's *Diary*, vol. v, p. 243.
6. *Young India*, 24 June 1926.
7. Dated 2 Feb. 1924. Quoted in Desai's *Diary*, vol. iv, p. 27.
8. *Navajivan*, 21 Feb. 1926.

9. Ibid., 21 Feb. 1926.
10. Dated 29 Oct. 1924. Quoted in Desai's *Diary*, vol. IV, p. 251.
11. *Gandhi Marg*, Apr. 1959 (rpt).
12. An undated letter written by C. F. Andrews, perhaps around 1920.
13. *Gandhi Marg*, Apr. 1959 (rpt).
14. Letter to Miss Esther Farring. Quoted in Desai's *Diary*, vol. I, p. 78.
15. Pyarelal's letter to C. F. Andrews dated 18 September 1931. Quoted in Hugh Tinker's *The Ordeal of Love*, p. 259.
16. The letter is dated 10 Nov. 1932.
17. The letter is dated 6 Jan. 1933. *Romain Rolland and Gandhi Correspondence*, p. 269.
18. *My Days with Gandhi*, Nirmal Kumar Bose, Nishana, Calcutta, 1953, p. 274.
19. Ibid., p. 275.
20. Desai's *Diary*, vol. VIII, p. 287.
21. *Harijan*, 23 Mar. 1940.
22. Desai's *Diary*, vol. VII, p. 111–12.
23. *Modern Review*, Oct. 1921.
24. *Young India*, 28 Oct. 1926.
25. Letter dated 1 Oct. 1918, Desai's *Diary*, vol. I, p. 258.
26. Letter to Jamnalal Bajaj dated 16 Mar. 1922, *Speeches and Writings of Mahatma Gandhi*, p. 99.
27. 1 Apr. 1905. I am grateful to Professor Paul Grimley Kuntz of Emory University, Atlanta, Georgia for drawing my attention to this article.

5 The Non-Violent Weapon of Suffering

1. *Young India*, 11 Aug. 1927, p. 251.
2. *Young India*, 31 Dec. 1931, p. 418.
3. *Young India*, 5 Nov. 1931, p. 341.
4. *An Autobiography* tr. Mahadev Desai, Navajivan, Ahmedabad, 1927, pp. 615–17.
5. Ibid., p. 616.
6. *To a Gandhian Capitalist*, Hind Kitabs, 1951, p. 49.
7. *From Yeravda Mandir*, Navajivan Press, Ahmedabad, 2nd edn, 1935, p. 68.
8. *Young India*, 29 Sept. 1921, p. 306.
9. Desai's *Diary*, vol. VIII, p. 203.
10. Desai's *Diary*, vol. II, p. 91.
11. Desai's *Diary*, vol. VII, p. 248.
12. Letter dated 2 Mar. 1924.
13. Letter dated 26 July 1926.
14. Address in Bombay, 18 May 1924.
15. Letter in *Modern Review*, Oct. 1916.
16. *Harijan*, Aug. 1939.
17. In a letter to Lord Irwin dated 28 June 1930.
18. See J. J. Doke, *M. K. Gandhi*, Natesan, 1909, p. 134.
19. *Harijan*, Apr. 1933.
20. *Young India*, 4 Oct. 1924.

6 Waiting On God

1. *Young India*, 14 Oct. 1926.
2. *Collected Works*, L, p. 326.
3. *Harijan*, 10 Dec. 1939.
4. *Harijan*, July 1933.
5. *The Bombay Chronicle*, Nov. 1932.
6. *Harijan*, 24 Dec. 1938.
7. Letter to Mirabehn, 6 Feb. 1947.
8. *Harijan*, 10 Dec. 1938.
9. For more on this theme see my *The Language of Philosophy*, Allied Publishers (India) and Martinus Nijhoff, 1981.
10. 30 Nov. 1944.
11. *Young India*, Aug. 1921.
12. *Harijan*, 16 Feb. 1934, pp. 4–5.
13. *Young India*, 25 Sept. 1924, p. 313.
14. *Young India*, 4 Dec. 1924, p. 398.
15. *Harijan*, 29 Aug. 1936, p. 226.
16. *Gandhi's Correspondence with the Government 1942–4*, Navajivan Publishing House, Ahmedabad, 2nd edn, Sept. 1945, p. 88.
17. *Gandhi Memorial Peace Number*, Viswa-Bharati, 1949, pp. 10–13.
18. *A Guide to Health*, translated from the Hindi by Rama Iyer, S. Ganesan, Triplicane, Madras, 1930, p. 129.
19. *Harijan*, 6 May 1933, p. 4.
20. *Harijan*, 8 Aug. 1936, p. 201.
21. *Young India*, 20 Dec. 1928.
22. In an interview, to S. K. Roy in USA in 1920.
23. From a prayer speech, 4 Jan. 1946.
24. From a prayer speech, 14 May 1945.
25. From a prayer speech, 26 May 1946.
26. *Harijan*, 21 Apr. 1946, p. 94.
27. *Harijan*, 20 Apr. 1935, p. 74.
28. Letter dated 12 Jan. 1931. Quoted in *Romain Rolland and Gandhi Correspondence*, p. 143.
29. *Young India*, 23 Sept. 1926, p. 333.
30. Desai's *Diary* vol. I, pp. 168–9.
31. From a prayer speech, 26 May 1946.
32. Press report, 22 June 1946.
33. *Mahatma Gandhi – The Last Phase*, Pyarelal, p. 163.

7 Diversities of Gifts

1. *Young India*, 25 May 1921, p. 162.
2. *Young India*, 3 Sept. 1931, p. 247.
3. See p. 50.
4. *Young India*, 11 Aug. 1927, p. 250.
5. *Young India*, 23 Oct. 1924.
6. *Young India*, 7 Jan. 1926.

7. Desai's *Diary*, vol. IV, p. 52.
8. Letter dated 10 Feb. 1918.
9. Desai's *Diary*, vol. I, 3 Mar. 1918.
10. Ibid., p. 67.
11. *Harijan*, 29 Sept. 1940.
12. *Young India*, 2 Sept. 1926, p. 308.
13. *Harijan*, 14 Sept. 1947.
14. *Harijan*, 29 Sept. 1940.
15. Quoted in *Mahatma Gandhi's Ideas*, C. F. Andrews, p. 71.
16. *Harijan*, 3 Nov. 1946.
17. *Harijan*, 29 Sept. 1940, p. 297.
18. 26 May 1946.
19. *Stray Glimpses of Bapu*, Kaka Kalelkar, 1960, p. 159.
20. Desai's *Diary*, vol. V, p. 48.
21. To the Council of the Federation of International Fellowships at Sabarmati, 13–15 Jan. 1928.
22. *Young India*, 5 Nov. 1931, p. 341.
23. *Mahatma Gandhi's Ideas*, C. F. Andrews, p. 71.
24. Cf. the 'reciprocal correction' referred to in the Amsterdam Assembly of the World Council of Churches.
25. *Harijan*, 28 Jan. 1939, p. 448.
26. *Mahatma Gandhi's Ideas*, C. F. Andrews, p. 306.
27. 26 Dec. 1924.
28. Desai's *Diary*, vol. IV, pp. 235–6, entry dated 22 Oct. 1924.
29. *Harijan*, 15 Sept. 1946.
30. *Harijan*, 24 Aug. 1934.
31. *Harijan*, 13 Mar. 1937, p. 39.
32. *Harijan*, 11 Mar. 1933.
33. *Harijan*, 13 Mar. 1937, p. 39.

8 The Vision Splendid

1. *Sabarmati*, 1928, p. 19. Report of the First Annual meeting of The Federation of International Fellowships held at Satyagraha Ashram, Sabarmati 13–15 Jan. 1928.
2. *Collected Works*, LXXVIII.
3. *Autobiography*, p. 366.
4. Ibid., p. 386.
5. Ibid., p. 414.
6. *The Selected Works of Mahatma Gandhi*, vol. III (Satyagraha in South Africa), Navajivan, 1968, p. 224.
7. *Autobiography*, p. 523.
8. Desai's *Diary*, vol. VII, p. 329.
9. *To Ashram Sisters*, 3 Oct. 1927.
10. Ibid., 25 Oct. 1927.
11. *Gandhi, his life and thought*, J. B. Kripalani, Publications Division, Government of India, 1970, p. 70.
12. *Autobiography*, p. 504.

13. Desai's *Diary*, vol. VIII, p. 276.
14. Letter dated 21 Dec. 1917. See Desai's *Diary*, vol. I, p. 4.
15. *Young India*, 13 Oct. 1921, p. 325.
16. Cf. Husserl's conversation with Dorion Cairns on 27 June 1932 when Husserl noted that the mystic 'neglects work'.
17. See G. Mackenrodt, *Sinn und Ausdruck der sozialen Formenwelt*, 1952, p. 200.

9 Mokṣa Rethought

1. K. Swaminathan, editor of the *Collected Works of Mahatma Gandhi*, tends to this opinion (in a personal letter to me).
2. *Harijan*, 22 Feb. 1942, p. 47.
3. *Collected Works*, XLIV, p. 444. From *Ashram Bhajanāvali*.
4. *Ibid.*, p. 454.
5. See *Collected Works*, XLIV for more in the same vein.
6. See article by Mahadev Desai in *Navajivan*, 21 Feb. 1926.
7. *Collected Works*, XLIV, p. 444.
8. *Young India*, 8 Dec. 1920.
9. *Harijan*, 25 Mar. 1939, p. 64.
10. *Young India*, 13 Oct. 1921, p. 323.
11. *Speeches and Writings of Mahatma Gandhi*, Fourth Edition, G. A. Natesan & Co., Madras, p. 685.
12. *Young India*, 27 Aug. 1925.
13. *Collected Works*, XIV, p. 201.
14. Article entitled 'Congress Position', 27 January 1948.
15. *Harijan*, 9 Aug. 1942. N.B. The Rashtriya Sevak Sangh is a Hindu rightist organisation with revivalist tendencies.
16. *Harijan*, 2 Mar. 1934, p. 24.
17. *Collected Works*, XLI, 21 July 1929, p. 11.
18. *Gandhi: His Life and Thought*, J. B. Kripalani, Publications Division, Government of India, Aug. 1970.
19. This phrase is used by Gandhi in an entry dated 9 August 1925, *Collected Works*, XXVIII, p. 50:

> The true cave is the one in the heart. Man can hide himself in it and thus protected can remain untouched by the world even though living and moving freely in it, taking part in those activities which cannot be avoided.

20. *Collected Works*, vol. XXXII.
21. *Ibid.*, p. 136.
22. *Ibid.*, p. 137.
23. *Ibid.*, p. 430.
24. *Young India*, Nov. 1925.
25. *Collected Works*, XXVIII, p. 320.
26. *Navajivan*, 21 Feb. 1926.
27. *Collected Works*, vol. XIV, p. 146.
28. *Harijan*, Aug. 1939.
29. *Collected Works*, vol. LXXVIII, p. 8.

30. *Harijan*, 28 Sept. 1947, p. 340.
31. *Arhat* means 'a liberated being' according to the Hinayana tradition.

10 Epilogue

1. *Collected Works*, XXXII, p. 155.
2. *Sabarmati*, 1928, p. 19.
3. *Harijan*, Feb. 1939.
4. *Delhi Diary*, Navajivan Publishing House, Reprint, Nov. 1960, p. 165.

Select Bibliography

The most invaluable and definitive source for all aspects of Gandhi's life and thought is *The Collected Works of Mahatma Gandhi*, Publications Division, Government of India, Delhi. (The series is as yet incomplete). See also *Romain Rolland and Gandhi Correspondence*, tr. of vol. 19 of 'Cahiers Romain Rolland', Publications Division, Government of India, 1976.

Further References

Andrews, C. F., *Mahatma Gandhi's Ideas*, Macmillan, 1930.
——, *Mahatma Gandhi at Work*, Macmillan, 1931.
Bose, N. K., *Selections from Gandhi*, Navajivan, 1948.
——, *My days with Gandhi*, Nishana, Calcutta, 1953; also Orient Longman, Delhi, 1973.
Desai, Mahadev *Day to day with Gandhi*, vols I–VIII, Navajivan, 1968–72.
——, *The Gospel of Selfless action or The Gita according to Gandhi*, Navajivan, Ahmedabad, 4th imp., 1956.
Doke, Joseph J., *An Indian Patriot in South Africa*, reprinted by Publications Division, Government of India, 1967.
Gandhi, M. K., *Hindu Dharma*, Navajivan Publishing House, Ahmedabad, 1949.
——, *An Autobiography or The Story of My Experiments with Truth*, Navajivan Publishing House, Ahmedabad, 2nd edn, 1940.
——, *Ashram Observances in action*, Navajivan, trans. published 1955.
——, *In Search of The Supreme*, vols I–III, ed. V. B. Kher, Navajivan, 1961.
Kripalani, J. B., *Gandhi, his life and thought*, Publications Division, Government of India, 1970.
Rolland, Romain, *Mahatma Gandhi*, Allen & Unwin, London, 1924.
Tendulkar, D. G., *Mahatma, Life of Mohandas Karamchand Gandhi* (8 vols) 2nd edn, Publications Division, Government of India, Delhi, 1960.

Index